MARK BRANDON READ

CHOPPER 8

MARK BRANDON READ

CHOPPER 8

A BULLET IN THE HEAD IS WORTH TWO IN THE CHAMBER

JOHN BLAKE

Published by John Blake Publishing Ltd,
3 Bramber Court, 2 Bramber Road,
London W14 9PB, England

www.johnblakepublishing.co.uk

First published in paperback in 2009

ISBN: 978 1 84454 760 9

British Library Cataloguing-in-Publication Data:
A catalogue record for this book is available from the British Library.

Design by www.envydesign.co.uk

Printed in Great Britain by CPI Bookmarque, Croydon, CR0 4TD

1 3 5 7 9 10 8 6 4 2

Papers used by John Blake Publishing are natural, recyclable products made from
wood grown in sustainable forests. The manufacturing processes conform to the
environmental regulations of the country of origin.

Every attempt has been made to contact the relevant copyright-holders,
but some were unobtainable. We would be grateful if the appropriate
people could contact us.

FOREWORD

AS a criminal, Mark 'Chopper' Read is a failure. He has spent most of his adult life in jail. He has been betrayed, shot, stabbed, lost his ears and has little money left because of expensive legal battles.

But the long-time stand-over man and self-confessed killer has embarked on a new career — as Australia's only celebrity gangster.

Read has already written seven bestselling books based on his life — books that have inspired shock, outrage and laughter at his exploits. With his first book now adapted into a successful motion picture, he has moved into writing crime fiction based on his three decades in the underworld.

Read can be funny, witty and charming, but it is impossible to ignore the fact that his life has been steeped in violence. He is a career criminal whose background makes him one of Australia's blackest cult heroes.

His background simultaneously repels and attracts. Like sightseers at a traffic crash, people are drawn to look and are horrified by what they see.

THE CHILD

Read was born the son of a war-stressed former soldier who slept with a gun at his side and a devout Seventh Day Adventist mother. He spent 18 months in a Melbourne orphanage as an infant before being returned to the family home.

Read has never used his childhood as an excuse for his later criminal behaviour, but admits he was subjected to violence at home and at school.

His parents split and he lived with his father, who told him, 'Don't ask for mercy from a man who has been shown no mercy.' At school, Read was slow, almost illiterate. He ran away from home six times between the ages of 10 and 15. As a teenager, he was diagnosed as autistic and was institutionalised. He claimed he received the controversial deep-sleep therapy and repeated shock therapy.

Bullied at school, Read found he had two skills: he could make people laugh and, as he grew stronger, he could make them frightened.

He was later to combine the two to turn himself into a feared underworld headhunter, a criminal who lives off the underworld, standing over, bashing and – if need be – killing other members of the underworld.

Read used his humour to make criminals, police and prison officers relax. He would often jolly his underworld targets into lowering their guard. Then he would strike.

But, as a teenage street offender, his criminal history was

unexceptional. He was in a northern suburbs street gang, which was slightly more ruthless and violent than most.

Many hooligans grow out of the adolescent culture of violence, but Read revelled in it. By the time he was in Pentridge, he was ready to graduate to what he considered the big league. He gravitated towards older criminals such as painter and docker and convicted murderer Billy 'The Texan' Longley and the notorious 'toecutter' Linus Patrick 'Jimmy the Pom' Driscoll.

Read may not have learned a great deal in school, but he was a keen student in jail.

THE CRIMINAL

Read learned early to stay on-side with prison officers. He made it clear he would never use violence against them. In return, in the 1970s, many officers turned a blind eye to his involvement in a vicious power struggle between two groups of prisoners in Pentridge.

The so-called 'overcoat war' was a five-year battle between prisoners, resulting in at least 100 attacks from 1975. It began over allegations that Read stole 60 sausages for Christmas dinner in Pentridge's notorious H-Division. 'Harsh words were spoken and blood enemies were made,' Read said later.

Read's group was called the 'overcoat gang' because they wore long coats, even in summer, to conceal their weapons.

It was not only Read's willingness and ability to inflict pain but also his tolerance of it – and his absolute indifference to the consequences of his actions – that made him feared by other inmates. He seemed to have no fear. Merely to fulfil a bet that he could get out of H-Division and into the prison hospital, he had his ears cut off by another inmate. Again, at his own request, he had his back slashed repeatedly with a razor during a prison riot.

He was eventually stabbed by another prisoner in a surprise attack and, in a bizarre display of 'warrior etiquette', actually complimented his attacker on his guile before collapsing, almost dead. He underwent emergency surgery, but lost part of his bowel and intestine.

The next morning a horrified nurse found him doing push-ups to prove that he was not cowed, with the result that the stitches in his stomach split.

Read's adult life on the outside was characterised by manic bursts of violence followed by his arrest and return to jail. In early 1978, after a few months' freedom, he tried to kidnap a county-court judge to hold as a hostage until his best friend, Jimmy Loughnan, was released from prison.

A policeman in the court said that, when Read produced a sawn-off shotgun and held it at the judge's neck, all the barristers hid under the bar table, the accused jumped in front of the jury to protect them and the judge, using a well-known four-letter word, yelled, 'Get this **** off me.'

Read was sentenced to 13 years for the kidnap attempt and was later stabbed by Loughnan in jail.

THE POLICE AGENT

When he was released in 1986, Read embarked on a campaign of terror against leading criminal figures: he demanded protection money from drug dealers, and became an underworld 'headhunter' who preyed on criminals, extorting a cut of their wealth. 'They were weak-gutted mice,' was his explanation.

Read has been portrayed as a real-life vigilante, a man who hates drug dealers, sex offenders and other lowlife members of the brutal underworld hierarchy. But he rejects any illusion of nobility being associated with his violence. To him, he says, it was business.

'Why would I rob a normal person? How much would they have in their pockets? A few dollars – and they would squeal to the law. A drug dealer can't complain and he carries thousands.'

He set up a base in Tasmania, returning regularly to Melbourne to conduct lightning raids on criminals. He stabbed, bashed and shot drug dealers, burned down the house of a major heroin seller and ran riot.

At the same time, he was regularly talking to members of the Armed Robbery Squad, giving them titbits of information on criminals he wanted out of the way. He regularly met Inspector Rod Porter at the Fawkner Club Hotel in South Yarra. The trendy crowd in the pub didn't seem to mind the heavily tattooed man with no ears.

'We were working on a particular criminal and wanted information from Read,' Inspector Porter said years later. 'He said he had a jumping-jack landmine and offered to place it in the crook's back yard to murder him. He didn't seem to understand that wasn't the way we worked.'

Police received information that several criminal syndicates, tired of being raided by Read, had offered a $50,000 contract on his life. 'There is no doubt, if he had kept going, he would have been killed,' Inspector Porter said.

Read persuaded detectives to give him a bulletproof vest for protection. He was wearing it early the next morning when he killed criminal Siam 'Sammy the Turk' Ozerkam in a Melbourne nightclub car park.

Even though it appeared a clear-cut murder case, Read argued in court that he had acted in self-defence. He was acquitted. 'Thank God for juries,' he said later.

He returned to prison in 1987, and in 1991 began to write hundreds of letters about his life, which were published in his first book, *Chopper: From the Inside*. He was released later that year and moved to Tasmania, vowing he was finished with crime.

TASMANIA

Within a few months of release, Read was a bizarre celebrity. He appeared on television around Australia and in the United States. Excerpts from his book were printed in Britain, New Zealand and South Africa. But, after six months, he was back inside, this time accused of attempting to kill a Tasmanian criminal connected with the drug scene in 1992.

Read's attempt to beat the charges was novel. He argued in court that, as a professional gunman, had he shot the man the victim would not have survived. It was an insult to his ability to suggest that he was involved, he said.

This allowed the prosecution to bring in his prior history, including reading sections of his book to the jury, in which he tells stories of using a blowtorch to torture drug dealers. The allegations in the book were matters over which he had never been charged or convicted.

The first jury failed to reach a verdict. He was convicted at his second trial, declared a dangerous criminal and given an indefinite sentence in 1992. He continued writing inside prison, smuggling out letters. Virtually all his royalties from the first four books were spent on legal fees.

In September 1995, the Supreme Court of Tasmania lifted the indefinite sentence and he was given a six-year term, which, according to Read's lawyers, should have made him eligible for parole late in 1995.

But the Tasmanian Attorney-General, Ron Cornish, disagreed, and Read was eventually released in 1998, his dangerous criminal tag overturned.

THE WOMEN

Read has received hundreds of letters from women around Australia. Many have included naked or semi-naked pictures of themselves. Others have written claiming to be victims of sex crimes and applauding Read for bashing sex offenders.

Mary Ann Hodge was in London on holiday when she first heard of Read. She was reading his first book when she got into a light-hearted argument with a group of Australians in a bar as to whether the criminal and author had any redeeming features.

'I decided to write to him when I got home and find out for myself,' the well-spoken, former private schoolgirl said later.

Ms Hodge began to visit Read and, in April 1995, they were married in Risdon Prison. The best man was Read's barrister, Michael Hodgman, QC, a former Fraser Government cabinet minister.

'I know that Mark is really a gentle man. I know that when he is released he will not break the law again,' the new Mrs Read said after the wedding. She said Read's books had given a false impression of her husband, and that he had given up crime. The couple moved to a farmhouse in Richmond, Tasmania, where they had a child, Charlie, but the marriage wasn't to last, and they split up in 2001 when Read returned to Melbourne with nothing but the clothes on his back. He has since married Margaret Casser, a friend of 30 years, in 2003.

CHOPPER INC.

Read was able to turn himself into a popular and marketable public figure while in custody in Victoria and Tasmania. He wrote manuscripts in his cell at night in his primitive handwriting, using the light from a television to illuminate the prison paper.

Criminologist Professor Paul Wilson once wrote of Read's first book, 'Nasty, vile, bloodthirsty and thoroughly revolting this book may be. But it is hard to put down. You will, however, feel the need to wash your hands after you have read it.'

Read was accepted as a member of the Australian Society of Authors in 1995. He remains unimpressed. 'Most writers and authors,' he writes, 'are bleeding hearts, greenies, commies, academic space cadets, alcoholic or junkie poofters from old-money families. They are the flotsam and jetsam of the anti-this and anti-that movement. I am a criminal and a heterosexual, I just don't fit in. Ha ha.'

He added, tongue in cheek, that some of the authors who had visited him in jail may have been seeking his advice, rather than the other way around.

'I am growing to distrust these literary scallywags. I've learned nothing from any of them. In fact, I feel it is the other way around. I am going to watch what I say to these word thieves.'

He has now turned to writing fiction, inspired by three decades of real-life violence and gunplay. As he said, 'All this stuff comes out of my head, even though I may be off it.'

His writing is crude, but tough, raw and funny, and it has the ring of authenticity.

The most frequently asked question about Read is: 'Are all the stories in the books true?' He has always maintained they are based on his life. But, characteristically, he adds that he has one favourite modern author: Helen Demidenko.

CONTENTS

1. No Tears for a Tough Guy   1

2. In a Pickle   31

3. Taking Care of Business   105

4. A Sweet Voice Calling   155

5. A Great Day for a Shoot 'em Up   213

6. A Hot Date   239

All of the characters in this book are made up, but some events
might take some scallywags down memory lane. Ha ha.

PART 1

NO TEARS FOR A TOUGH GUY

I've known a hundred good street fighters and a thousand not so good ones.
But in a lifetime I've met only a handful of freak street fighters, the best of the
best. They all died young. The freaks always do.

This is the story of one of them…

HIS name was Billy, but they called him 'Blueberry' for short. There
was no choice, really. His real name was William Hill, so it just came
naturally that he'd get 'Blueberry' while he was still a little kid.

Not that Billy stayed little for long. He grew fast, and by the time he
was 16 he stood an even six feet tall. He was a thin kid with an
abnormally thick 'bull' neck. He had long skinny arms with giant hands
hanging on the ends of them. They looked as big as dinner plates.

Billy seemed to be born with the makings of a professional boxer's
face, and soon picked up the optional extras – the classic pug nose

and the flattened top lip. His ears were slightly cauliflowered and both eyebrows were thickened and scarred. He had a rich olive complexion but his hair was light brown, almost blond, and curly. The vivid green eyes stared out into nothing. Those eyes didn't smile, even when he did. When he grinned, the missing top tooth gave him a look that was a sort of a cross between a naughty schoolboy and a grey nurse shark.

Billy didn't so much walk, as swagger. He had an arrogant air mixed with a streak of dark violence that warned anyone near him the full-of-himself look was backed up with a heap of dash. The big hands were covered in a patchwork quilt of scars. And he hadn't got them chopping up rump steak.

They used to say around Collingwood, 'If Blueberry Hill isn't a nutcase, he'll do till one comes along.'

The fact was, Blueberry was not a nutcase. He was just tough, a freak street fighter. That's why, at 15, he was arrested for killing a 27-year-old man in a fist fight.

Peter Stavros was a black belt fourth dan karate expert with a criminal record as long as your arm. Fourteen convictions for assaulting police and one conviction for rape. He never did a day's jail for any of his assaults on police.

Times had changed. Only a few years earlier anyone who raised his hands against a copper would get a flogging for his trouble and jail time to boot. Then, when he got to the Big House he would have to have to walk the 'liquorice mile' – getting whacked by a line of prison officers with truncheons. But for Stavros it was fines, fines, probation and more bloody probation. And, for some unknown reason, he served a lousy 16 months of a four-year sentence for rape.

He'd been out of jail and working as a bouncer at the London Tavern Hotel in Lennox Street, Richmond, for about nine weeks when he hit a snag. One night he told a big 15-year-old kid he couldn't come in. The skinny kid with the big neck just stood there, looking at him with a gap-toothed smile. Stavros threw a punch at the kid to back up his words. He wasn't in the mood for arguing.

The Coroner's report showed that Peter Stavros was dead from blows to the head before he hit the ground. The self-defence plea was accepted and a Supreme Court jury found Billy Hill not guilty.

Nine months later the death of Peter Stavros and the publicity it generated took a little-known teenage Richmond street fighter from being a nothing to being something. The Press went mad.

'Billy "Blueberry" Hill Not Guilty!' ... 'Fifteen-year-old Kills Karate Expert' ... 'Greek Rapist Dies At Hands Of Schoolboy.' And 'Princess Di's Amazing Broccoli Diet'. Some things never change.

For the public, it was another case of 15 minutes of fame. Like the kid who took the gun from the Melbourne docks after Freddie 'The Frog' Harrison had his head removed from his neck per medium of a shotgun blast, it was just a jolly good read for a little while. But, to the underworld, it was a lot more.

The public might not have remembered Billy Hill's name, although no one who'd seen his smile would forget it. But to every drunk, pimp, slut and would-be gangster he was a dead-set instant legend.

Every rung up or down the ladder in the underbelly of any city in Australia was always stained in blood. Stavros was considered a top-line fighter in every way. He was a national kick-boxing champion, light heavyweight division, and one of the most feared stand-up street fighters ever to come out of Brunswick. He was backed up by a 20-man mob of nutters from Albert Street, Brunswick, and their blood battles with the Coburg boys in Bell Street were famous.

Stavros was so well known that the fact he had been killed by a 15-year-old kid with a strange nickname created a sensation. How could the Press avoid paying special attention to such a kid?

Of course, anybody from the back streets of Tigerland already knew that young Blueberry Hill was a rising star in the street-fighting caper. Born and bred in Lennox Street, West Richmond, he'd been punching his way up the ladder from the age of 14, when he opened his innings by biting the nose off Reggie McKee outside the Royal Hotel in Punt Road.

Reggie may not have had a nose any more, but he still had mates. Two weeks after McKee lost his sense of smell, it was payback time. The 22-year-old street fighter from Fitzroy with the nasal problem had half a dozen boys, all armed with iron bars, to back him up. Billy spent 14 weeks in the Epworth Hospital in Erin Street. Then he discharged himself, walked into the Lord Newry Hotel in Brunswick Street, Fitzroy, pulled Reggie McKee's right eye out, then set about the bar with a broken Irish whiskey bottle. They reckon the blood was so thick on the floor they had to rip the carpet up and burn it.

Billy was a young lone wolf but since the Stavros unpleasantness he had taken to walking about Richmond with his own crew: two teenage criminals, Leigh Kinniburgh, nicknamed 'the Face', and Bobby Michieletto.

At 16, Billy Hill looked like a 20-year-old tent fighter who'd learned to fight in jail, and his two mates didn't look much better. But they could have been in nappies and be sucking on dummies and no bouncer would have blocked their way into any pub or nightclub after Stavros bit the dust. Everyone knew it was healthier to stay on the good side of the boy with the grey nurse smile.

Bobby Michieletto had tried to buy a handgun from a crew of nutters who drank in the Morning Star Hotel in Hoddle Street, Collingwood. Being young and foolish, he had paid $700 in advance, then got lashed on the deal. It was this small matter of business and honour that captured the attention of Blueberry and his two companions.

As they drank in the Citizens Park Hotel in Church Street, Billy said, 'You're a bloody mental case, Bobby – $700 up front and you get lashed. Any mug could see that lot coming.'

Bobby Mick, as his friends called him, was a fast-thinking but slow-talking kid, built like a small bull. At 16, he could bench press 280 pounds, in sets of a dozen, all day long. And he had a punch like a sledgehammer. His only trouble was, he trusted people.

Leigh Kinniburgh, on the other hand, trusted no one and was slow thinking and fast talking. He wasn't physically strong at all but tossed punches at a hundred miles per hour and used his face as a battering ram. He was totally fearless in a fight and quite psychopathic when it came to inflicting or taking injury. But, as good and as game as both kids were, they knew they were so far behind Blueberry they couldn't hear the band playing. Hence their total loyalty and devotion.

It was up to Billy what action was to be taken, and they waited for his decision on the matter. No correspondence would be entered into.

Billy was making the most of his chance to bag Bobby Mick. 'What the bloody hell made you want to do business with them rat bags from Hoddle Street? Bloody Collingwood. They are all nutcases over there,' he sneered.

Bobby Mick looked a bit shamefaced. 'Sorry,' he muttered.

'Sorry indeed,' said Leigh Kinniburgh. 'Ya stupid dago.'

'Shut up, Face,' said Billy. 'Insulting people won't get things even.' The Face returned to his beer in silence.

'Yeah, well,' said Billy. 'I don't like going out of Richmond for any reason, but needs must be met and when the devil calls and all that sort of shit. Ha ha.'

'So what are we doing?' asked Bobby Mick.

Billy looked down at his little mate as if he was a pup that had just pissed on the carpet. 'We are going to bloody Hoddle Street. That's what we are doing,' he said slowly, with exaggerated patience.

'Collingwood,' said the Face, breaking his silence. 'We'll need a fucking army. Jesus Christ. Collingwood.'

He shook his head. 'Hoddle Street. That's seen more bodies than the Western Front.'

'Well,' snapped Billy, dropping the patient routine. 'We either go to the Morning Star Hotel, or we cop it sweet. Whether it's 700 dollars or 70 cents, they lashed Bobby, and that means they lashed me. And no one lashes me.'

'Who are these turds anyhow?' said Billy.

'Skinny Kerr and his crew. Peter Thorpe, Kevin Toy and Rockin' Ronnie.'

'Rockin' Ronnie,' Leigh Kinniburgh yelped. 'Rockin' Ronnie the Nazi. Shit, he's got a crew of at least 60 backing him up alone.'

Bobby continued, 'Ray Bennett, Terry Taylor, Steve Finney, Ronnie Cox and Fatty Kane.'

Blueberry Hill looked at his mate with a look of comic horror. 'Is that all?' he asked.

'Yeah,' said Bobby Mick.

Nine men in all, thought Billy.

'How we going to handle that?' asked Leigh.

'I think,' said Billy, 'it's safe to say we'll be relying heavily on the element of surprise. Ha ha.'

'How do ya mean?' asked Leigh.

'Who owes you the money?' Billy asked Bobby Mick.

'Skinny Kerr,' said Bobby.

Billy had a think. 'He lives in Cambridge Street near the Collingwood State School,' he said after a while. 'So let's not bother with the pub, let's just go and see him at his joint.'

Leigh smiled. He was relieved. 'Can I wear a mask?' he asked.

'I think we'd all better,' Billy said.

They didn't know that what was to take place would haunt them all.

Skinny Kerr lived with his mother in a little single-fronted, two-bedroom, brick workman's cottage, built in the last century. Cambridge Street was an old bit of Collingwood, and at night it was a very dark part of town.

When Mrs Kerr answered her front door at 9.30 at night, the fist that hit her on the chin put her to sleep for a full three weeks. It wasn't a full coma but near enough to it.

Skinny was watching TV with a pie in one hand and a bottle of beer in the other. He heard his mother hit the floor and turned to look down the dark hallway as three masked men came down it.

Skinny was as hard as nails, a tough hood in his late twenties. He smashed his beer bottle over his own skull as he rose to his feet screaming with rage. He swung a savage blow into the face of Bobby Mick as Billy Hill rained blows down on him. Skinny went down. Leigh Kinniburgh put the slipper in and the fun started. Bobby Mick held his bleeding face in pain and rage and helped the other two as they kicked and kicked and kicked the unconscious body. After about three minutes Billy was getting tired and pulled up. Skinny didn't move. He couldn't. He was quite dead.

'Search him and go through the house,' Billy ordered.

Skinny was soaking wet from neck to knee in his own blood and the $1,200 he had in his pockets was also red and wet. The boots Leigh 'the Face' had been wearing had dug into Skinny's chest and into his heart and lungs. They had literally kicked holes in him. Billy ransacked his mother's bedroom and found cash to the tune of $2,200 and jewellery.

Bobby located a bag full of guns in Skinny's room. Two sawn-off double-barrel shotguns and cartridges, and six handguns with boxes of ammo. Leigh removed the rings and personal jewellery from the sleeping body of Mrs Kerr and the three walked out.

They took their masks off and walked through the night back to Elizabeth Street, Richmond, to Bobby Mick's place. His Italian mother went crazy when she saw the damage to his face and she rushed him to the Epworth Hospital in Erin Street, the Accident and Emergency Unit.

Billy took all the loot and gave Leigh $200 and sent him home.

'Meet me at the corner of Church and Victoria tomorrow,' he said. 'We'll whack this lot up then.'

'But I want to check it all out.'

'That $200 comes out of your whack.'

Leigh wasn't pleased, but he wouldn't question Blueberry Hill, let alone defy him.

Billy Hill wasn't too interested in firearms, but he wanted to keep them out of the hands of his two friends. Billy was a fist fighter, pure and simple. But he knew Bobby Mick and Leigh Kinniburgh both wanted to step up the criminal ladder into the deadly world of the gunnie.

They were both a bit mad, and if they got armed up to the eyeballs they would grow away from him and either run headlong to a small box in the graveyard, or a slightly larger one in Pentridge. Billy decided to hide the guns. They could be of great use when needed, but carting loaded guns on you all the time was a bit out of the league of a 16-year-old, no matter how tough he was. Anyway, Billy didn't like them, and didn't trust people who carried them so he hid them away. He counted out the money. There was $3,200. He hid the jewellery; he knew it could be traced. Then he kissed his Auntie Muriel good night and went to bed.

Every night before he went to sleep in his bedroom in his auntie's place on Lennox Street, he would say a little prayer. His late mother had taught him this prayer. She had died when he was ten years old. He'd never met his dad.

Billy closed his eyes and mumbled the words he'd recited every night that he could remember. 'And now I lay me down to sleep, I pray the Lord my soul to keep, and if I should die before I wake, I pray the Lord my soul to take. Amen. Good night, Mum, wherever you are.'

• • •

The homicide squad couldn't operate a three-seated shithouse without getting one of the pans blocked up, it seemed to a lot of people who took an interest in the violent end of Skinny Kerr. It had been six months since the murder, and Blueberry Hill had been arrested, questioned and let go five-times.

The Press was screaming. It made front page every time he was taken in and let go.

Keith Kerr wasn't impressed. He was Skinny's uncle and he was sitting in the lounge of his home in Lithgow Street, Abbotsford, talking to Peter Thorpe and Kevin Toy.

'My bloody nephew gets his heart and lungs kicked out his arsehole, my sister-in-law is nearly turned into a vegetable and Blueberry Hill and his mates are laughing,' he spat. 'It's even-up time.'

Peter Thorpe nodded. Kevin Toy sat quietly. He looked thoughtful.

'He's got a birthday party coming up in about a week. The fourth of November. He'll be 17,' he said.

Keith Kerr shook his head. 'Seventeen years old. Holy hell, he's a freak. Best street fighter in Richmond at 17 years old — it's bloody hard to credit.'

'Yeah,' said Peter Thorpe. 'Once in 20 years one comes along, rare as hen's teeth. Goodfellow was the same, he could flog half of Melbourne by the time he was 16 years old. Harris Morrison, Kingdom West, Kane. They were all freaks.'

'Ya right,' said Kevin. 'And they're all dead.'

'Yeah, well,' said old Keith Kerr. 'We may have to give Billy Blueberry a bit of a helping hand, fate wise.'

'Happiness for me,' said Blueberry Hill to Bobby Mick, 'would be to own a thousand-room hotel and to find Chief Inspector Graeme Westlock dead in every room. Ha ha. The bugger's been picking on me ever since Stavros. It's not fair.'

'Yeah,' said Bobby Mick. He wasn't big on conversation. Especially since his face had been cut up with Skinny Kerr's beer bottle. The scars didn't do a lot for Bobby's good looks, or his good nature, not that he had started out with much of either.

The two tough teenagers were standing in the piano bar of the Chevron Night Club on St Kilda Road. It was 4.30 am on a Sunday morning. They were about to finish up and go and meet Leigh Kinniburgh at the Cadillac Bar in Carlton when the shooting started.

Blueberry Hill didn't notice Bobby Mick fall dead to the floor. All he felt was a heavy punch and a red-hot pain in his neck. He turned, and like some insane wild machine started swinging sledgehammer punches into the head of the man carrying the gun. Peter Thorpe fired one more wild shot into the darkness as he fell to the floor, dying.

Then Billy started to kick the bouncers at the club as they stepped in and tried to restrain him. He was pissing blood from a .38 bullet wound to the neck, but they found themselves facing an onslaught of punches that rendered two bouncers unconscious and two others running for their lives.

The self-defence laws are pretty clear. A man who kills another man with his fists after being shot in the neck is pretty hard to prosecute successfully. But Chief Inspector Graeme Westlock was most happy to formally charge Blueberry Hill with the murder of Peter Thorpe as Hill lay in bed at the Alfred Hospital, conveniently located behind the Chevron Night Club.

A week later, before Billy checked out of hospital, the Director of Public Prosecutions dropped the case against him. A gunman murders an unarmed youth, then tries to kill a second, but gets punched to death, and the police charge the man who was defending his life after being shot in the neck. It seemed to some in Richmond that the police and newspaper vendetta against Blueberry Hill had taken on comic proportions.

Mr Mario Bonnanno QC, Director of Public Prosecutions, personally went to visit Billy Hill in hospital to tell him that the murder charge was no more. The Press went crazy.

'Blueberry Hill Beats It' ... 'Murder Charges Dropped' ... 'Teenage Tough Guy Gets Off Again.'

When Billy Hill walked out of hospital he was 17 years old. It was 17 November. He had missed his birthday party, but Leigh Kinniburgh and the Richmond boys had arranged a big piss-up at the French Knickers Hotel at the corner of Church Street and Victoria Street, Richmond. The joint was Billy's favourite hangout.

You don't have to be told. The Press found out about it and took a hidden camera into the hotel to film Blueberry drinking with well-known Richmond criminals, professional boxers, football players, gangsters and gunnies, strippers and prostitutes.

The next day the morning paper carried photos and a headline that ran 'Birthday Thrill For Blueberry Hill'. That was all right, but the story underneath it went on to condemn local authorities for allowing Billy Hill to indulge in underage drinking. Such criticism was not considered fair play in Richmond social circles, but what could a poor boy do but cop it sweet.

'I mean to say,' said Billy's Auntie Muriel, 'if they can't hand ya for murder, Billy, ya gotta expect 'em to try and pinch ya for underage drinking. Ha ha.'

Billy Hill sat at the kitchen table and spread a lavish helping of marmalade on to his morning toast – the first of a dozen slices he knocked off every day. Tea and marmalade on toast was Billy's breakfast routine. Meanwhile, he read the morning paper and that big gap-toothed smile slid across his dial.

'It must be a slow news day, Auntie M,' he snorted. 'Underage drinking indeed. They gotta be kidding. Too young to drink. What a lot of flap doodle. I'm not too young to get pinched on murders when I'm only defending me bloody self.'

'Too bloody right,' said his Auntie Muriel. 'That's perfectly correct, Billy.' She was very supportive of her favourite boy.

Muriel Hill was devoted to her nephew and would not hear a bad word said about him. How dare the police and Press pick on a young innocent lad. It was a bloody disgrace. She would complain to the neighbours.

Muriel was a well-built, attractive 32-year-old woman. She had the same rich dark olive complexion as Billy, the same light-brown, almost blonde hair and the same vivid green eyes. She was the baby sister of William Hill, Billy's dad, the dad Billy had never ever known because he had vanished before Billy was born.

Muriel was not only his auntie but also his late mother's best friend. When Jeanie Hill died, Muriel was delighted to take charge of the little boy. Muriel worked in a flower shop in one of Richmond's best-known streets, but she knew her way around. She was a former prostitute and stripper but had given it all up to care for young Billy. She'd gone from fucking to plucking and from horns to thorns.

What the Tax Department didn't know was that Muriel Hill actually owned the florist's shop that she supposedly only worked for. Muriel was no fool. She had inherited two houses in Lennox Street and had bought two more houses as well as the shop. But no one knew this, not even Billy.

She had worked for eight years as a high-paid stripper and call girl before giving the game away to look after young Billy when she was 25. And unlike most other working girls she'd looked after her money, and now it was looking after her. And Billy.

She truly loved young Billy and it was fair to say Blueberry Hill loved his Auntie M more than anybody else in the world, now that his mum had gone. Not that it was much of a contest. Billy didn't like many people.

'You should eat more than marmalade on toast, Billy,' she told him.

'But I like marmalade on toast,' said Billy.

'You should let me cook you ham and eggs,' said Auntie M. 'Your father always liked me to cook him ham and eggs.'

'Well,' said Billy with a sneer, 'I hope that wherever that cocksucker is he is enjoying his ham and eggs. As for me, I like marmalade.'

'I'm sorry,' said Auntie M, frightened that she had incurred his wrath. 'I didn't mean to upset you. I'm sorry Billy.'

Blueberry Hill reached over and gave his auntie a big marmalade-covered kiss on the mouth. She giggled, happy that he was no longer cross at her mention of the long-vanished father and brother.

Billy didn't go outside the front door until about midday. He had a luncheon appointment with his la-di-dah lady lawyer at Rhubarb's Bar and Restaurant in Gertrude Street, Fitzroy.

Anita Von Bibra had been with him since the Stavros fiasco and their relationship had come along very nicely since then. There was trouble coming his way and a pre-bloodshed legal chat with Madam Von Bibra was a must. The lunchtime restaurant meeting in the courtyard at Rhubarb's had become a regular event.

Anita Von Bibra was a wealthy, south-of-the-river socialite barrister, who lived with her property developer husband in a $3.5-million mansion in South Yarra. At least, that was what they'd paid for it in the property boom in the 1980s, when every yuppie in town used lines of credit the way they used lines of coke. By the time the 1990s came around, the Von Bibra shack was probably only worth a flat $3 million. Life can be cruel like that, but it seemed to Billy that Anita was bearing up bravely.

She cruised about town in a Mercedes sports coupe worth 100 grand. She was old enough to be Billy's mother, but he was only 17 and she was very well preserved, and looked thirty-something. She was a neat, petite, elegant lady with long hair dyed jet black, big sparkling dark eyes and a wide smile that gave some people ideas when they looked at her lips.

Anita had once been a model, and still had the body and legs to prove it. She was only five feet nothing tall, hence the high heels that added at least four to five inches to her height. She always wore a well-cut suit with the shortest skirts she could get away with cut tight around a wiggle of an arse that looked like two apples tied in a silk scarf.

Her only drawback was a shrill high-pitched squeal of a voice that could travel across a courtroom and burst the ear drums of an already half-deaf judge. Even when she whispered her voice could travel 100 metres on a windy day. She was quite famous in legal and criminal circles for her outrageous conduct, and the Press loved to hate her.

Anita's running public battle with the Director of Public Prosecutions had caught the attention of the national media after she screamed at him from the steps of the Melbourne Supreme Court, 'Hey, Mario, if I'd sucked the Attorney General off at the last law-society dinner, I'd be a QC too, ya dog.' She was a toff with a knockabout sense of humour and a painter and docker's vocabulary.

One of her best-known cases had involved defending a notorious conman. The police crown witness was a well-known Italian criminal. Anita was claiming that the crown witness had stolen her client's cheque book. In her summing up to the jury, she made one of the outrageous throwaway remarks that had captured the attention of the national media a few times before.

'Well, ladies and gentlemen,' she said, 'if this case has taught us anything, it is that none of us can ever trust a dago with our cheque book.'

She had been married three times and made a small fortune on each divorce. Why she bothered defending every psychopath from Richmond to Collingwood was a mystery. She certainly didn't do it for the money. The truth was Anita was an armchair left-winger – and anyone who knew her could tell she got a bit of a thrill dealing with young tearaways like Billy Hill. She couldn't help going for that James Dean rebel without a cause stuff: tattoos, muscles, scars and the whiff of violence.

'If I don't fight for the little Aussie battler, who will?' she'd scream at the Press and anybody else who'd listen.

The trouble was, obviously, that Anita's idea of the little Aussie battler was every head-banging, gun-toting psychopath and raving mental case in Melbourne. Oh, and Billy Hill. Except that he was different. He didn't carry guns.

Billy walked into the restaurant and out into the courtyard at about 12.30 pm. Anita called out to him, 'Billy! Here I am.' It was a fair bet they heard her in the next suburb.

Her diamond rings flashed and glittered in the sunlight as she waved her hand. Billy walked over and sat down.

'What?' Anita pouted like a bad soapie actress. 'No kiss hello?'

Billy reached over and kissed his lawyer on the cheek. Anita didn't invite all her clients to lunch, very few of them in fact, but she had a genuine soft spot for Blueberry Hill. Lunch proceeded and Anita's legal advice flowed freely.

'Billy, as long as they hit you first or they use a weapon and you use your fists, we can plead self-defence till the cows come home and win hands down every time. But we have to be able to show we were acting in the defence of our own life or the life of another. If we do that, we can kill the Queen of England and beat the blue.'

Billy looked thoughtful. 'I think I've got some shit coming up with old Keith Kerr and Kevin Toy and that lot from Collingwood,' he said.

'Hmmm,' Anita mused. 'The ghosts of Christmases past and all that. Skinny Kerr and his mother come back to haunt you?'

Billy nodded. 'Yeah,' he said. 'That's what that shit in the Chevron was all about.'

'I knew that,' she answered. 'Strangely enough, I defended Peter Thorpe on a rape blue ten years ago. I spent three months telling a jury he was innocent. We won the case. I took him back to my chambers for a celebratory drink and he belted me in the mouth, bent me over my office desk and committed a foul rudeness upon my person.

'What could I do? I'd just spent three months telling the world he was innocent, and there were no witnesses. You're the first person I've confessed that to, Billy. And I'm bloody overjoyed to know the low dog is dead.'

For once, Billy looked shocked. 'Fair dinkum, Anita' he said, his voice full of genuine sympathy and concern.

Anita took the boy's hand, touched. 'Not to worry, Billy,' she said with a wink. 'Being up-ended over the office desk wasn't the point. The bloody ingratitude of the low bastard, that's what hurt me. He certainly had a different idea of how to handle a hand-up brief.'

Billy was quite shocked at some of the remarks Anita made. In matters sexual Billy was a total innocent. Anita was a woman of the world, and some of the things she said made him blush red. She took a certain delight in teasing the lad, sitting with her legs crossed in front of him with her short skirt sliding around and rippling in the breeze, accidentally on purpose giving him a gander at the upper thighs that had made Anita a hot item in the bikini-modelling caper when she was at law school.

Billy was very correct where the ladies were concerned. He might have been a bare-knuckle killer, but Anita's well-honed instincts told her he was a virgin. The prospect of correcting that small matter for him filled her with a certain evil delight. It was a little fantasy she indulged in after the third drink. Which is one of the reasons alcohol is rather popular, even if not many people would own up to it. But

Anita's plans for a little extra-curricular tutoring in client–lawyer liaison would have to wait. Billy had other things on his mind. He went back to Richmond with his head buzzing with plans, as well as a few belts of champagne Anita had pushed at him. Between that and Anita's mini-skirt, it had been a very good lunch indeed.

'We gotta hit them before they get us,' Leigh Kinniburgh said.

Billy didn't say anything straight away. He was thinking.

The pair had decided to avoid regular drinking haunts like the French Knickers Hotel and had taken to drinking at the Vine Hotel in Bridge Road and Squizzy Taylor's Pub in Gertrude Street, Fitzroy.

Blueberry Hill had let the Face carry a handgun. Two, in fact: a .38-calibre automatic and a sawn-off double-barrel shotgun. Leigh Kinniburgh walked about with the handgun on him, and saw himself as Blueberry Hill's personal bodyguard.

Billy, on the other hand, was a realist. He saw the Face as a mental case with a loaded gun.

Leigh was rattling on about the coming blue. He was half nervous and half bloodthirsty, which meant he was as toey as a broken sandal. 'Needs must when the devil drives. We gotta attack the bloody Morning Star and get in first,' he said for the third time in two minutes.

'Anita said as long as I act in self-defence she can get me out of anything,' Billy said.

'That old nympho,' laughed Leigh, putting a hole in his manners. 'She got my old man out of a shooting charge 15 years ago. Shit, I was two or three years old and she was 25 or 30 then, I reckon.'

Billy scowled. 'Anita Von Bibra is a very lovely lady and I'll break the jaw of any man who speaks ill of her,' he grated. He had a thing about her the way some blokes in the boob were bent about Ita Buttrose.

Leigh back-pedalled at 100 miles an hour. He was no fool. 'Oh, sorry, Billy. I didn't say she wasn't a nice lady – just a bit long in the tooth, that's all.'

Billy looked down at Leigh. 'Long in the tooth, eh? You'll have no teeth if ya keep going. OK?'

'Sorry, Billy,' Leigh said meekly.

'Anyway,' said Blueberry, trying to look dignified, 'as I was saying, as long as we can claim self-defence we can beat any blue in the book.'

'Yeah, well,' said Leigh. But he was a bit drunk and he couldn't help tossing in a smartarse remark. 'I guess we can always attack 'em with Anita's walking stick …'

Leigh didn't see the punch. And he didn't feel it. So, when he woke up in the back of an ambulance, he didn't remember it. All he knew was that his .38-calibre handgun and all his top teeth were missing. Then he fainted again.

Billy, meanwhile, had decided to face the music alone and unarmed. One man against a small army. Of course, he'd swear that he was the victim of a gang attack, thus maintaining his self-defence. He knew that Leigh Kinniburgh was in hospital falling in and out of a coma, and he felt a bit concerned and hoped he hadn't hit Leigh too hard. Shit, one left hook to the top teeth shouldn't cause that much damage.

Leigh Kinniburgh must have a paper-thin skull. Bloody pansy. Poor little Bobby Mick, he thought. Billy really missed Bobby Mick. Why couldn't it have been Leigh instead of poor Bobby? He was getting angry again, thinking about it. These turds in Collingwood had to be dealt with, and the sooner the bloody better.

Billy rang Anita at home and warned her he could be facing arrest within the next few hours. That's if he was lucky. Otherwise he would be in hospital, or dead.

Anita was what lawyers and police describe as 'gravely concerned'. In this case, for her favourite client's skin. Apart from anything else, she hadn't had a chance to have her wicked way with him yet.

'Please don't do anything rash, Billy,' she pleaded. 'As your lawyer, I must advise you against rash action.'

'But if they attack me, Anita, I can act in self-defence, can't I?' Billy asked.

'Of course, darling,' she cooed in the sort of voice that $200 an hour buys. 'Act in self-defence only and all will be well.'

Billy wasn't a brilliant conversationalist at the best of times. And right now he was preoccupied. 'OK,' he said woodenly. 'Thanks, Anita.'

'Be careful, Billy,' Anita said, then hung up.

She sat on the end of her bed, wondering what Billy Blueberry was up to. She doubted he would be careful. It wasn't in him.

Melanie Wells lived next door to Billy Hill in Lennox Street. She was heading out her front door the same time Billy was walking out of his. She stopped to look at him. He was her hero. She had secretly loved Blueberry Hill since she was a little girl. She watched him kiss his Auntie M on the cheek and then closed the door.

'Hi ya, Mel,' said Billy.

'Hi ya, Billy' said the starstruck 15-year-old.

'Where are you off to all dressed up this time of night?' asked Billy. 'Ya look good enough to eat.'

Melanie only wished he meant it. She'd sit on his face at a moment's notice, but Billy treated her like a baby sister, always polite, thoughtful, kind, protective and so very politically correct, much to the girl's annoyance.

'I'm going to the end-of-year dance at school,' she said. 'Where are you going, Billy?'

'Ah,' said Billy with a cheeky grin, 'you don't want to know. Ha ha.'

'Ya gonna blue them dogs in Hoddle Street?' she asked.

'How did you know about that?' asked Billy, surprised that his plans were being broadcast all over the neighbourhood.

'Shit,' said Melanie, 'every man and his dog knows ya gonna blue the Hoddle Street crew.'

'Yeah,' said Billy, winking mysteriously. 'But no one knows when, hey, kid?'

Melanie wasn't so smart after all.

'Ya wanna come to the dance with me, Billy?' she wheedled in her cutest little voice.

Blueberry laughed. 'I'd look good dancing at the Richmond Ladies College,' he said.

'Nah, Billy. You'd be OK, you'd be with me.'

Billy didn't want to offend his cheeky hot-pants little neighbour. 'Maybe I'll pop in later tonight,' he said. 'What time does it go till?'

'Midnight,' she said.

'OK, cheeky chops, maybe later. I gotta go and do something now.'

'OK, Billy.' She was excited. The prospect of Blueberry Hill showing up at her school and impressing hell out of all her school chums filled her with a delicious anticipation. 'See ya later, Billy,' she purred. She'd seen them do it on the soaps a million times.

'Yeah, see ya, Titch,' said Billy. Such a smooth-talking bastard.

Melanie pouted. I wish Billy wouldn't call me Titch, she thought to herself, as she pushed her chest out to show him that she was anything but a titch these days. But Billy was blind to her ample charms. He put his giant hand on the top of her head and ruffled up her hair, then turned and walked away.

God, what a fantastic bloke, she thought to herself. He was everything she ever wanted and he didn't even know she was alive. Well, he did, but not in the way she dreamed of, and that cute little-boy habit Billy had of ruffling up her hair made her feel like the fish John West rejected with all the goodies to go with it. But, instead of Billy taking her in his strong arms and holding her close and kissing her, all he did was call her Titch and ruffle her hair.

Melanie sighed, then turned and headed off towards Gleadell Street and the dance. 'This will be fun,' she groaned to herself. Six hundred schoolgirls all dancing together, no boys allowed. It will be like a fish market by the end of the night.

Rockin' Ronnie MacSladdon, Ray Bennett, Terry Taylor, Steve Finney, Ronnie Cox, Fatty Kane and Kevin Toy put their drinks down and walked out of the Morning Star Hotel. The night was still a pup and they were out to make the most of it. They started walking down Hoddle Street.

They were on their way to meet Keith Kerr at the Clifton Hill Hotel in Queens Parade. There was a full moon out and the night was clear and warm. Everyone was in high spirits. Plans had been set in place to even up on Blueberry Hill once and for all as a payback for Skinny Kerr and Peter Thorpe. He'd be dead in the next 24 hours — if all went well.

Old Keith had it all in hand. His motto was that no one went against Collingwood and lived, no matter how good they could fight … That's why God invented guns.

Ray Bennett was the first to notice him get out of the car. He couldn't believe it. 'Hey, boys, cop a look at this,' he hissed to his mates.

'Jesus,' said Kevin Toy, who had a remarkable grasp of the obvious. 'It's Blueberry Hill.'

Billy had caught a lift with old 'Chang' Heywood, a local Richmond knockabout. Chang was always willing and ready to drive Billy any place he wanted to go in his old 1967 Hillman Arrow.

Billy walked straight across Hoddle Street and towards the group. Even though there were seven of them, the whole crew went into a state of shock.

'He's not going to fight us all, is he?' whispered Rockin' Ronnie, as if he suspected that's exactly what was going to happen.

Terry Taylor pulled out a small handgun.

'Put it away,' snapped Kevin Toy. 'We can take him. Seven against one, for God's sake.'

'Bullshit,' yelled Taylor, who didn't give a shit about the odds. 'Kill the bastard.'

He aimed the little .32-calibre revolver at Billy Hill and pulled the trigger. The first two shots missed, and Billy just kept walking towards them, as cool as you like. The third shot clipped his cheekbone but still he kept coming. The fourth slug hit him in the upper right side of the chest and the fifth went wild. The piece only held five shots.

They were all gone, but Billy wasn't. He was still coming straight at them.

Now the crew was really worried. 'What now?' yelled Ronnie MacSladdon.

'Let's get him,' said Kevin Toy.

The gang charged forward towards Billy Hill. Their mistake was in trying to take on a freak on his own terms. Blueberry smiled like a grey nurse in a school of tuna. As the gang reached him, Billy's fists swung like Jack O'Toole swinging his axe on *World of Sport*, and they were about as deadly.

Kevin Toy hit the ground first, out cold with a broken jaw and cheekbone, then cracked his skull on the footpath.

Then there were six.

Rockin' Ronnie ran a knife into Billy's guts but a left hand that would have dropped a bullock shattered his skull. MacSladdon fell down dead. Billy could kill with either hand once he got speed up.

Then there were five.

Ronnie Cox grabbed Billy from behind and gouged his left eyeball, while Fatty Kane moved in with a broken bottle, cutting Billy's face to ribbons. Steve Finney stabbed Billy in the chest with another broken bottle, but it was a mistake. Billy reached out and put his right hand around Finney's neck and squeezed, and caught Fatty Kane on the chin with a left hook. Fatty lost interest, and went to sleep on the spot.

Then there were three. Billy still had Steve Finney's now unconscious body, flopping around like a rag doll in a washing machine.

Terry Taylor and Ray Bennett had been standing back. Billy spun around, still holding Finney by the neck, and smashed Ronnie Cox three crashing blows to the skull with his left hand. Ronnie was no different from anyone else; he went to the ground, and stayed there.

Then there were two.

Billy looked down and realised that Steve Finney was dead. He'd strangled him. Then he looked at Terry Taylor and Ray Bennett and smiled. Bennett froze, but Taylor turned and ran.

Billy started to laugh then spat blood into the face of a now crying Ray Bennett. He fell to his knees and begged, 'I'm sorry, Billy. Don't hit me! Don't hit me. Please, Billy, please don't hit me.'

A crowd of onlookers had gathered, and Billy knew he'd won in front of witnesses. Ray Bennett was the luckiest man in Melbourne.

Billy Blueberry turned and staggered back to Chang's old car and got in. Old Chang took off.

'Jesus, Billy, you fuckin' killed 'em,' he babbled. 'You beat 'em all. God, I never seen nothin' like it. Billy, you're a fucking legend. You'll go down in history.'

Billy coughed up blood.

'Hell, Billy, you're pissin' blood. You're fuckin' dying. Don't die on me, kid, don't die. Hang on, I'll get you to hospital, hang on.' Poor old Chang was panicking, and you couldn't blame him.

'Nah,' said Billy. 'Forget the hospital, take me to Gleadell Street.'

'What are ya talking about, kid?' Chang yelled over the howl of the motor and the whine in the gearbox. He was wringing the revs out of the old Hillman, trying to get his mate to the hospital.

'I promised a little girl I'd take her to a dance,' said Billy with what passed for a smile. It wasn't a good look. His face was covered in blood already, and there was plenty more where that was coming from.

'Kid,' said Chang, 'you're dying and you need help.'

'Just get me to the dance on time,' said Billy with a laugh that made an ominous rattle in his chest. It was filling with blood. 'The girls' school. C'mon, ya silly old bugger. Drive.'

Chang put his foot down to the metal even harder and got the old Hillman Arrow up to its top speed of 60 mph. Billy was holding his guts and chest. He knew he didn't have long to go, but he didn't want his Auntie M to see him like this and he didn't know where to go. Why not go to the dance? He smiled to himself. Titch would be glad to see him.

Chang pulled his old car up outside the college. Billy opened the door and stumbled out. Chang took off, heading for Lennox Street to tell Billy's Auntie Muriel. She had to be told.

Billy walked into the school ground, trying to keep the stagger out of his gait. A bunch of girls were standing in a group outside having a sneaky smoke.

'Hey, it's Blueberry Hill,' said one girl. Then she looked harder and yelped, 'God, look at him, he's bleeding.'

'He's bleeding to death,' said another.

'Get Titch,' Billy ordered. His voice was rattly from the blood in his throat.

'Who?' asked one of the girls.

'Melanie Wells,' Billy croaked. He was trying to yell.

Two girls ran inside as Billy fell to his knees, then slumped backwards. His eyes went up towards the big full moon. It was a nice night to die, he thought. Warm summer's night. Full moon. Only he was starting to feel a bit cold.

Melanie came out. 'Billy,' she shrieked.

She ran to him and knelt down and held his head in her hands. He lifted himself up and rested his head in her lap. The blood got on her party dress.

'Hi ya, Titch,' he said. 'I won the blue. Ya should have seen it.'

The music had stopped and the schoolyard was filling up with schoolgirls, all either crying or whispering the name 'Blueberry Hill'. They all knew he was dying.

Teachers called the police and the ambulance. Billy coughed up more blood and Melanie tried to wipe his bleeding face with her little lace hanky.

'Don't die, Billy, the ambulance is coming,' she whispered.

'Nah, Titch. I'm dead,' said Billy.

'Don't say that, Billy. No one can kill you. Ya can't die, please, Billy. Don't die, please, Billy. Don't die.'

The girl was sobbing. She held her face to his. 'Don't die, Billy, please don't die,' she recited over and over.

Billy coughed and started to recite the prayer his mother had taught him. 'And now I lay me down to sleep,' he mumbled.

'No, Billy, stop it!' screamed the girl. Her face was wet with tears.

But Billy kept going. He was gasping now. 'I pray the Lord my soul to keep, and if I should die before I wake ...'

'I love you, Billy,' cried Melanie. 'I love you.'

'I pray the Lord my soul to take,' he whispered.

Melanie shook Billy's head. 'Wake up, Billy. Don't die.'

Blueberry Hill opened his one good eye, his right eye, and looked up at the moon. Then he opened his left eye.

'Mum, is that you, Mum?' he said softly.

Then he closed his eyes. He was dead.

Chief Inspector Graeme Westlock pulled his car up and got out. The phone call he received from Anita Von Bibra sent him to the Morning Star Hotel. He had just left the carnage in Hoddle Street. Three men dead, two in hospital. Chang Heywood under arrest at Richmond Police Station. The copper couldn't believe that Billy had been driven to a girls' school instead of a hospital.

He got out and walked through the crowd of schoolgirls to where Billy was lying dead.

'Ahh, Billy,' said Westlock, who was a hardnosed bastard. 'Not a bad way to die, kid. Lying in the moonlight surrounded by a couple of hundred wobbly-bottomed schoolgirls. Yeah, kid, ya always were a show-off.'

Melanie put Billy's head on the ground and got to her feet. 'Piss off, you bastard. Go on, piss off.'

The girls all began to yell. 'Go on, ya dog, piss off.'

Most of them were crying. Melanie ran forward and began to punch the big policeman, crying, 'Go away, go away.'

Graeme Westlock held the girl and his mood softened. 'C'mon, now, sweetheart, stop all this fuss. C'mon, you lot, cut all this bloody nonsense out.' Then he looked down at young Melanie. 'C'mon, sweetheart. Dry them eyes. That's Blueberry bloody Hill down there and, whatever else he was, he was a tough bastard and ya know what they say ... no tears for a tough guy.'

PART 2

IN A PICKLE

RUSSIAN Suzi was a tall, well-built lady with a beautiful but unfriendly face. She was as graceful as a panther, and about as friendly, unless there was money involved. Her charm was strictly by the hour.

Suzi had an air of arrogance. She was good-looking but she knew it, and she was quite happy to make sure you knew that she knew it. She was what some would call a female Venus Flytrap. Everything about her – the way she looked, acted, moved, walked, talked and teased – was aimed at attracting and trapping men. Her whole personality was sexual. She was a sex-show girl and took great personal pride in the fact that she was greatly in demand.

She knew that as long as men were men and they liked to look she would only ever see a dole office from the outside, and then only from a chauffeur-driven limo.

It hadn't always been that way. As a kid, Suzi had been the school fat girl, nothing more than a great mass of wobbling butter in a school tunic. But, like a lot of fat girls, she had a wonderful face. In Suzi's case, a wonderful sexy face sitting above the biggest set of boobs any young girl ever had to lug about. But, unlike other fat girls, Suzi didn't shy away from the boys, nor did her weight stand in her way or embarrass her. She had an arrogant, cheeky manner even then.

She was 13 years old and on her way to school in Collingwood when a gang of schoolboys, aged from 14 to 16, waylaid her and proceeded to call her 'Fatty'. She stopped and looked at them. There were nine of them. She looked at her watch, then stared at an evil-eyed young psycho, about 14 years old, who appeared to be the head of the crew.

'OK, Mickey, I tell ya what,' she said. 'I reckon I could gobble you all off in half an hour flat.' She always had a healthy appetite.

Mickey Van Gogh was a bit shocked at this. Then he looked at the fat girl's face. Jeez, she had a really beautiful, sexy face.

Suzi started to run her tongue around her lips. 'C'mon, dickhead. Make up ya mind.'

Mickey lashed a backhander across the fat girl's face that stung her cheek and made her ears ring. She tasted blood inside her mouth. But instead of crying she gave him a look that would blister the paint on a Kingswood at 50 feet, defying him to do it again.

'Do you want ya doodle sucked or don't ya, you fucking nutcase?' she snapped. She was such a romantic.

Mickey Van Gogh and his mates started laughing. This Suzi chick was new in the Collingwood area, but they could see she'd fit in, no problem at all. They nicknamed her Russian Suzi and, yes, she did handle the nine of them in half an hour. And no one ever, ever, ever called her Fatty again.

Suzanna Polanchoishnavich was indeed Russian, hence the nickname. She sat quietly at the bar of the Caballero Night Club. It was 2 pm on a quiet Monday afternoon. She lived in one of the flats on the third storey of the building that housed the club.

Suzi was no longer a little fat girl but a big, tall, beautiful woman. It was hard to pick her age. Her brown hair was bleached so blonde it was almost white, and her green-blue eyes looked as if they had seen a thousand years of life, the way even the classiest whore's eyes always do.

Having been fat as a kid, she was determined never to go down the lardarse track again. She took up weight-lifting, and what had once jiggled now rippled.

She said the hours in the gym were for her dancing, but what she was really after was power. The power that comes from being stronger than any other woman. The power from sexiness, which would make men obey her. Pussy power.

She looked so good she could have been 18. No one knew her age and no one was game to ask.

Suzi had just finished an hour lifting weights in the club's gym. She was going to take a sauna but, as was her habit, she liked to knock off at least half a bottle of straight vodka with a full salami sausage sliced thinly, along with a small jar of Mexican hot chillies and a jar of olives. It seemed to cover all the food groups.

This and reading the morning paper was her daily routine. Sunday night had been a big one. She had danced from 9 pm Sunday night until 4 am Monday morning. She didn't do tricks unless it was for big dough, but another dancer, Kerry Griffin, had taken on more than she could chew again, and that had nearly caused a riot.

Kerry had seven guys in one of the dressing rooms all on her own. Anyway, to cut a long story short, Suzi pulled three of them out to take some of the strain and then got stuck with servicing all three for no money at all as they reckoned they had already paid Kerry – and Kerry, true to form, hadn't actually collected any money at all. Meaning that Suzi got double deckered with one to follow for nothing. And all silly Kerry said was, 'Thanks, Sally.'

Needless to say, being screwed for no money to help someone who couldn't even remember your right name was not Suzi's idea of a good time, let alone professional etiquette.

Suzi was very big on etiquette. She decided to complain to the boss yet again about Kerry. The big nutcase went through the mugs like a vacuum cleaner on roller skates – and still came out broke in the morning.

Kerry was a scatterbrained hard case. She'd threaten to punch ya lipstick up ya bum if you didn't lend her a thousand bucks – then forget your bloody name ten minutes later. She had to go. This was the conclusion Russian Suzi had come to over her newspaper and her third glass of vodka. She was a natural at the tough business decisions.

She made Kerry Packer look like Mahatma Gandhi.

Kerry Griffin walked down the stairs from her small flat above. 'Hi ya, Simone,' she said to Suzi, who had long since given up trying to correct Kerry's bad memory.

'Someone pinched all my money,' said Kerry. 'Can I snip you for $500?'

'No problem,' said Suzi. 'I'll get it for ya after I've had my sauna.'

'Thanks,' said Kerry.

Suzi had learned this trick a while ago. She smiled to herself, willing to bet Kerry would forget she'd put the bite on her, and snip someone else for the dough.

Tashliene and Samantha came down the stairs, then Angela. Three of the four Bennett sisters.

Tashliene, Samantha and little Angela worked at the club. Michelle had vanished overseas with some dago to the 'Costa Del Arse Sol', never to be seen again outside a Spanish brothel. Evidently, the heroin in Spain had been coming over mainly on the plane ever since. Thank you very much, Michelle.

Johnny Go Go was fond of saying to the three remaining Bennett sisters, 'Ya know, girls, selling your numb-nut friggin' little sister to them dagos was the best thing I ever did. Ha ha.'

Merchant seamen from Spanish, Greek, Turkish and Arabic cargo ships would pay five to fifteen thousand dollars cash for a girl, and a blonde girl with big tits gets the best price. Michelle was blonde with a big set of hooters and the Spaniards went mad over her. Anal sex is a popular pastime with the wops and dagos, and a blonde 17-year-old with big boobs who can speak fluent Greek from the waist down is worth her weight in gold.

Michelle had to go. She was part of a heroin deal, and there were no ifs or buts to it. Only tits and butts.

The proposal had been hard to refuse. It went something like this: 'Darling, you can get rich in Spain with a needle up your arm and a dick in ya bum, lying in the sunshine on the beach, or you can go into a 44-gallon drum and lie on the bottom of the Yarra. Which one do ya want?'

Michelle was no Einstein, but even she could see it wasn't a trick question. She went.

She loved sex, heroin and the beach, and the guys on the cargo ship seemed OK to her. That was a year before, and Johnny Go Go had made three million profit on the deal to date.

And you know what? Tito Carrasella, the Spanish end of the deal, was in love with Michelle Bennett. So this story did have a happy ending, even though Tito hadn't as yet removed his Aussie toy girl from the brothel he'd put her into. Love is love, but business is business. Tito was a businessman, but sooner or later he would take Michelle home to the happy hacienda that heroin built. Collingwood girls don't stay down for long. Not unless their mouths are full, or they're wearing cement boots.

'Did ya cop a look at this shit in the paper?' Suzi said to the Bennett girls.

'What's that?' asked Tashliene. She always was a stickybeak, one way or the other. Usually the other, if you get the drift.

'Some 17-year-old kid killed three men in a fist fight last night in Collingwood, then died in some schoolyard over in Richmond,' said Suzi.

'Fair dinkum,' exclaimed Kerry, who may have been an expert in French and Greek, but she spoke good old Aussie strine when it came to talking, not working. 'Who was he?'

Suzi read on. 'Billy Hill. They called him Blueberry Hill.'

'Shit,' said Tashliene. 'The bloke who killed Peter Stavros.'

Suzi read on. 'Yeah,' she said. 'I think I've heard of this kid, must have been a hell of a bluer.'

Suzi looked thoughtful. 'Anita Von Bibra gets a mention – and Graeme Westlock, the copper.'

'Who's Von Bibra?' asked Angela Bennett.

'She's a lady lawyer,' snapped Kerry. 'Geez, even I know that. God, you're a dumb moll.'

Angela went quiet, and decided to ask no more questions. Then Kerry would be right on both counts.

'Billy Hill,' said Suzi to herself. 'Billy Hill.'

She got up and went to look at one of several hundred framed photos hanging on the club walls. 'Billy Hill,' she kept repeating quietly. She was looking for someone called Muriel. Eventually she found the photograph she was looking for.

'Yeah,' she exclaimed, 'Muriel Hill. She danced here about seven or eight years ago. Good friend of Raychell Brown. Shit, I knew her myself when I was 15 years old, when I first started here.' In their game eight years was a lifetime, most were either retired or dead within five.

'Hey, Kerry,' she said loudly. 'You remember this chick?' She was pointing to the photo. It was the women in the clubs who would remember a face. To the punters they were all just legs and tits. The mugs rarely looked them in the eyes.

Kerry came over and looked. 'Oh yeah. Mary Ann. I remember her. Top worker, then gave it all up to look after her sister's kid.'

Suzi said nothing, and just nodded. Even though Suzi knew that Muriel gave up work to look after her brother's kid, and Mary Ann was the name of a barmaid who hanged herself in the toilets at the club about two years before, Kerry's scattered identification was confirmation of what Suzi was thinking. Kerry never forgot a face – it was just that she never remembered a name.

Muriel Hill, she thought. Karen Phillips would want to know this, and earning Brownie points with the Rabbit Kisser was one of Russian Suzi's favourite pastimes.

As Russian Suzi turned to return to her stool at the bar, she saw Tashliene and Samantha up on the bar in a 69 position, with Kerry and Angela looking on giggling. It was rehearsal time.

God help us all, thought Suzi to herself, lesbian sisters and psychopathic whores, I gotta get out of here. And Karen Phillips, she knew, was the only one with the power to promote.

Girls didn't just leave the Caballero these days. Under Karen's rule you got promoted out, or put off, but no one got out alive without her permission. She didn't want any of her girls learning the business and then setting up in competition.

It may have been restraint of trade, but a corpse can't go to the Trade Practices Commission. Suzi hoped the Rabbit Kisser's new baby had mellowed her attitude. The baby was the only thing that had been near her tits without paying a big quid for the privilege.

Suzi returned to her stool and wondered about this and other matters. She had always been curious. For a whore, she was a heavy thinker.

On 12 July 1979, while the Orangemen were banging their drums on the streets of Belfast, Big Billy Hill sat in the back of a spotless black Cadillac with three other guys on a hot afternoon on Knickerbocker Avenue in Brooklyn, New York. Big Billy had a sawn-off shotgun in one hand and a photo of a baby boy in the other.

Little Billy, I wonder what will become of him, he thought. Ahh, I guess it's better for him to just grow up and think his old man is dead.

These fucking dagos, how I hate them. I kill them, I work for them, I take their money, I run from them, I hide from them and I work for them some more. I even leave my wife and child for them. Ha ha. Big Bill gave a sardonic laugh.

Not that the dagos with him would understand that. They'd think a sardonic laugh was a small fish with a sense of humour.

Little Caesar Bonventre said, 'What ya laughin' at, Aussie Bill?'

Big Bill replied, 'How come the best hitmen you dagos have got are all fucking Irishmen?'

Bonventre looked sour. 'Cos youse guys ain't got enough smarts to make money any other way, that's why. Killing people – that's all you stupid Irish are any good for.'

Little Caesar liked to act tough and pretend he was named after the great Roman leader Julius. The truth was he got the nickname because he liked salad and no one was game to call him Waldorf.

'Yeah,' snorted Big Bill. 'So how long has Meyer Lansky been a fucking Italian?'

'What do ya mean by that?' asked Little Caesar.

Big Bill smiled. 'What I mean is, you stupid wop dog, if you dagos are so fucking smart, how come you all work for a Jew?'

Little Caesar nearly choked on the rage that welled up inside him. The truth hurt, but Baldassare Amato and the Bonanno family were going to change all that.

'Listen, Aussie boy,' he snarled. 'You're here to do a job, not to make smartarse remarks about things you don't understand.'

'Ah, eat shit, Caesar,' grinned Billy Hill. 'You import help from Ireland, South Africa and Australia and you reckon I'm the one with problems. The so-called Mafia is a fat old whore with a terminal case of the pox. When Hollywood stops making movies about you, there'll be no more Mafia. You're yesterday's men.'

Caesar screamed, 'We will always be here.'

'Yeah,' said Big Bill. 'Tell that to the Chinese and the Colombians. Ha ha.' The shotgun in his lap dissuaded any further heated geographical and ethnic debate.

Meanwhile, the big Cadillac had glided to a halt outside a little joint called Joe and Mary's Italian-American Restaurant. In the tiny courtyard out the back, the boss of the Bonanno crime family sat having lunch. This was Carmine 'Lilo' Galante. He sat with a bodyguard called Leo Coppolla.

Caesar Bonventre got out of the Caddie. 'Give me five minutes to get in, then hit the place,' he ordered.

Bonventre shook hands with another man Big Bill recognised as Baldassare Amato. Shit, thought Big Bill, these dagos are treacherous, lowlife dogs. Amato and little Caesar are personal bodyguards to Carmine Galante and they are going in to have lunch with him – then they're going to watch me and two Italians all the way from South Africa kill him. Shit, these guys can't even do their own killing any more. Big money and imported help is their caper. They can't trust any of their own any longer. Today was an example. Evil, treacherous dogs.

The three men walked into the restaurant. Frank Sinatra was singing in the background on some well-worn LP record. The front wall of the place was covered with a large painting of Leonardo da Vinci's *The Last Supper*, which was always a nice ironic touch in Mafia haunts.

The walls were decorated with photos of various local American-

Sicilian identities stuck between photos of various dead popes, which probably made sense, what with the Church racket being the only one bigger than the Mafia. Both organisations had a strict hierarchy and scared little people shitless. The difference was one gang used to have more sex but, then again, the Mafia sometimes got a bit as well.

Gee, I love killing these fucking dagos, thought Big Bill. It was great to have a job you loved. I'd nearly do it for nothing, he chuckled to himself.

Galante and Coppolla sat at a courtyard table eating fish salad and drinking red wine. As they'd got fatter, they'd lost their taste for blood – and had been ordered off red meat as well, as if they thought they should worry about living to a ripe old age. Fish salad, snorted Big Bill contemptuously. A meal for gay boys and dancers. And soon-to-be corpses. Big Bill smiled a bleak smile, like a grey nurse shark.

The lunchers sat under a checked yellow umbrella. There were tomato vines growing all over the courtyard. It was just like home in the old country – except the Empire State Building wasn't sticking up half a mile into the sky in some one-horse village in Sicily.

Christ, thought Big Bill, all we need now is for Marlon Brando to come out humming the theme music to the *Godfather* movie, and the whole comic production will be complete.

Little Caesar and Amato had vanished. No doubt they'd excused themselves to go to the lavatory, the way the weak mice do in all good dago set-up jobs.

It wasn't hard to guess where Hollywood got all its plots from. Big Bill almost felt embarrassed as he raised his sawn-off. His two companions opened fire. Galante copped a head full of slugs to go with a mouth full of fish salad. He should have complained. Slugs in the salad was not a good look. Even if it was good roughage.

Big Bill took the top off Coppolla's head with one shotgun blast. The dagos liked to spray a few shots around when they got excited, but Bill knew that, when it comes to gunplay, less is more. For him it was a very ordinary day's work.

Big Bill had seen more blood shed on the Melbourne waterfront in one month than he had in the New York Mafia wars in a year, but would anyone believe it? No way. Why? Because Hollywood doesn't make movies about Melbourne, that's why.

Let's get out of this panty-waist shithole of a town and back to Aussie land, Bill thought. He was sick of Yankee Doodle dago gangsters and their Al Capone lookalike false pretence.

After the shooting party was over, the three gatecrashers left suddenly, leaving someone else to clean up the bodies, the blood and the fish salad. And nobody would be picking up the bill, let alone leaving a tip. Unexpected gangland executions can make life hard for a small restaurant business, especially if the health inspector gets to hear about it.

They drove the big Caddie over to Menlo Park and walked into the Roma Restaurant to meet Little Caesar Bonventre and Baldassare 'Baldo' Amato. There was still ten grand each to collect. Ten up front and ten after. That was the deal.

Big Bill and his two mates were greeted by two shifty-looking wops with shiny shoes and oily smiles. Gaetano Mazzara and Frank Castronovo.

Bill knew Castronovo. He was a cousin to the Corsetti family, or at least had some connection with the Corsetti clan from back home in Lygon Street, Carlton. Mazzara had a Melbourne connection, too. He had a brother who helped run the Victoria Market.

Immigration split families three ways. They could choose Canada, America or Australia, which meant a Sicilian crime family could reach from Lygon Street in Melbourne to Hester Street in New York. And speaking of Hester Street, that's where Castronovo told Big Bill to go.

Bill didn't like this. It was a change in plan and he didn't want to play. Big Bill had one dago friend, a Sicilian named Filippo 'Jersey Phil' Sinatra. His older brother, Pat, lived in Carlton.

Jersey Phil had a small club in Belleville, New Jersey. Big Bill would ring the Toyland Social Club on Hester Street and get Little Caesar and Amato to come to him. He knew one thing these New York boys didn't like was driving over to New Jersey, but Big Bill knew Caesar would come.

When he got to Jersey Phil's club over in Belleville, Bill walked in and held out a package to him. 'Hey, Phil, do me a favour,' he said. 'If something fucks up, post this money and this letter for me, will ya?'

Jersey Phil looked at the thick letter and said, 'Sure, Billy, but nothing will go wrong. Caesar's a good guy.'

Big Billy Hill was never seen again. It was as if he just vanished into the smoke, smog and fog of a steamy New Jersey summer night.

'Big Bill was right about one thing,' Little Caesar said to Jersey Phil a while later. 'He said we import all our hitmen.'

'Yeah,' laughed Phil Sinatra. 'But he forgot the most important thing. Ha ha ha.'

'Yeah,' laughed Amato Baldassare. 'We don't fucking export them. Ha ha.'

'What about this letter he gave me?' said Phil.

Caesar looked at it. 'Money for the family, hey? Shit, I'm a family man. Billy wasn't a bad guy. Post it.'

'Ya know,' Amato said, 'Caesar, you got a big fucking heart. That's a nice thing to do.'

'Yeah, well,' said Little Caesar. 'Like I said, I'm a family man myself.'

'Aren't we all,' said Jersey Phil. 'Ain't we all.'

Motherhood wasn't something Karen Phillips had exactly planned on. She had many plans but being Mother of the Year was not one of them.

Johnny Go Go had taken her to visit the graves of Mickey and Raychell Van Gogh and Ripper Roy Reeves, and one thing led to another and Johnny ended up humping her on top of Ripper Roy's grave with Mickey Van Gogh on one side in his grave and Raychell Van Gogh on the other side in hers.

As she was in the throes of passion she started to yell, 'Mickey, Roy. Yeah, I can feel you both.'

She was a sick bitch. When she found she was in the family way she would have terminated the pregnancy, only she was convinced that somehow the spirits or ghosts of Ripper Roy Reeves and Mickey Van Gogh had entered her body and that the baby she carried was part of them.

'God,' said Johnny Go Go. 'Karen is so possessed with the memory of Ripper Roy and Mickey the Nut and Mad Raychell she'd crawl into their graves and kiss their corpses if she could.'

Karen had a baby boy and, true to form, she named him Michael Roy. What outraged Johnny was that she told the doctors at the hospital that the father was one Michael Van Gogh, not Johnny Go Go, and insisted the child's last name be registered as Van Gogh. Johnny was deeply hurt and offended.

It was his little baby boy, not a dead man's, and he planned to take the child from Karen. But the Rabbit Kisser was a dangerously psychopathic lady and the only way to remove the child from her would be to kill her, before she killed him. To top it off, Karen had started a war with the Carrasella family.

This was a complication: the leftovers of the Corsetti clan had regrouped and, along with the Mazzaras and the Castronovos, had regained control of everything they'd lost at the hands of Mickey the Nut, Mad Raychell and Ripper Roy.

Karen didn't know that Johnny was in business with Tito Carrasella, who was mixed up with the other Italians. God, he thought, the Rabbit Kisser is turning into a bigger mental case than Mickey Van Gogh, Ripper Roy and Mad Raychell put together, and now the baby. He had to get that poor baby, his son, away from her.

Karen Phillips and Russian Suzi sat in the plush office of Anita Von Bibra, baby Mickey lying quietly in Suzi's arms. Karen held a cigarette in her left hand; Anita couldn't help but notice a heavy blue spider's web tattoo that covered her hand and appeared to run up her left arm under the sleeve of her leather jacket.

Anita switched her mind back to the business at hand. She was in her brisk, meet-the-new-client mode. 'Who told you about me?' Anita asked.

'I read ya name in the paper and it seems you're a friend of a friend,' was the blunt reply.

'Oh?' said Anita coolly. 'And who might that be?'

'Muriel Hill.'

Anita stopped. 'Oh yes, poor Billy's Auntie M. Oh yes, indeed.' Her eyes started to go all moist.

'Look, I want a trust fund set up for my son and I want him placed into the care of Muriel Hill,' Karen said. 'Muriel was an old friend from long ago, and she has agreed to do it for me. I am unable to care for and protect my son. Muriel has agreed. I've got a million dollars to go into a trust fund for my son.'

Anita Von Bibra knew exactly who Karen Phillips was. The Carrasella family and the Mazzara clan had hired Anita on small matters from time to time.

Anita had carefully avoided handling any matter to do with the Caballero Night Club and the crew of deranged killers connected with it, and now she had the Rabbit Kisser herself in full psychopathic living colour sitting in her office.

There was a small but definite silence. Anita cleared her throat daintily. 'I'm afraid that I am unable to help you, Miss Phillips,' she said in her most neutral voice. 'Conflict of interest, you know.'

'Listen,' hissed Karen. 'How would you like to vanish, just disappear one night and reappear about a month later with a raging heroin habit, getting your ring gear jack-hammered by twenty Turks a night in a brothel a mile north of Istanbul?'

Anita shifted in her seat. So did her ethics. By the time she'd controlled the nervous tic in her cheek, she seemed to have it all worked out.

'A trust account, you say?' she said brightly. 'Yes, and having this beautiful baby placed into the loving and protective care of Miss Muriel Hill, a wonderful woman, by all accounts. And all in secret, naturally. Yes, well, I think I can handle that.'

Karen smiled, got to her feet and shook Anita's hand. Anita smiled too, but there was something about her body language that said she'd rather be picking up a tiger snake than Karen Phillips's hand.

But she hadn't lost her poise, or sense of humour. 'No need for Turkish brothels for me, my dear,' she said. 'I'm quick on the uptake, if nothing else. I fully understand your requirements in this matter.'

'Make sure you do,' Karen said, thin-lipped. 'Or else I'll put you in a brothel and sell your daughter to a pet-food factory. Fuck me around and I'll make mince meat of your whole friggin' life. Dogs and cats will be shitting bits of your family out all over Footscray.'

Anita swallowed hard. 'Miss Phillips, you have my sworn word all will be done and all will be correct. I swear it.'

Karen and Russian Suzi walked out into the street.

'Remind me to have that old moll killed once she fixes all this legal shit up,' Karen said.

'Why sell her to the Turks?' said Suzi.

'What?' said Karen. 'Black dyed hair and a flat chest. We'd be lucky to get enough money to cover the taxi fare to the wharf. Nah. Not worth worrying about.'

'We will just vanish her, like a German backpacker,' Suzi said. Being European herself, it was a pretty ordinary crack to make, but that didn't worry Suzi. She was a pretty ordinary cracker, when it came to matters of taste and delicacy.

'Yeah,' said Karen, with a giggle. Nothing worried her, except not getting her own way. That didn't often happen these days.

Karen took baby Mickey. 'OK, now listen, Suzi. Get yourself over to Lygon Street. You know the drill, wear something short and low cut. These bloody dagos can't help themselves. Tits and arse. God, have we put some dagos off with this old trick. And remember, we want the prick with the American accent.'

It was back to business.

'OK,' Suzi smiled. 'I'll doodle shake his brains out. Ha ha.'

Karen snapped, 'Just get him back to the club. His brains will be coming out another way.'

Suzi turned and walked away. She had her orders, and she knew what she had to do. You didn't argue with Karen Phillips if you knew what was good for you. And, so far, Suzi had shown a high instinct for knowing what was good for her. The Rabbit Kisser was about as sympathetic as Joseph Mengele. But she had better legs.

Old Salvatore 'Sally' Castronovo was visiting Melbourne. He'd come all the way from New York city. He'd become a major force in the Bonanno crime family and had branched out to work also for the Carrasella clan in Palermo, Sicily, and the Mazzara clan in the small seaside town of Castellamare del Golfo, Sicily. This place was also the home headquarters of the now powerful Bonventre clan.

Old Sally Castronovo was in Melbourne to strengthen ties and to pull the Spanish connection together. Tito Carrasella handled that from Melbourne. Sally was to fly to Spain, but there was something he wanted before he left: a memento of his trip to the city beside the Yarra. And he knew exactly what he wanted, he cackled to his young nephew Benny, 'But I just don't know how to wrap it.'

It was an old joke but a goody; Sally had been most amused to hear some Aussie DJ called Ross Patterson crack the gag on a Melbourne talkback radio station called 3AW. What dear old Uncle Sal wanted for a going-away present, he told young Benny, was to be set up with some Melbourne pussy.

Benny promised the old guy he had just the ticket. He'd met a sex-crazed, bleached-blonde Amazon about a month before who would fit the bill very nicely indeed. She was a female body builder with a body that had to be seen to be believed, and he knew his old uncle would be greatly impressed with his thoughtfulness and judgement in this matter.

Benny had arranged to meet Suzi at the Bowling Green Hotel in Carlton, one of his favourite haunts. He hadn't mentioned his uncle to her, but he didn't think it would be a problem. Suzi once said that she'd gobble a racehorse and break the jockey's jaw for a thousand dollars and Benny had two grand in his pocket. According to his calculations, that meant his uncle was in for a good night. Any way you looked at it, it certainly sounded a better idea than going to have a perve at the penguins at Phillip Island with a busload of gooks.

There were no prizes for guessing how Suzi would be dressed. Or almost dressed. She was wearing a skin-tight micro-mini dress that clung tight around her body. It did little to hold her love jugs in, and it just managed to cover her tight muscle-bound arse. She had a high-cut thong G-string affair on under this, and nothing else. If she leaned over, you could see through her cleavage right to the floor. She was fully waxed and polished like a new Mercedes, and looked like a porno star on steroids.

Suzi didn't like to wear stilettos during normal hours, because they were her work clobber. She danced in them, and did some tricks wearing them, which drove the punters out of their horny little minds. The poor saps got so hot when she strutted around in those high heels that they'd give her their rent money for just a quick peep at her pussy.

But she rarely wore the high heels in public because she was so tall she stood out, and the coppers would pull her over and accuse her of hooking. Most of the time they were after a perve or a feel, but sometimes it would go further. She'd blown away more coppers than Ned Kelly, and all without the rusty helmet.

Tonight she didn't want to be too identifiable, so she slipped on a pair of white Chinese kung fu slippers. They went well with the white dress and knickers.

She put on her lipstick and walked out of the Caballero Night Club and got into her white Mazda RX7. She was on her way up and out. The Rabbit Kisser had bought her the car, given her a mobile phone and a small high-standard .22-calibre handgun and told her not to do any more tricks, unless of course Karen ordered it herself.

Suzi was on four grand a week. Karen also insisted she do more body building, which Suzi loved, and to continue with her karate lessons. Suzi already had her black belt, first degree. Suzi suspected Karen was grooming her for some sort of personal Girl-Friday bodyguard role, and wondered if tonight's adventure with Poppa Castronovo was the tester.

She was determined not to let Karen down. The Rabbit Kisser had called a Collingwood war council for Tuesday night at the Caballero. All the Aussie crime families from Collingwood would attend. They were the old-school-tie brigade of the Melbourne underworld, a respected group who had controlled the criminal scene for the past 100 years.

Through marriage and de facto relationships that produced children, these 11 families had really become one giant clan with 11 different surnames shared out between them. If they weren't rooting, they were probably related – and in some instances they were both.

They had become scattered throughout Melbourne but they all sprang from the same street in Collingwood 100 years ago. Its name was East Street. For 40 years these 11 families had watched their city and the crime world they controlled become perverted and corrupted and then controlled by the dagos, and later the Asians. Some people considered them yesterday's men, but they refused to lie down. Suzi was a Russian, but she was part of Collingwood in her heart. And she was always prepared to do the business with one of the old crew, with her knickers in her handbag and her legs in the air. It was called integration.

It was only sex. It was all good fun. Yeah, OK, she copped a few kickings along the way. And there was that bullshit with the German Shepherd while Mickey the Nut held a gun in her mouth. But, hell, she was only fifteen years old and she never told the police. She had proved herself. She was a staunch solid chick and most street chicks from Collingwood get kicked about like a footy until they start to kick a few goals themselves. Which was what she was doing tonight, she thought.

Suzi parked her car in Lygon Street, and made her way to the Bowling Green Hotel.

'Here she comes,' said Benny to his Uncle Sally. They were sitting in the bar, having a quiet drink while they waited.

'Jesus, kid,' said Sally Castronovo as he took in Suzi's body, which reminded him of the 100-metre sprinters at the Olympic Games, except that she was as white as they were all black. 'She'll fucking kill me,' he breathed, but he didn't look as if he'd mind going out that way. 'Shit, look at the size of this bimbo. Mamma mia, Holy Mother of God.'

When Sally saw Russian Suzi, he knew the cold war was over. He grabbed his dick with one hand and crossed himself with the other. Luckily he didn't get mixed up.

'Thank you, God,' he said.

'What about me?' said Benny.

'Yeah, yeah, you too, kid,' said Sally. 'Now, introduce us, make sure she knows this ain't no date, this is bingo, bango time and fuck off, OK?' He always was such a romantic Italian gent.

Benny smiled. 'OK, Uncle Sally.'

Benny walked up to Suzi and slipped twenty $100 bills, tightly rolled up, into her hand.

'There's two grand there, Suzi. And that old guy's my Uncle Salvatore, he's from America and I told him yours is the best pussy he's ever gonna get.'

Suzi smiled. 'Well, little Benny,' she said, 'you know that's true.' She laughed, then looked at the short, thickset pot-bellied old man. 'I reckon a good fuck and a green apple would nearly kill your Uncle Salvatore,' she remarked.

'Don't call him Salvatore, call him Sally,' said Benny. 'And, yeah, go easy on him.'

Benny walked Suzi up to Salvatore Castronovo.

'Uncle Sal, this is Suzi. She's a good friend of mine and she'd like to be a good friend of yours.' Smooth talker was Benny. He was even slick with a hooker he'd just paid.

The old man wasn't so smooth. He stuck his paw up Suzi's skirt and into her panties and grabbed hold. He was much older than her. Was this the generation gap he was feeling? He left his hand where it was. 'Suzi, you and me is gonna be real good friends,' he growled. At his age he couldn't waste time.

Suzi smiled and reached forward and down and kissed the little fat pig on the mouth. She acted the part but she hated it. Deep inside she wanted to kill this little dago. Unlike a lot of hookers who felt the way she did, she could do it easy.

It was Monday night. The Caballero was closed, but inside the strobe lights flashed in the darkness as a lone, long leggy blonde danced on the bar. She wore white stilettos, suspenders and white stockings. She was not rehearsing for *The Sound of Music*. Suzi came through the door with Sally Castronovo. Before he had been a fat little dago pig. Now he was a drunk, fat dago pig. It wasn't an improvement.

'What's this place?' he demanded.

'I live here,' said Suzi, still playing her part, but without much passion.

'Ya live in a strip joint?' exclaimed Sally.

'Yeah,' said Suzi. 'There's flats upstairs.'

Sally was transfixed by the blonde glamour girl dancing on the bar.

'Jesus,' he said. 'She can dance, but what's that all down her freaking arm. It's like some sort of spider's web.

'It's a tattoo,' said Suzi.

Old Sally walked closer to the dancing girl. 'Holy shit, I ain't never seen nothing like that.'

Suzi stood back. She had spent a half-hour bent over the bonnet of her Mazda RX7 letting this little pig screw her and then he wanted a blow job afterwards. She could still taste the little pig in her mouth. She wanted to watch the dog suffer. As Sally drew closer to the bar, he looked up.

'Spider web tattoo,' he said suddenly, as if he'd just realised something. 'Hey, you're the crazy whore who's been causing all the trouble with my people. I'm gonna rip your arse out, you fucking whore.'

Sally didn't see the kick but he felt it, the white pointed toe of a stiletto high heel came swinging out and hit him dead centre in the throat. Sally choked and tasted his own blood. He gasped for air but none came. The dancing girl pulled her foot out of his neck and returned to her dancing and Sally Castronovo fell to his knees holding his neck and croaking for the air that wouldn't come.

Blood spurted out of his neck and up into his mouth. His lungs were beginning to fill with blood. He fell forward on to his face, choking to death.

Suzi turned the club lights on and the strobe lights off. Karen Phillips grabbed a towel and flicked a switch that killed the music and jumped down off the bar.

'What do ya reckon, Suzi?' she asked. 'Ya wouldn't guess I'd just had a baby, would ya?'

Suzi looked Karen up and down. 'Nah, Karen, you're right. Ya lookin' a million dollars. Now what about this dog?' she asked.

'They teach you to snap necks at them karate lessons?' asked Karen.

'Yeah,' said Suzi.

'Well then,' said Karen, 'let's see ya do it. Give him a head job he'll never forget.'

Suzi walked over to the still choking man, reached down, grabbed his head and with a giant twist upwards and to the side broke Sally Castronovo's neck like a chook's.

'What do you bench press?' asked Karen.

Suzi looked puzzled. 'I'm only pushing 250 pounds at the moment.'

'What do ya reckon this little slob weighs?' asked Karen.

Suzi looked down and gave the body a nudge with her toe. 'Ahh, I reckon 230–240 pounds.'

'OK,' said Karen. 'Carry him down to the keg cellar then tell silly Kerry and them snatch-sucking stupid Bennett sisters to mop up this fucking blood, then run out and find me a really big pickle bottle, big enough for a human head.'

'Where will I get one of them?' asked Suzi.

'I don't know,' snapped Karen. 'Jesus Christ, do I have to think of everything? Just do it.'

Suzi looked hurt. She was just concerned at how to ask at the all-night deli for a head-sized pickle bottle. Karen softened, walked over to her and said, 'Ya did good tonight. From now on you're with me all the time, OK?'

Suzi beamed a big smile and said, 'I reckon one of them giant pickled-onion bottles would do. After all, he smelled like one.'

'OK,' said Karen. 'Fix all this up then get me one, there's a good girl, OK.'

Muriel Hill sat beside the baby's cot at her house in Lennox Street. Young Melanie Wells sat beside her.

'He's a lovely baby,' said Melanie.

'Yes, he is,' said Muriel. 'You know, he reminds me of Billy when he was a baby.'

'I'll always be here to help you look after him,' Melanie said.

Muriel took the young girl's hand and squeezed it. 'You're a good girl,' she said.

'He's such a quiet little boy, isn't he?' Melanie said.

'Yes he is,' said Muriel. 'Very quiet.'

What's his name again?' asked Melanie.

'It's Michael Roy,' said Muriel. 'Van Gogh is his real surname but, if any one asks, his last name is Hill.'

'Good,' said Melanie. 'Then I'll call him "Blueberry".'

Muriel had a tear in her eye. 'Yes,' she said. 'Little Blueberry Hill. Who will ever know? People mind their own business in Richmond. No one will ever question it.'

'So he's our baby, is he, Auntie M?' asked Melanie.

Muriel smiled. 'Yes, sweetheart. He's our baby.'

Melanie threw her chest out and jutted her chin. 'And no one is gonna kill this little fella on us, not while we're around to protect him, hey, Auntie M?'

Muriel liked Melanie to call her Auntie M. It reminded her of her Billy. 'That's for sure, kid,' said Muriel. 'Over our dead bodies.'

The two women took each other by the hand and swore to protect little Mickey.

Now, dagos can be cunning and Aussie males vicious. The Jews are cold blooded, the Chinese will kill for cash and the Irish for fun or a cause, good or bad. But women will walk to hell and back to bite out the devil's nuts when it comes to protecting a baby.

'No one's ever gonna hurt our baby,' swore Muriel again. 'Hang on,' she said. 'He's just about to go to sleep.'

Muriel knelt beside the cot and young Melanie joined her and Muriel started to pray: 'And now I lay me down to sleep, I pray the Lord my soul to keep, and if I should die before I wake, I pray the Lord my soul to take.'

Melanie had tears in her eyes. 'That was Billy's prayer,' she sobbed.

Muriel nodded. 'Yeah, well, it's little Mickey's now.'

It was Tuesday night and the Collingwood clan was gathering at the Caballero Night Club. The Rabbit Kisser was late. Johnny Go Go greeted the guests with a smile that barely concealed his concern. He and Karen had barely spoken for the past month and no longer slept together. Each thought the other could stab them in the guts while they slept.

Johnny was trying to find out where she had hidden baby Michael – and at the same time he wanted to stop the bloodbath Karen wanted so badly. He was no peacenik but he knew that blood in the streets meant newspaper headlines, and that meant pressure on the cops.

The jacks couldn't give a stuff if every crim went on the missing list, but there was an election in the wind and the politicians knew that headless corpses in the street made the voters windy. People might start muttering about law and order, and next thing they would be asking all sorts of tricky questions. Who knows where that sort of thing might end up? Victoria had a reputation as the cleanest, most law-abiding state, with the 'best police force in the world', and the government and the cops didn't want to rock that particular boat.

Most nights when Parliament was sitting you could find back-bench hacks — half-pickled from dining-room port that they put on each other's bills and never paid for — sneaking down to the Caballero and stuffing their electoral allowances down the knickers of the willing dancers.

Most of the Honourable Members were holding theirs while watching the pussy parade. But when they had to front the voters they all of a sudden became concerned about the popularity polls — not the ones threatening to poke out of their Y-fronts.

At least half the old Collingwood crime families went along with Johnny Go Go. The Collingwood crew had been pulled from the ashes by Johnny Go Go and Karen Phillips, and now the Rabbit Kisser wanted to launch it back into a bloodbath that would surely outdo anything even the late Ripper Roy, Mickey the Nut and Mad Raychell had ever imagined.

They wanted to make money, not war. All crims eventually lose the blood lust. As they get older they want to be comfortable. Which is why they are always open to being walked over by a new group of ethnic crooks willing to die to get to the top of the dung heap.

In America the Colombians were determined to take over from the Mafia and the Italians would rather a bowl of linguine followed by a dish of cunnalinguine than fight for what they believed was theirs, handed to them by their hard old Sicilian forebears.

Karen had surrounded herself with her own personal crew. Sure enough, Russian Suzi had realised her ambition of being promoted rather than given a .38-calibre redundancy. She acted as a sort of driver, personal bodyguard and Girl Friday to Karen – as well as running the million-dollar-a-year prostitution empire for her. Karen had filled the Caballero with strippers and whores, all blood loyal to herself, as well as mentally insane nutters who could stab or bottle a customer to bits at a moment's notice.

She had Hank Hitchcock, nicknamed Hankster the Gangster, a 30-year-old tank of a man who carried a sawn-off double-barrel in an overcoat wherever he went. It was a good idea in winter, but in summer he lost 25 kilograms and had the complexion of a beetroot.

There was Aaron Guzzinburg, a Jewish killer from south of the river, a legend in the world of shadowy killers. His arrival on the scene came at a cost of two grand a day as a retainer, and he'd been on the scene for the past five weeks.

There were two more Jewish hitmen who spoke only Yiddish to each other and talked to no one else, except when Karen spoke to them. They worked for Guzzinburg at a grand a day each, at Karen's expense. No one knew their names, and no one was game to ask.

There was also a tall black Jamaican chick with a massive set of tits working as a dancer at the club. She was as black as night but had dead seaweed-green eyes. She seemed to be in a zombie-like drugged-out state as she danced non-stop for hours without a break. She could be lathered in sweat but wouldn't pull up.

This Jamaican had big, thick sexy lips and a face that just stared out into nothing, but when Karen walked into the club the black princess would come to life, as though coming out of a trance. They called her the Jamaican at first, then someone asked who 'the spook' was so they just called her Spooky – but not to her face.

There was something quite strange and deep about this lady. No one wanted to see this dark woman in a dark mood. She didn't do tricks, she just danced. No matter what money was offered, and there was plenty, she just danced for the punters.

Then there was a young 16-year-old total fruit loop, a kid named Johnny McCall. He was nicknamed 'Jack', and would proudly tell one and all that Black Jack McCall was the name of the man who shot the great gunfighting legend James Butler Hickock, otherwise known as Wild Bill Hickok. History has it that McCall shot Hickock in the back of the head as he sat playing cards in the Mann and Lewis Number 10 Saloon in Deadwood, Dakota, in 1876.

Karen had given young Jack McCall a .38-calibre Colt Peacemaker revolver and the kid had shot three people in the past month – not dead, but not for want of trying. He saw himself as a gunslinger in the American Wild West style. Karen liked the kid's style, and he in turn loved Karen. He was quite dangerously insane.

They were a good pair.

Kerry Griffin was a company girl, and as far as she was concerned Karen ran the company. She would fuck or fight anyone if Karen so wished it. But her habit of forgetting who people were wasn't getting any better. She often mistook Johnny Go Go for the bloke who cleaned the nightclub, and had once shown him where the vacuum cleaner was and abused him for not cleaning up properly.

Johnny was a trifle miffed by this, but everyone else thought it was the height of good humour.

The Bennett sisters gave blind loyalty to Karen and no other. Lee Lee, the tall sultry Chinese stripper with the savage scar under her bottom lip, obeyed Kerry.

Lee Lee was a Chinese wet dream except for the scar where her lip had been sewn back on after Kerry bit it off. A small point that Kerry had since forgotten about.

Lee Lee was near brain dead and could be described as a Chinese sexual public toilet with a smack habit, just waiting to die. She was little more than a slave who got her ring gear jack-hammered 20 times a night at 100 bucks a pop with the club taking nearly every cent. All Lee Lee got was a needle in the arm three times every 24 hours. She slept with Kerry in her flat and was little better than a walking corpse, but she would blindly obey any command from the boss.

The clans gathered for the big meeting. It was a regular Camp David for Collingwood crims.

There were the Kellys, the Browns, the Pollocks, the Phillipses, the Griffins, a smattering of various odd-looking fellows whose last name was Van Gogh, the Peppers, the Bennetts, the Bradshaws, the Rebecca clan, the Finneys, the Maloneys, the Lawsons, the Featherstone gang, the Taylors, the Wells family, the Cartwrights, the Crawfords, the Gilmores, the Vintons, the Rooneys, the Slatterys, the Brasco boys and, last of all, what was left of the Reeves family.

It was the *Who's Who* of old-fashioned crime.

There was roughly 200 people in the club drinking and one way or another through marriage or de facto relationships involving children everyone in the room was somehow related. In spite of the fact that some of these families had been killing each other and trying to kill each other for the past 60 years, this was the Collingwood crew. Karen had pulled them together for this because she knew that, pound for pound, Collingwood could put together more sheer firepower than anything the dagos had to offer, any place or any time.

Karen arrived with her small army in tow. As soon as she entered the club, she pointed to Keith Kerr and screamed, 'Who invited that tip rat? Jackie, shoot the dog.'

Young Jackie McCall might have been bred and born in the gutter, but he understood etiquette. He pulled out his Colt Peacemaker and shot Keith Kerr stone dead. This was an invitation-only affair, and according to the lady of the house Kerr hadn't been invited. Inexcusable manners.

Johnny Go Go was a bit alarmed about this. 'Holy shit,' he yelled. 'He's with the Peppers.'

'Yeah well,' said Karen. 'Not any more. Maybe I was a bit hasty, but I owe someone a favour.'

The crowd went silent. Karen could do that to a crowd, one way or another.

'Right, you lot, cop a look at this.'

Kerry Griffin came into the big room and sat a large pickle bottle on the bar. But it wasn't pickles inside it. It was the head of Salvatore Castronovo. He was an ugly prick when he was alive, but he was a shocker in a pickle jar.

Then Karen yelled, 'OK, Boo Boo.'

Another stripper walked out with yet another pickle bottle with a human head in it. It was the head of Tito Carrasella. Johnny Go Go went pale. He had been doing business with the late Tito. All of a sudden it looked as if he had a corporate partnership problem.

'Bookends,' someone yelled.

'Cancel the antipasto,' mumbled someone else.

'That's right, Johnny,' said Karen. 'All the way from Italy. I should have put the prick in olive oil. Hey, Michelle,' she yelled.

Michelle Bennett walked into the room. Her family rushed to greet her.

'Tell 'em,' yelled Karen.

Michelle cried, 'Johnny sold me to the dagos.'

The Bennetts went crazy. Russian Suzi went for Johnny. She hit him across the throat with a sideways right-hand karate chop. Johnny hit the deck, choking for air. What used to be his Adam's apple was getting in the way in his windpipe. It was not a healthy look.

'He's been doing big smack business with the dagos,' yelled Karen. 'I love him, but there's no shades of grey.'

Johnny was proving her wrong because his complexion was turning a distinctive greyish tinge, the colour that precedes death.

Evidently, Karen did have some sympathy in her. It seems she didn't want to see Johnny suffer, so she pulled out a .32-calibre automatic and emptied the six-shot clip into Johnny Go Go's head and chest. He looked like a cross between Swiss cheese and sausage meat.

The truth was that Karen knew all about Johnny's business matters, and she thought the selling of the young Bennett girl to the dagos was both highly comic and good business. It also helped the nation's balance of payments problems – and, although Karen may have been a psychopathic slut, she was a dinki-di Aussie. But she was prepared to use any advantage in the present small business and domestic matter because no one was going to get her baby. When it came to matters of child custody, she didn't mess about.

'Fuck the family court, Johnny had to Go Go,' she said with a giggle to Russian Suzi.

Meanwhile, the Jamaican beauty was up on stage, oblivious to the gunplay, dancing smoothly to gentle rock and roll music. She was wearing white stilettos and matching satin French knickers. She looked out into nothing, as usual. She had long black hair like a Chinese girl. It hung down nearly to her arse.

Big Frank Bradshaw was standing looking at the body of Johnny Go Go. He was horrified. 'You're fucking insane,' he yelled at Karen. 'What's this shit all about?'

'We go to war with the dagos tomorrow,' she answered. 'You're either all with me or against me.'

'You can get fucked,' said Big Frank.

But, as he said it, the big Jamaican girl bent down, took a razor blade from her mouth and ran it almost gently across his neck. Big Frank grabbed his throat and fell to his knees. It was a fatal case of shaving rash.

'You know the drill,' Karen said to Russian Suzi.

The big blonde stepped forward and grabbed his head and snapped it hard to the left side and Frank fell down dead. The two unnamed Jews and Aaron Guzzinburg and Hankster the Gangster all pulled out guns. Some members of the crowd did likewise, but not against Karen.

The Rabbit Kisser started to laugh.

'Now, why don't we clear these stiffs away and let's all nut this shit out. OK.'

Half an hour later the club was jumping. The girls were all dancing. It was a full-on party. Seven of the Bennett boys were so glad to see their distant young cousin Michelle again they were gang-banging her across one of the club tables, much to her apparent delight to be welcomed home so warmly.

Sick pack of monkeys, them Bennetts, thought Karen. Considering that nearly all the people in the room were somehow related through marriage, there was a lot of sex going on.

Kerry Griffin was up on stage doing the business with Pop Finney. It was a case of pop goes his weasel. Shit, thought Karen, Pop Finney was married to Kath Brown, Kath was Jenny Brown's sister, Jenny was Kerry's mother. That made Kerry Pop's niece by marriage, sort of. Depraved bitch.

There was young Angela Bennett copping it the Greek way over in the corner of the club, courtesy of Normie Taylor. Oh well, at least Normie wasn't a relative, she thought. Only her stepfather. Ha ha.

Karen signalled and a team of about 20 of the family heads went up to the penthouse on the sixth floor to talk business.

Kenny Pepper spoke first. 'What if the Corsettis and the Mazzaras and Castronovos start to import Sydney hitmen?' he asked.

Aaron Guzzinburg giggled. For a Jew, he had mad blue eyes. Rumour had it he was the black sheep of a respectable shopkeeping family, and had once gone to one of the poshest private schools in Melbourne. But that was a long time ago. Now he killed people.

Russian Suzi smiled.

'Where do they keep all the Sydney hitmen?' asked Karen.

Kenny Pepper looked puzzled. 'I don't know. I just asked what if they started importing Sydney gunnies.'

Karen continued, 'I'll tell ya where they keep all the Sydney hitmen, in the same cupboard as they keep all the Abo brain surgeons.'

The men laughed their guts out. Except Kenny Pepper, who looked a bit shamefaced. Then he spoke up, going for the historical angle. 'Snowy Cutmore was a Sydney gunnie – and he killed Squizzy Taylor.'

Ray Taylor, head of the Taylor family, pulled out a gun and shot Kenny Pepper in the kneecap. Evidently, he disapproved. 'Squizzy was our great-great-grandfather and we don't need turds like you reminding us of that shit,' he said reprovingly. It wasn't good manners to talk like that about people's forebears.

'Anyway,' said Karen, 'the bloody Cutmores lived in Smith Street, Collingwood, before they moved to bloody Sydney.'

The men all nodded.

'Oh,' said Kenny, 'I didn't know that. Can I go to hospital please?' His manners had improved dramatically but his walking hadn't. He had developed a pronounced limp in the previous 30 seconds.

Karen nodded. 'Yeah, go on. Someone take him.'

When Kenny was carried out, Ray Taylor said, 'I didn't know that about the Cutmore family.'

'Yeah,' said Karen, 'I thought everyone knew that.'

'Oh well,' said Ray. 'That makes everything all right.'

Karen had just made up the Cutmore story on the spot, but she knew that by lunchtime tomorrow Snowy Cutmore would be an old Collingwood boy along with Ned Kelly, Les Darcy, Banjo Paterson, Henry Lawson and fucking Superman.

Anyone from Collingwood could tell you that Ned Kelly was born in the backroom of the Tower Hotel. He was Collingwood through and through. Pinched his first horse from some mug in Forest Street, Collingwood.

Legends, she thought to herself. They hanged all the good ones and told lies about the rest. Ahh, Collingwood, God bless it. Good old Collingwood forever. Hardly won a footy match for years, yet pound for pound outnumbered every other fan club in Australia ten to one. Collingwood had pride, guts, many a drunken lie told in pubs and the ability to bury anyone who dared question it. Snowy Cutmore, indeed. She smiled to herself.

By Wednesday lunchtime, the streets of Melbourne ran red with blood. Or, at least, that's the way the media splashed the story. In fact, a few inner suburban streets got the odd splash of Italian blood.

Tommy Novella, Carlos Popovic, Mario Delucca and Danny Boy Mazzara carelessly got in the way of shotgun blasts. They had just left the bar of the Dan O'Connell Hotel in Canning Street, Carlton, when Ray Taylor and his crew hit them.

Meanwhile, as Jerry Carrasella and young Benny Castronovo walked out of the Kent Hotel in Rathdowne Street, Carlton, Vincent Rooney and Pat Slattery took their heads off with four blasts from sawn-off pump-action shotguns.

Toto Corsetti escaped death, but lost his left leg from the knee down as he ran up Wellington Parade, East Melbourne, trying to escape the shotgun of Albert Vinton.

Maria Lamberti was killed by accident when she got in the crossfire in a shoot-out between Aaron Guzzinburg and Charlie Mazzurco, a Corsetti family strong man. Mazzurco did cop three slugs in the guts and chest before being dragged into a car by Kiki Lucharas.

Return fire was sent in the direction of little Peter Gilmore and Neil Crawford as they walked out of the Curry Family Hotel in Wellington Street, Collingwood.

'No great loss,' said Karen to young Johnny McCall. 'All in all, it's been a bloody good start to things. I'm well pleased,' she said, patting Russian Suzi on the back. 'Let's go to the Telford. C'mon, Coco,' she yelled to the big Jamaican girl. 'Let's go. We had better close the Caballero till this lot is over.'

The Telford Social Club in Victoria Street, Abbotsford, was a shotgun blast away from the Terminus Hotel. It had been a small billiards club built in 1927 and later named after H.R. Telford, the trainer of the world's greatest racehorse, the magnificent Phar Lap. There had been an ugly rumour that the great horse was born and bred in New Zealand. The truth, of course, was that the beast was born in Collingwood. In a small stable off Hoddle Street, to be exact. Collingwood was well known for its thoroughbred breeding.

The old social club had had been closed up since 1952, but Karen Phillips had bought it about a year before and done it up a treat. It was now used as her own private hangout for personal friends and the inner circle of the crew.

It had case-hardened steel plate two centimetres thick on the inside of the front door, and the front windows were covered by thick red velvet curtains that were lined with bulletproof material. It would nearly break your arm to pull those curtains – but no one pulled them, no matter how nice a day it was outside. While they were across the window, no one could look in, and no one could shoot in.

Security bars ran across the outside of the door and windows. A small red and gold sign above the front door simply read 'H.R. Telford Social Club – members only'.

The inside was small but it had been decked out with the Karen touch. It wasn't what you'd call a light touch in the style department. There was plush red deep-pile carpet and red and gold velvet wallpaper, and the ceiling was painted black. It seemed the decor was not inspired by a nunnery.

A full-size billiard table stood near the front door with a big covered light hanging low over the table, straight out of *Pot Black* on television. All that was missing was whispering Ted Lowe, Eddie Charlton and Hurricane Higgins, but it's a fair bet they might not have been keen to play at the Telford Club – at least to win – once they saw the regulars there.

Behind the billiard table stood a big, highly polished wooden table with 12 heavy chairs around it. Behind that was a massive timber bar with fridges and freezers and a fully equipped kitchen attached to it. The toilets and bathroom were upstairs, along with two bedrooms and a lounge and another small kitchen. There was a lock-up garage out the back, leaving enough room for a small courtyard. All in all, it could have been 'Property of the Week' in the real estate pages, although the armour plating might have been a bit hard to explain away.

The bar was fully equipped with enough booze to get a small army drunk, or two members of the armed robbery squad, and the kitchen held enough food to feed the same army before it got on to the booze. There was an old 1960s-model jukebox near the billiard table that played all Karen's favourites – 1950s rock and roll, country music and some modern stuff. It was like some sort of gangsters' time warp.

The walls were covered with probably 100 or more framed photographs. Photos of Ripper Roy Reeves, Mickey Van Gogh, Raychell Van Gogh, Leon and Deon Pepper, Fatty Phillips (Karen's dead and never seen again brother), and Raychell's dead brother Bryan Brown. There was a photo of the old world billiards champ Walter Lindrum, a photo of Phar Lap and Collingwood-born jockey Jim Pike, after the 1930 Melbourne Cup win. And a photo of famous Collingwood boxer Lionel Rose when he beat Fighting Harada, who was not born in Collingwood, for the world title in 1968.

Naturally, there were photographs of the Collingwood Football Club, the 1953 and 1958 Premiership teams, photos of Aussie cricket greats Victor Trumper and Don Bradman and jockeys like Pike, Darby Munro and Scobie Breasley. Not to mention the boxing legend Les Darcy, criminal legend Squizzy Taylor, Hollywood movie-star gangsters Jimmy Cagney, who wished he was born in Collingwood, Humphrey Bogart, who barracked for Collingwood, Edward G. Robinson, and the sex goddess Jayne Mansfield.

There were photos of the famous London gangsters Ronnie and Reggie Kray and, most strange of all, a large photo of the old country singing legend Smoky Dawson right next to a photo of the Queen of England.

One thing there wasn't. There were no photos of Yank basketball players and no one wore baseball caps back to front. It was like stepping back to a time when Australians were happy to be themselves and not poor imitations of people from another country. This was Collingwood, not New York.

As far as Karen was concerned, Manhattan was a drink drunk by hairdressers and rich poofters.

The whole place had a magic look and young Johnny McCall, the 16-year-old gunnie, loved it. They walked in. The big Jamaican girl had never been there before but Suzi and Johnny McCall were regular visitors. They sat at the table and Suzi went and got four extra-large glasses of Scotch whisky.

'Hey, kid,' said Karen, 'have you met Coco?'

Johnny McCall looked at the big smoky-eyed Jamaican lady and said, 'Well, yeah, but no, not really.' What he meant was that he'd seen her in her role as an exotic dancer, but had not yet had the pleasure of being formally introduced. The kid smiled and held out his hand and stood up.

'I'm very pleased to meet you, Coco,' he said.

The big stripper took his hand and smiled. It was like a scene from *My Fair Lady*.

'My name is John McCall but you can call me Jackie for short, if you like,' he said.

Suzi and Karen both laughed and Coco sort of melted a bit and shook his hand. 'You nice baby boy. You can call me Coco or Joeliene,' she said in a husky West Indian accent to die for. Some blokes already had.

'I'm not a baby boy,' said Johnny, his ego quite bruised.

'Yes, yo is, boy,' said Coco with a smile, 'but you a real pretty baby, so don't be cross.'

Johnny sat down.

'Take it as a compliment,' said Suzi.

Both Suzi and Johnny had seen the big Jamaican chick take life as casually as if she was shelling peas, but it was the first time either had heard her speak.

Johnny was really curious about Coco, but bit his tongue as he was smart enough to know that questions weren't welcome in this sort of company.

Johnny McCall had known Karen Phillips most of his life. His idols when he was growing up had been Mickey Van Gogh, Ripper Roy Reeves, Raychell Van Gogh, and then the famous Collingwood legend herself – Karen Phillips, the Rabbit Kisser.

It was a dream come true when he was invited to get around with her and she gave him his own handgun with 50 boxes of ammo and $1,000-a-week walking-around money. To top it off Karen had taken his cherry about a week before. The very first sex he ever had. It was fantastic, but she had explained she could do it only the once as she was having women's problems after having the baby. He wouldn't trouble her again, unless he was asked, because he fancied himself a gentleman.

Johnny didn't realise that the truth was a little more than simple 'women's troubles' and Karen had every intention of showing both Suzi and Coco exactly why, when she got the chance. Karen had given birth to a healthy boy and got the doctor to put an extra stitch in to keep her nice and tight, but Johnny could have done real damage if he'd got up a full head of steam, so to speak.

It was hard to believe that a 16-year-old with the face of a 14-year-old boy, roughly 5 feet 7 or 8 inches tall in the old measure, could be so well equipped in the trouser-snake department. Both Coco and Suzi towered over him. He was built like a tuppenny skun rabbit, as skinny as a rake, but hung like a draught horse.

He also had a young gun madness in him. A Wild West cowboy gunslinger fixation. Shades of Ripper Roy with a loaded gun in his hand. He was totally kill crazy but, without it, either Suzi or Coco would snap his skinny little neck like a twig. But he was a cute, sweet-faced kid, real cute.

'Suzi, Coco,' said Karen. 'How big was the biggest you ever seen in your life?'

Karen got up and brought over the bottle of scotch. Johnny was a bit embarrassed at this line of questioning.

Suzi wasn't. She answered, 'Probably Ripper Roy. I never had him myself, but I have seen him pull the monster out a few times.'

Karen nodded. 'Yeah, Ripper Roy for sure. That was a bloody whopper.'

Coco spoke in that lazy Caribbean drawl. 'Herman the German, he would come to see me twice a week in a whorehouse I worked in in Amsterdam about four years ago. Now, he made my eyes water but, ohhh, I loved that thing.'

Karen was waiting for the cue to talk about Johnny's. 'Well, girls. About a week ago I copped the biggest monster God ever hung on any man. I was saddle sore for a week. It was like trying to ride a mad bull in a rodeo. I walked like Wyatt Earp for a month.'

Suzi and Coco looked at Karen in surprise. This was the Rabbit Kisser talking, after all. She could take on a herd of donkeys and blow a bloody elephant. Any man who got her to send up the white flag was a freak.

All of a sudden, young Johnny McCall went as red as a beetroot. Suzi saw Johnny's face and pointed at him and looked at Karen. 'You're kidding,' said Suzi.

Karen smiled. 'I took his cherry and it turned out to be a fucking coconut. That monster nearly killed me doing it.'

Coco's eyes went wide. 'Show me,' she purred, like a black panther on heat.

Suzi started to giggle. 'Yeah, c'mon, kid. Let's have a gig at this.'

Johnny turned to Karen, covered in embarrassment. 'Karen,' he pleaded.

'C'mon, kid,' said Karen. 'It's only us here. No one will know. Show 'em. These girls have seen more dicks than an army doctor.'

Johnny sat still. If they thought he was going to stand there in a public place and put on some sort of sick floor show, they had another thing coming, or so he was thinking …

This was a new and novel experience for the three girls. Men had always begged to get their gear off whenever they were anywhere near these walking wet dreams. Now they had a bloke who really was shy. What on earth could they do? It was a fair bet they would think of something.

Karen winked at Coco, and the big Jamaican girl seemed to know exactly what she meant. She took off her leather jacket and dropped it over a chair, then removed her tank top and unleashed a big black set of watermelons. Then she took off her high heels and her jeans. Then her panties. Then put her high heels back on again. This was a master stroke. Johnny thought he was going to have one. But his heart managed to stay in one piece and, despite his embarrassment, he felt himself rising to the occasion.

'Coco knows what little boys like,' she whispered in that throaty voice.

Suzi and Karen sat there as Coco went to the jukebox

and looked down at the selection panel. 'Ahh, yeah,' she purred. 'A little Elvis.'

She pressed B17 and Elvis started to sing that old striptease classic 'Little Egypt'.

'Little Egypt came out struttin', wearing nothing but a button and a bow, dar dar dar dar ...' Coco mouthed the words suggestively and swayed to the music, gradually dancing over to Johnny.

Karen and Suzi sat and smiled, totally entertained at the sight of the blushing young kid who, only a few days before, had gunned down Keith Kerr in cold blood in front of 200 Collingwood criminals without batting an eyelid. Now he was almost rigid with nervous embarrassment. It was quite comic. Coco swayed back and forth and bent forward and jiggled her massive tits into the kid's face and, sly as a pickpocket going the dip on a bankroll, she reached down and started to undo his pants.

Johnny jumped, but Coco purred to him like a big cat. 'Take it easy, baby, relax,' she whispered as she worked on those pants.

Johnny's handgun dropped heavily to the floor as it fell out of his belt. Then Coco reached into his underpants and took hold of the contents, and it was her turn to be shocked. She stopped dancing and looked down at the giant thing in her hand. 'Ohhh, my sweet Mary,' she groaned. 'I don't believe this.'

The big Jamaican got to her knees in front of the boy and held it in her hands like an axe handle.

Suzi was on her feet. 'Oh, God,' said Suzi. 'That's not for real. No wonder you're so thin, kid, all ya blood is in ya dick.'

Coco ran her wet tongue up the length of it and the young lad jumped to life and the semi-erect member began to grow to full throbbing size. Coco tried to take the massive tool into her mouth but only managed to engulf not quite half of it.

'Give me a go,' said Suzi, always prepared to try to meet a challenge. The big blonde bent down but could only take not quite half its full length into her mouth.

'That's outrageous,' said Suzi. 'I've never met any man I couldn't deep throat.'

Coco agreed. Personal pride was on the line. Coco had worked in whorehouses from London to America and she had yet to come across any man she couldn't take, but here it was in front of her, attached to the skinny little body of a baby-faced 16-year-old kid.

Coco began to suck up and down till she gagged and choked on it, but she still couldn't take any more than half the length.

The big Jamaican whore got angry at herself and stood up with one foot on either side of the chair Johnny was sitting in and, with her hand guiding the young lad's dick into her, she lowered herself on to it with a look of surprise on her face. After about halfway, she moaned and then Johnny couldn't control himself any longer and he gave his hips a little thrust upwards and the big black girl eyes began to bulge. He wasn't able to sink his full length into her but the big girl held the lad's shoulders and pushed his face into her massive bosom and held her weight on her legs, unable to allow herself to take any more than the half a length she had or to sink any lower down on to the giant pole.

She moved up and down on to the length of meat she could take without doing herself any medical injury, and still she was only humping on a bit over half of the skinny kid had to offer.

Then Johnny yelled out 'Ahhhh' and Coco felt better. She had popped his cork in roughly 100 seconds, maybe 120 seconds. Even if she couldn't take it, neither could he. She climbed off and looked down at the kid.

'You gonna be one hell of a big boy when you grow up, kid. Johnny, you stay here and zip ya pants up and don't bother lookin' at my arse either. You're a bloody freak, kid.' Then she smiled. 'But a cute one.'

A Collingwood boy, of course.

Jersey Phil Sinatra spoke quietly into the phone. 'The two boys will be there in about three days. Listen, Pat. Keep quiet about this. Don't tell none of the family you're importing help to help our friends because our friends get excited. We don't want no loose talk, so say zip till they get there ...

'Yeah, Pat. Chips off the old blocks. Little Caesar's kid, Angelo and Amato's kid, Tony. Both top boys. They took care of that Benny Zito problem in Clifton, New Jersey. Gee, Pat, I wish you was with me. I miss ya, brother. Anyway, they are on their way. Get Palazzolo to meet them. Don't you pick them up from the airport. Jesus, all this shit over some Irish whore with a gang of "skippy drunks" backing her up. I can't believe it, this fucking Collingwood sounds like the South Bronx on a bad night. Holy shit. Anyway, the boys will fix it. See ya. I love ya.'

Jersey Phil Sinatra hung up. He hadn't drawn breath for three minutes. He was thinking ...

The sons of Baldassare Amato and Little Caesar Bonventre had, like their fathers, climbed the ladder and were now middle-ranking killers, guys on their way up the Bonanno crime-family ladder.

Angelo Bonventre had married the granddaughter of the late Vito Genovese himself. That made him an up-and-coming Mafia prince, if he stayed alive and on the right side of his in-laws, neither of which was guaranteed in his line of business. Meanwhile, life was sweet.

The Genovese name was almost mob-land royalty. The Aussie connection in Melbourne, Australia, was worth six million a year to the Bonanno clan. Johnny Zippo, Tommy Palazzolo, Mickey Morelli, Georgio Lucchese, Lucky Lauricella, Bobby La Barbera, Nicky Gambino, Jimmy Catalano and the Buscetta brothers had all invested big money in the Aussie smack trade.

OK, six million a year ain't no big deal, but it grew by a million each year and, with the Colombians holding the big share of the coke market in the States, the Italians knew they had to invest offshore.

Australia could be the new land of opportunity. Here the whores were legal and there was a million or two a year to be made by getting a few sluts to lie on their backs or on all fours. And the beauty was you didn't have to take on the locals. It was all handled hand in hand between brothers and cousins, from one country to another, with no outsiders.

They had the same set-up in London, Canada, Spain, France. The only country the mob couldn't get into was Ireland and, let's face it, no one with half a brain would want to get into Ireland anyway. The mad Irish had been killing Italians for years, just for practice half the time, from London to New York, from Boston to Melbourne.

The Irish had never beaten the Italians, and never would when it came to financial muscle, but the mad Irish bastards team up with the freaking Jews and go to war with the Italians at least once every ten years.

When was the last time in New York? thought Jersey Phil to himself. Yeah, that nut Mickey Featherstone and his crew. Jesus, the mad Micks nearly tore New York apart. Well, young Angelo and Amato will fix this shit down under, once and for all.

Things went quiet for about a week. It was as if the whole Melbourne criminal world was in a state of shock. Not a single shot fired. The police were raiding clubs and private homes all over the city, but not finding much. The newspapers were running headlines about a 'wall of silence', the way they usually did. Chief Inspector Graeme Westlock had been placed in charge of the organised-crime division and for once the homicide squad was not heading the investigation.

The Caballero was empty when the police smashed its front doors in. There was no sign of trouble, but the smell let the coppers know there had been foul play in the joint not too long before.

No wonder there was a smell. There were seven rotting corpses in the keg cellar. The victims were identified by what was left of their fingerprints, tattoos and teeth. A warrant had been issued for the arrest of Karen Phillips, but the Rabbit Kisser had vanished. It was as if the war had started on Wednesday and then everyone had forgotten what the hell was going on.

Anita Von Bibra pulled her car up in front of old Pat Sinatra's house. She got out and walked to the front door and knocked. After a minute, she heard footsteps inside, then the front door swung open, and she saw Pat Sinatra standing there, squinting out at her through the screen door. It was a quiet Thursday morning. The sun was shining. The streets of Carlton seemed almost asleep. But as Pat opened the screen door a car pulled up in front of the house and a thickset man got out carrying a double-barrel sawn-off shotgun. He ran up and screamed, 'Hey, Pat!'

The first shot hit Anita Von Bibra in the back and blew her lungs and heart out and all over Pat Sinatra's white shirt. The second blast blew Pat's eyes and nose right back through his head along with his brain and sent the whole bloody lot splattering down the hallway.

Hankster the Gangster got back into the old blue Ford Falcon with young Michelle Bennett behind the wheel. She planted her high-heeled foot to the floor. The V8 answered the call like it was the start of the big one at Bathurst, with Alan Moffatt in the pilot's seat. The screech of the tyres blotted out the sound of the flywire door, sprayed with blood and guts, banging in the breeze.

Michelle, along with her mad sisters, had been put to work in a small brothel run by Russian Suzi, but managed by Hankster the Gangster. The Collingwood crew had sliced up its empire and fortune.

The Bennett family would gain control of nearly 50 per cent of the prostitution, as it was the largest criminal family in Collingwood, no mean feat in itself. There were some big families in Collingwood, and most of them were criminal in some form or another. Anyway, as most of the whores in the parlours were either related to a Bennett or going out with a Bennett or married to a Bennett or named Bennett, it only seemed fair that the Bennetts got the biggest whack from the local parlours.

The only fly in the soup was Normie Taylor, who would regularly show up at parlours and not only shag the arse off his stepdaughters and nieces, but also pocket the takings while he was at it, from force of habit. So, when Normie showed up dead in Smith Street,

Collingwood, with his backbone filleted very roughly with a 12-gauge shotty, the unfortunate occurrence was naturally blamed on the dagos.

This made Hankster the Gangster almost smile, as he had been dispatched on the little errand to lay Normie to rest. Not that it worried anyone, much, especially the police. Old Normie was a sick, perverted lowlife who had to go one day. He was not missed, except by his young stepdaughter, Angela Bennett, who loved the old nut for some strange reason, even if he did plonk her as regular as clockwork.

The lesson to be learned from Normie's timely demise was this … an underworld war was always a good time to cull a few from your own team. The other side would always be blamed. It was like a free hit.

Poor Angela always was a bit of a nut, and showed up for work at the brothel dressed all in black out of respect for Normie.

Aaron Guzzinburg and his two Yiddish-speaking helpers had been sticking close to Karen for the past week. Young Kid McCall, as the girls had begun to call him, was holed up at the Telford Social Club with Russian Suzi and Coco Joeliene, the big Jamaican girl with the sore pussy.

No one knew where Karen or Aaron Guzzinburg and his crew were hiding. She just rang and gave orders, and when she said 'jump' people just said 'how high?' If there had ever been any doubt about her, there wasn't any more. Not after the cold-blooded exhibition at the club on the night of the meeting, followed by the slaughter of the Italians. It was the biggest defeat suffered by armed Italians since Tobruk.

The truth was, Karen had won the war on the first day. There wasn't much more to do except to hit a few stragglers. The Sicilians and their Calabrian lackies had vanished, or so it seemed, but Karen didn't take a victory for granted and prepared herself for the Sicilian payback that she knew would come. They would either use outsiders or use the police but the payback would be delivered. It was the Italian way.

Russian Suzi put the phone down. 'That was Karen. We have to go and see some turds in Errol Street, North Melbourne,' she said.

'What's going on?' asked Johnny McCall.

'Ahh, a couple of Yankee Doodle dagos are meeting with Pino Castronovo and Gaetano Mazzurco at the Limerick Castle Hotel tonight,' said Suzi.

'Dagos at the Limerick Castle,' said Kid McCall. 'That's a bit funny. That would be like an Irish birthday party held at the bloody Luna Bar in Lygon Street. Most odd.' The Kid had a most odd way of talking sometimes. He said things like 'most odd', as if he was bloody Sherlock Holmes or something.

'Yeah,' said Suzi. 'It is, but who cares? Are you a gunman or a tourist guide? Keep your mind on the main game.'

Coco Joeliene was wearing a white body suit, with press studs at the crotch and white stay-up stockings with her trademark white five-inch stilettos. Suzi was dressed the same, but in black. They were trying to teach young Johnny to do the *Rocky Horror Show* dance. Coco pressed A14 on the jukebox and the music blared out.

'Let's do the time warp again, let's do the time warp again,' went the lyrics.

Johnny yelled out, 'It's just a jump to your left, now a jump to your right.'

The two girls and the Kid had become quite good friends over the past week and had taken to sleeping in the main bedroom upstairs, which had a giant queen-size bed. Johnny would sleep between the two girls like a little kid snuggled between two big mothers.

Mind you, their idea of mother care was to smother KY jelly all over the pointy end and keep trying him on for size. Both girls seemed hell bent on taking the lot even if it killed them. It drove them insane. Professional pride was on the line. They were both workaholics.

Meanwhile, down at the Limerick Castle, Pino Castronovo and Gaetano Mazzurco stood in the bar with two short thickset young men. Angelo Bonventre and Tony Amato spoke with tough clipped New York accents. There was a fifth man with them, an Aussie named Terry Kerr. He was doing a lot of talking.

'Listen, Pino, I'm telling ya I can set Karen up. We kidnap the Kid's mother, you know, Johnny McCall's mum. She lives in the Collingwood Commission flats. That will bring the Kid out. I know she likes that kid. Shit, she's known the little mental case since he was a baby. She'd follow him to hell to make sure he's OK.'

The two American mob guys liked this idea, but Pino shook his head. It was bad enough that they were working with a traitor like Terry Kerr at all, let alone allowing him to suggest battle plans, he reckoned. Still, Angelo Bonventre couldn't help being attracted to the idea.

'Ha ha. Between the Irish and the Sicilians, it's a wonder anyone's got a fucking mother left,' Angelo said.

'Ha ha ha. Yeah,' said Tony Amato. 'Remember Mothers Day 1977?'

'Shit, yeah,' said Angelo. 'How could I forget? The whole Trafficante family woke up to find that there wasn't a mother, grandmother, wife, sister, or daughter left. Kidnapped the lot. They made peace before lunch. Ha ha. That fucking Gambino, he was a cunning old rat.'

'Yes,' said Pino, who didn't have the faintest idea what his second cousin was talking about. 'I'm sure we are all very interested in your sentimental yarns of Mafia adventures of yesteryear, but this is here and now and half our people got whacked on the one day. Are you now suggesting we run about town on some giant hunt for mothers and grannies?' There was a trace of sarcasm in his voice.

'You talk a bit fancy, kid,' Angelo growled to Pino. It was not meant as a compliment.

'University,' grunted Gaetano Mazzurco, a man of few words. 'Pino is a university graduate.'

'Yeah, well,' said Tony, 'if he talks like that to us again, he will be a broken-jaw graduate, OK?'

Pino said, 'Sorry,' but nevertheless he'd made his point.

'Nah,' said Angelo. 'Ya right, we will lay off the mothers.'

The men continued drinking. Both Angelo and Tony thought that Australian beer was the best they'd ever tasted and planned on drinking more. After some ten minutes, Pauly Della Torre, another Castronovo cousin, walked into the pub with a fantastic-looking whore who worked as a dancer in one of his clubs. She was legs and tits made by the hand of God. The men turned to look.

'Angelo, Tony,' said Pauly. 'I'd like to introduce you to a good friend of mine, Miss Carolyn Woods.'

Carolyn put out her hand and said, 'I'm very honoured to meet you, gentlemen.'

They were no gentlemen, but, then again, she was no lady, either.

Angelo took her hand, and showed no signs of letting it go for a while.

Pauly continued, 'Ya see, fellas, little Carolyn's got this problem.'

'What's that?' said Tony, running his hand across the girl's bottom as she gave him a big smile.

'Well,' said Pauly, 'Carolyn here don't like one guy at a time, she likes two at a time, and she has a lot of trouble finding two guys who want to play.'

Angelo looked at Tony and Tony nodded.

'Carolyn,' said Angelo. 'This is your lucky night, ha ha.'

Kid McCall, Coco Joeliene and Russian Suzi sat in a beat-up old Jag across the road from the Limerick Castle Hotel, quietly waiting. Coco Joeliene had been answering Kid McCall's questions as she'd got to know him. Like him, she'd opened up more and more.

Suzi was also curious about the big Jamaican beauty, and sneaked in a few innocent questions about her past.

'I was born in a small seaside town called Rio Bueno near Montego Bay, baby,' Coco said in that sensational West Indian accent. 'Baby, it a beautiful place, but we were dirt-poor folks. My brothers sell me to whorehouse in Kingston. I was 10 maybe, 11 years old. Big girl for my age. The whorehouse kept me till I was about 13, then sold me to sailors who took me to Haiti and sold me to brothel in Port Au Prince. Same story again about a year later and I was working in whorehouse in Costa Rica. Then I ran away to America. Mexico first, a few whorehouses there. Then New York. Strip club and whorehouse in Queens, then I meet nice man. He fix me with papers, passport. I go with him to Copenhagen in Denmark and do porno movies.

'I like that, he treat me good. Then he take me to Netherlands, to Amsterdam. Two years window girl, then to London, then to Australia. I like it here and that's it.'

Coco seemed to have run out of story.

'What happened to the nice man?' asked Suzi.

Coco answered, 'Oh I marry him. He travel with me all the way to Australia.'

'Well, where is he?' asked Kid McCall.

'Oh, he sold me to Karen, twenty-five thousand dollars. Karen shot him and gave me the money. He was just a pimp. I'm free now but I'm gonna stay with Karen. She's a good lady, treats Coco good.'

Kid McCall gave Russian Suzi a sideways look and Suzi tapped her head with her finger. The Kid nodded. Poor Coco was quite mad but also quite lovely. She'd be OK with a bit of love and loyalty and attention and simple common friendship.

The Kid took the big Jamaican's hand and kissed it. 'You stick with us, Coco.'

The big black princess reached over and took the boy's head and kissed both his eyes. 'I'm gonna, baby. Where you go, Coco goes.'

McCall was a bit taken aback at that remark.

'Hang on,' whispered Suzi. 'Here they come.'

'Shit,' said Kid McCall. 'There's six of them. Who's the moll?'

'I don't know,' said Suzi. 'There was only meant to be four of them.'

Suzi handed Kid McCall a .45-calibre gold cup automatic handgun. 'Here, kid, it holds seven rounds. Forget the .38 revolver.'

'Nah,' said the Kid. 'I'll use both. I'll whack the whole fucking six of 'em, that's what Wild Bill Hickok would do.'

Coco Joeliene was sitting at the wheel of the Jag and Russian Suzi sat in the back. McCall was sitting next to Coco.

'OK, Coco, start the car, do a U-turn in front of the pub and I'll jump out. Go, go, go.'

The old Mark-10 Jag started on the first kick. Coco Joeliene gunned the motor, dropped it into gear and took off, leaning hard on the wheel and spinning the car around. It was like something out of the movies, which was fair enough, because they all thought they were in one.

Angelo and Tony had their guns out as soon as the Jag's wheels squealed. But before the car screeched to a halt Kid McCall was out the door and firing, with a gun in each hand. A slug from Tony's gun hit the windshield of the Jag and shattered it but the bullet didn't hit anyone. His next slug hit the Kid across the right side of the face, but then Tony Amato fell down dead. Carolyn Woods hit the footpath with a .38 slug through her neck.

Pino Castronovo, who didn't carry a gun, was hit with a .45-calibre slug in the chest that shattered his heart.

Angelo Bonventre, who was shooting like a wild man and hitting nothing, fell with two slugs in the chest. Gaetano Mazzurco fell to the ground with two in his guts and Pauly Della Torre ran up Errol Street faster than he'd run for a very long time. Kid McCall took aim and dropped Della Torre with one shot in the centre of the back at 150 feet with his .38-calibre revolver.

'Fantastic,' said Johnny McCall. 'Just like the movies.'

Mazzurco was still alive and Kid McCall sat back in the car.

'Hey, Suzi, do that thing with the neck again, will ya. I want to see that again.'

Russian Suzi said, 'Sure, Johnny,' and got out of the car, then walked over, bent down and took Gaetano Mazzurco's head in her hands. Mazzurco looked at her and saw the beautiful face and the snow-white blonde hair and said, 'Help me please, help me.'

Russian Suzi ripped the head back and to the side. There was a cracking sound, like a door being hit with an axe, and Mazzurco lay dead. His eyes were wide open, and still registered amazement.

Kid McCall was really pleased with the savage-looking scar that ran across the right side of his face. He didn't like the fact that he had a pretty, almost girlish face. The scar did give him an older, more brutal look. But the girls still thought he looked like a little cute kid, except that he now also had a cute scar. They didn't tell him this because they didn't want to hurt his feelings.

Poor Johnny couldn't win.

News of the Limerick Castle shootings swept through the criminal world and the deaths of Angelo Bonventre and tough Tony Amato made headlines in the American papers.

Karen turned to Aaron Guzzinburg. 'That's the trouble with importing hired help,' she said.

'Yeah,' said Aaron. 'They don't get exported.' They had a little giggle at this. It was a cross between Jewish humour and gunnie humour. Just the thing if you happened to run into Meyer Lansky.

They were sitting by the swimming pool of Guzzinburg's South Yarra home. Karen had been staying with the Jewish hitman for the past week, keeping an extremely low profile. As the crow flies, Collingwood wasn't far across the Yarra, but she could have been in another country, for all anyone suspected. Which is where Guzzinburg's two Hebrew helpers were, in fact. They had taken a plane for Palermo, Sicily, to do a little business. What with short hours and frequent-flyer points, it was a good job. Providing you didn't get shot, of course.

The Boss who controlled all others, at least as far as the Australian connection went, was Don Pepe 'Little Toto' Della Torre. The Jewish gunmen's overseas assignment was to kill his grandson, Pauly 'Peppe' Della Torre, who lived in a seaside town named Marsala on the western end of Sicily. The two hitmen would never return. You don't kill a Mafia Don in his hometown and get out of it alive. But the two Jewish comrades, who both spoke Italian as well as French and German, had felt sure that all would be well when Guzzinburg kissed them farewell at the airport.

Guzzinburg, however, strongly suspected he'd never see the pair again. Oh, well, he thought, that's war. Sending them to kill Pauly Della Torre was more a message of psychological fear than anything else: from Collingwood to Sicily, with love from the Rabbit Kisser. Next time New York. Guzzinburg doubted the tactical logic but remained silent on the matter.

Aaron had never been much of a romantic, but now he found Karen Phillips in his bed every night teaching him things that would probably kill him. She was simply the hottest sex he had ever had – and she was paying him. He might have been a gunman, but he was a good Jewish boy at heart, and brought up to love a bargain, and it all seemed too good to be true. But Guzzinburg wasn't swept away with love, just lust. If someone else came along and paid him more, he'd work for them. Until then, any time Karen spent checking out his circumcision with her tongue was a bonus.

From her point of view, playing the lollipop game with Aaron seemed a good way of securing not only the physical loyalty that cash was buying, but his emotional loyalty as well.

Poor Karen thought that love and a blow job were the same thing. She didn't know any better. In the emotional gutter she lived in, where men visited their daughters-in-law twice a week in the brothels they worked in, where 16-year-old boys held their 14-year-old sisters down so that six or seven of their mates could gang-bang them in return for a gram of heroin, in a world where sex and drugs and death seemed the norm, a blow job was the closest thing to love you'd get. Karen was attempting to secure Guzzinburg's emotional loyalty in the only way she knew how.

In one way the cynical hitman was right, but in another he was wrong. Karen did have real love for the dead and love for the people who backed her in her war to the death. How could Guzzinburg or anyone attempt to understand the Rabbit Kisser?

'How goes the investigation, Westlock?'

Chief Inspector Graeme Westlock looked up. There, standing in the doorway of his fifth-floor office in the St Kilda Road police complex was the Assistant Commissioner for Crime, Frank Doolin.

'Very good, sir,' muttered Westlock, scrambling to his feet.

'Re these mental cases in Collingwood,' said Doolin, getting straight to the point. 'Running about the fair streets of Carlton shooting the olive oil out of our ethnic brethren. It just won't do, Westlock. The bloody media seem to think it's our fault. What they want to know, and therefore what I want to know, is just what are we doing about it?'

'Well,' said Westlock, 'I thought if we waited for a while they would eventually kill each other.'

'Oh yes,' said Doolin. 'Very droll. A vain attempt at comic relief, I'm sure. Ha ha. But what am I to tell the bloody media?'

Westlock thought about it for a moment. 'Tell them we are hoping to make an arrest within 24 hours.'

'Oh yes,' asked Doolin. 'And who are we arresting?'

Westlock smiled. 'I thought the editor of the *Herald Sun*. He's the one causing all the trouble.'

Doolin turned on his heel and started to walk away. But he couldn't resist a parting shot over his shoulder. 'One day, you'll joke yourself all the way back to traffic duty, Chief Inspector, or the Lost Property Office,' he said. 'I just can't decide which, yet.'

As the Assistant Commissioner walked away, Graeme Westlock thought to himself, Paul bloody Doolin, you precious old poofter, you wouldn't know a crim if you woke up and found Ned Kelly sitting at the foot of ya bloody bed.

It was 9.15 pm at night. Graeme Westlock took the lift to the ground floor and walked around to the small park behind the police complex and sat on a bench. He needed a bit of air to clear his thoughts and let him do some thinking without stray Assistant Commissioners sneaking up on him.

Westlock was aggrieved. He could do without men who had fought their way up the police ladder with a knife and fork and a

Masonic handshake suddenly screaming at him to personally end the biggest gang war in Melbourne's history since Ripper Roy had run riot years before.

He was no fool. He knew Karen held the key to the whole shooting match. But where was she? 'I know you're out there, Karen,' he mused. 'But where?'

While all this was running through his head, a car pulled up about 20 feet from where Westlock was sitting. It was an expensive 1993 Mercedes Benz 500 SL. A man stepped out of the driver's seat and walked over towards him. With a car like that, he could almost have been a stockbroker. He wasn't.

'Hi ya, Graeme.'

Westlock blinked and looked up. 'Hello, Aaron,' he said, deadpan. 'Long time, no see.'

Guzzinburg sat down next to the policeman.

'Well?' said Westlock. 'Is this a social visit, or business, or just an accident?' He somehow doubted it would be an accident. Guzzinburg had a habit of knowing exactly what he was doing. The only accidents around him happened to other people.

'Well,' said Guzzinburg pleasantly, the way a dangerous man can afford to be, 'it's business that may involve an accident.'

'I'm listening,' said Westlock. He was all ears.

Guzzinburg sighed a long sigh and said, 'As our dago friends are so fond of saying on all them mafia movies, "Business is business".'

'Get to the point,' said Westlock. 'Where is she?'

For Guzzinburg, the tide had turned when he received a phone call from Sicily. He had listened in stony silence to a description of how his shadowy Jewish companions had made it to Palermo and then to the town of Marsala. It was no coincidence that soon afterwards Don Pepe 'Little Toto' Della Torre and his wife, his son and three of his grandchildren were shot dead. The Jewish hitmen had not returned to Palermo, but travelled overland to the southern end of Sicily to the seaside town of Licata, on the Gulf of Gela, and from there hired a boat to Malta. But after only 36 hours in Malta they were both machine-gunned to death as they drank coffee outside a cafe in the town of Valletta.

The phone call was simply to let him know that the hands of the Della Torre family were attached to very long arms. Guzzinburg knew then for sure that it was no longer a local gang war between Collingwood and Carlton. It had taken on much larger, darker proportions, and it made him very thoughtful, indeed.

Aaron Guzzinburg always played the odds, and the odds as he saw it were now against Karen Phillips and her drunken collection of street fighters, gunmen, psychopaths and bloodthirsty whores. It was time for him to swap sides and survive. It was the smart thing to do.

It was the only thing to do.

Kid McCall walked out of the tattoo studio on St Georges Road, North Fitzroy. He had his leather jacket on but under it his left arm from the shoulder all the way down to the fingertips of his left hand was covered with a dark-blue spider's web tattoo, just like Mickey Van Gogh and Raychell Van Gogh once had, and just like the one the Rabbit Kisser had. The Kid had another tattoo on his neck. It was the motto of the French Foreign Legion, 'Je Ne Regrette Rien' – I regret nothing.

It was true. Johnny didn't regret anything. In fact, he was in hog heaven. He was on his way to pick up some jewellery he had on order: two thick 18-carat gold chains, 120 grams of gold in each, and with a solid gold engraved medallion on the end of each chain. On one medallion it read 'Coco Joeliene loves Kid McCall'. On the other it read 'Russian Suzi loves Kid McCall'. The chains were to cost $4,000 each, but to Johnny the girls were worth it.

He was also to collect a Rolex watch for himself for a rather reasonable $5,000. And a big gold chain, the same design as the others, which read 'Coco Joeliene' on one side of the medallion and 'Russian Suzi' on the other. This was another four grand.

The Kid had $18,000 in his pockets to pay for his little shopping spree. Hankster the Gangster had delivered what was supposed to be 20 grand to his mum's place. The money was to be given to Karen, but when he counted it there was 38 grand in the bag. Mistakes were always being made with drug and whore money. Shit, Karen collected 100 grand a month in drug and moll money at various addresses. She didn't even count it. Everyone robbed everyone.

The Kid had heard a story once about a big roll of cash being flushed down a toilet by a speed freak who was so out of his brain with paranoia he thought the flat he was in was about to be raided any minute. It took him an hour to flush all the money, and when someone did knock on the door later that morning he shot himself in the head rather than be taken alive.

He was a little hasty. The bloke at the door was the plumber who had come to unblock the dunny.

They had to unblock the toilet a week or so later and found the mulched-up cash in the pipes.

What it all meant to the Kid was that 18 grand going missing was chicken shit.

When he got back to the Telford Club, he found Russian Suzi upstairs in the big bedroom giving Coco Joeliene a fast and furious rogering with a huge buzzing vibrator. Johnny stood in the doorway of the bedroom in amazed silence until the two girls noticed him and, like naughty children caught out, covered themselves and hid the battery-operated monster away.

Johnny the Kid didn't say a word. He just walked in and gave each girl a heavy gift-wrapped parcel and went back into the lounge and poured himself a drink.

After about a minute he could hear excited noises as the two girls tried on their gold chains and came running into the lounge in their dressing gowns with their gold chains around their necks. Both girls had tears in their eyes. Then Johnny showed them his watch and Russian Suzi squealed when she saw his bandaged hand. He took off his jacket and shirt and removed the thin bandage, soaked in blood and ink, and showed off his arm-length spider's web tattoo, his neck tattoo and his big gold chain.

They were all like excited children. Neither Russian Suzi nor Coco Joeliene had ever really been in love – true emotional mental and physical love with any man. But both girls agreed that they truly loved this cute skinny kid. They couldn't stop the tears as they admired the expensive gold chains hanging around their necks. It wasn't the junkie gold – they'd seen plenty of that in their time – but the sentiment that had prompted the Kid to act the way he did. It was the thought that counted.

A strange, unique and lasting emotional bond had formed

between these three lost souls. They had become a little gang of three. Their own little family. It was something they had and only they could understand.

'How big do ya reckon her tits are?' asked Hankster the Gangster.

Michelle Bennett was mixing up a full gram of heroin in a large spoon. She was in much consternation, and the Hankster's questions were annoying her.

'Whose tits?' she snapped, her voice as jagged as broken glass.

'Spooky's tits,' said Hank. 'The big black chick.'

'Why do ya wanna know that for?' asked Michelle, a bit jealous at Hank's interest.

'I was just wondering,' said Hank. 'How big do ya reckon?'

Michelle thought. 'I reckon at least 120 centimetres,' she said.

'What's bloody 120 centimetres?' asked Hankster. 'What's that in the old money?'

Michelle thought again. 'Oh, about 48 inches,' she said.

'Shit,' said Hank, 'I'd slip her on like a wet soapy sock.'

Michelle put the needle into the spoon and sucked up a small quarter. Hank couldn't take much more. She would use the rest.

'Yeah,' said Hank. 'I'm gonna sneak a go at that black moll one night and wop a bit of the Hankster right up her. Ha ha ha.'

'But I thought I was your girl?' said Michelle.

Hank laughed. 'You, ya slut?' he snorted. 'You're anyone's girl. Hey, Michelle, how many brothers you got?'

Michelle looked at Hank with hurt in her eyes. 'Four real brothers, three stepbrothers,' she answered, bottom lip trembling. She knew what was coming.

'Yeah,' sneered Hank, looking to wound the best way he knew. 'And which one of them hasn't been up ya? Ha ha.'

He nearly fell over laughing. Michelle protested, 'What can I do? I've been getting bashed and up-ended since I was 12 years old. That don't mean I like it.'

Hank laughed. 'Oh yeah, what about ya bloody cousins? There's about a dozen of them and they spend more time up you than a tampon. Ha ha.'

Michelle was now in tears. 'Yeah, well,' she sobbed. 'I don't know. It's just the way it is.'

Hank snapped, 'You're a slut moll, what are ya? Go on, say it.'

Michelle sobbed, 'I'm a slut moll.'

Hank held out his arm and grated, 'And don't forget it, slag. If I tell you to jump, you say "how high", OK?'

Michelle nodded as she sucked all the heroin up out of the spoon and into the needle. 'Hold your arm, baby,' she said to Hank.

The big thug gunman held his arm to pump a vein up and Michelle tapped the needle with her finger; she found a vein in his arm, sank the needle in, and pushed the plunger. All the way.

The liquid disappeared up into the vein. Hank said, 'Oh yeah,' and dropped back on to the bed and breathed in, then out, deeply. And didn't breathe again.

Michelle whispered, 'At least my cousins don't call me names, ya bastard.' It was no use abusing him. He was gone.

Michelle went into the lounge of the parlour and spoke to her sisters Tashliene, Samantha and Angela. 'I think the Hankster is dead. What should we do?'

'Check his pockets,' said Angela, quick as a flash. 'And search his car. Clean out all his money first.' A NSW copper had taught her that, and there were no better teachers anywhere north of St Kilda. They used to turn on the lights and sirens to be first to reach a body. Angela had been a quick learner when it came to matters of currency.

'Hang on,' said Tashliene, 'I want the prick's jewellery.'

'Nah, fuck you,' said Samantha, the smooth one. 'We whack what he's got up even between us.'

'No,' said Michelle. 'I mean, should we tell someone?'

'Tell who?' said Angela.

'Tell Suzi,' said Michelle.

'Oh yeah, great,' said Angela. 'And we all end up dead too. Just dump the dog.'

'He wasn't a dog,' said Tashliene.

'Oh yeah, he used to make me bark like a dog whenever he got up me,' said Angela.

'I didn't know he was screwing you,' said Michelle, a strange look on her face.

Tashliene and Samantha looked at Michelle. 'He was plonking all of us and he used to pull that bark-like-a-dog bitch trick on Yolanda as well,' Samantha said.

'What?' said Michelle.

'The big Spanish moll. Well, she is a dog.'

'Whatever,' said Angela. 'Let's take what he's got and ring the boys and get him dumped some place in Carlton.'

'He's got a half-pound of smack hidden in his car somewhere,' said Yolanda as she walked into the room. 'If we are gonna do it, let's do it right.'

Michelle looked at the Spanish whore with the big boobs. 'How long you been listening in, ya sly slag?' she hissed.

Hankster the Gangster was found in Canning Street, Carlton. The girls had shot him in the chest with his own shotgun to make it look like murder. Poor Hankster, gunned down in the line of duty. All wore black at his funeral and cried the loudest. Michelle Bennett even fainted and nearly fell into the open grave with grief. It was a beautiful touch.

That night after the funeral Michelle was unable to service clients and the parlour the Bennett sisters ran was closed as a sign of respect. They sat inside at the kitchen table cutting half a pound of pure heroin up into three pounds, then into lots of three grams.

'God,' said Angela, 'this is hard work.'

'Yeah,' said Michelle. 'And if Yolanda had told me about the half-pound before, I would have killed him sooner. Ha ha ha.'

> *No criminal venture or enterprise can last the distance*
> *without force of arms.*
> Ripper Roy Reeves, 1973

It was a lesson the Rabbit Kisser was learning the hard way. She was trying to carry out a blood war and hold together a multi-million drug and sex empire at the same time. But when she killed Johnny Go Go she blew away half her force of arms and nearly all her drug connections.

She had killed the major part of her own power base and her vanishing act allowed the various Collingwood criminal families to seize control of her empire in return for their physical help in her war with the dagos. She accepted this as fair payment and compensation. Her baby was safe and sound with a million dollars in trust for him, and she had another two million and a massive armoury of weapons hidden in a secret underground cellar under the floor of the Telford Social Club in Victoria Street, Abbotsford.

The Caballero Club had been Johnny Go Go's and as far as Karen was concerned it could die with him. She was all alone. She didn't see Guzzinburg as a part of her crew. He was expensive hired help.

Young Johnny McCall was a cute kid on his way up and a vicious little killer and his love for her and his loyalty touched her, even if he did tickle the kitty when he had to collect money for her. So what. He was a good kid. You can't expect thieves to back you up without losing a little petty cash along the way. The little bugger had touched her pocket for about forty thousand in the past month and bloody Russian Suzi had run financial riot. There was an easy $100,000 missing at her end but what of it? The war was everything. The money was only the grease that kept the wheel moving.

Melbourne had approximately 5,000 whores, and about 1,000 had been controlled by her. The Italians controlled another 1,000. The rest ran free range, like wild chooks. Karen controlled all the smack and speed from Collingwood to Abbotsford, Clifton Hill and Victoria Park. And she was pushing into Carlton and parts of Brunswick and North Melbourne.

Karen had $127,000 in cash on her and two .38-calibre automatic handguns, loaded, and six spare clips. She had a pound of pure meth amphetamine for party use in the back of her 1986-model Porsche 911 Carrera Turbo. She felt safe here in South Yarra with Guzzinburg. She had her police scanner and her mobile phone. To hell with the brothels, massage parlours and escort services and the speed drug factory and the smack connections. If she lost it all, who cared?

She put a full gram of near pure speed into the spoon and mixed it with water. Yeah, she thought savagely, killing Johnny Go Go might have been a tactical error. But it was him or the baby.

Which reminded her of the fear that was never far from her thoughts. If anything happened to her, what of baby Mickey? Muriel Hill and young Melanie Wells won't be much protection, she thought. Russian Suzi would be there, but the bloody Hankster had got himself killed.

Some members of the family would remain loyal. What about the Kid? He was getting close to Russian Suzi and Coco Joeliene. He'd keep an eye on the baby. He was loyal and he could only get bigger with time.

Ideas welled and spun into Karen's head as she put the needle into her arm. Yeah, the Kid. I'd do well to invest a bit in him for the future, she thought. He was a stone killer now, on his way up. When young Mickey grows up, he will need a friend if his mum's not around.

With these dagos, every father has a son and every son a brother and every brother a cousin and every cousin an uncle and every uncle a brother who's got a son with a brother, who's got a cousin with an uncle; it's never ending.

Killing these Sicilians is like mowing the lawn: a few rainy days, a bit of sunshine and a month later you're knee deep in dagos all over again. 'Jesus, and I thought the Collingwood clans were inter-related,' Karen mused. 'No wonder these dagos all looked alike. They've spent the last 2,000 years interbreeding. That's what the Bennett clan will end up like if they aren't careful.' Karen smiled at her own comic thoughts. Then she wondered about the meeting Guzzinburg had set up.

He had arranged to meet with the Turks at Queen Victoria Market. A Jew with Turkish criminal connections – it had to be fair dinkum because it seemed too far-fetched to be a lie.

The story was that the Turks wanted to side with her against Carlton – something to do with a ten-pound heroin rip-off and the Ilhann brothers getting whacked by two of the Corsetti clan last year.

If she allowed the Turks in, she'd have a whole new heroin connection and the Turks had the best connections next to the Chinese. The Sicilians were only really middle men in the smack caper. The Turks and Chinese had direct access to the supply. So a meeting with Abdul the Camel and his sons might be a good idea.

She couldn't help wondering. A little healthy paranoia went with the territory in her line of business. Jesus, she played sink the sausage with that cold-blooded Jew Guzzinburg every night. If he was out to betray her, he could kill her any time.

Karen headed for a shower. She had a lot to consider. Yeah, she'd set up Kid McCall and the two girls, and swear them to loyalty about baby Mickey first. At least little Mickey would grow up with some sort of family and crew of friends to watch over him. A man without a crew in Melbourne was a man totally alone. It was Johnny McCall's birthday soon. Kill two birds with one stone, she thought.

Downstairs, Aaron Guzzinburg picked up the phone. 'It's on for Sunday morning, 2 am. Just me and the Rabbit Kisser. Yeah, yeah,

OK. No problems. Yeah, I understand. And this squares us up, OK? Yeah, I know, it's not personal. Business is business. We both get what we want. OK, see ya.' And he hung up.

He could hear Karen, upstairs in the shower. She was singing.

'Born Free, as free as the wind blows,
'As free as the grass grows,
'Born free to follow your heart ...'

PART 3

TAKING CARE OF BUSINESS

IT was no ordinary Saturday morning for Johnny 'the Kid' McCall. It was his birthday, and he was as proud as a boy with a broken arm. Russian Suzi had spent the past week teaching him to drive a car. By the end of it all, her poor white Mazda RX7 was fit for the junk heap, but he had finally got the hang of the driving caper.

Karen had come out of hiding and taken Johnny to Lennox Street, Richmond, to show him her baby son and introduce him to Muriel Hill and Melanie Wells. Afterwards, she had made him swear an oath not to reveal what she was going to show him. Then she had taken him to a secret trapdoor that led to a cellar underneath the Telford Club.

Johnny had never seen such a collection of arms and ammo. It made the nuffies from Gympie look like peacenik hippies. There was also more money in that cellar than the average crim would see in a dozen lifetimes.

They had some photos taken together and hung them in frames on the walls. Karen had given him a white 1987 Ford Mustang Dominator car, and she gave Russian Suzi a 1991 Chevrolet Corvette and the ownership papers to the H.R. Telford Social Club.

Karen also owned a vacant shop across the street with a two-bedroom flat above it. She gave the ownership papers to Suzi with the understanding that, although, legally, Suzi now owned both buildings, in fact they belonged equally to Johnny the Kid and Coco Joeliene. There was also a list of names marked for death – to be carried out if anything happened to her.

Karen had been in a happy mood when she took Kid McCall around and made all these arrangements. But it was as if she had lived too long and wanted to rest. She had been tapped on the shoulder by the bony hand of death, and she knew it was getting impatient. It was as if she was settling her affairs before she went. You can't live a life like Karen's and expect to end up in an old people's home knitting socks for the grand kids.

Karen had always been matter-of-fact when it came to death. She had seen so much and ordered so many that to her it was no big deal.

She had paid a visit to members of the Van Gogh and Reeves families with expensive gifts and secret instructions. There were tears as they waved her goodbye. It was a bit like planning a long trip, except there's no return ticket from hell. She did her best to smile, but the air was heavy with sadness. In the underworld, people who are marked have an air about them, almost a smell.

Karen had spent her whole life racing headlong towards the grave at 1,000 miles per hour, without a care. But, now the time had almost come, Russian Suzi could sense that Karen's flame was puttering and was nearly out. She was using three full grams of speed a day and was growing more and more insane.

One night they found silly Kerry Griffin and Chinese Lee Lee working Fitzroy Street, St Kilda, on a Thursday night. Both were smacked out of their brains and totally lost. Karen insisted they stay in the spare room at the Telford Club.

Spanish Yolanda had been found wandering the streets of Collingwood, homeless and terrified. The Bennetts had bashed her and turfed her out. She had an interesting tale to tell.

So it was Russian Suzi, Coco Joeliene and Kid McCall in one bedroom and Kerry Griffin, Chinese Lee Lee and Spanish Yolanda in the other. Neither Russian Suzi nor Kid McCall used heroin, but the rest of the girls loved it and it was needles up arms and tongue kissing all day and night. Unlike the others, Coco Joeliene was very strong and, heroin or not, she was on deck mentally at all times, even if she did have this stoned, dead-eye look.

Suzi wanted to spend some cash and get the shop across the road renovated and secure and poshed up – into a real Mink-de-ville, la-di-dah set-up, so she could turn it into a brothel. As Kerry, Lee Lee and Yolanda were only cluttering the place up, they could live and work across the street.

Yolanda was still a stunning, dark-eyed, olive-skinned beauty with a pouty face like a Spanish doll. She would take it any way she was told to, a passive and submissive young lady with a meek personality. But Russian Suzi didn't trust her one bit.

Lee Lee was a brain-dead imbecile. She didn't have much of a brain to begin with and the scag had killed that long ago. The only asset she still had she sat on. Still, she was too stupid to backdoor anyone so she could be trusted.

Kerry was so out of it she had trouble remembering her own name, but each of the girls had something in common: long legs, curvy bodies and big boobs. And they were sex machines, so putting them to work was not only a must but a kindness. It was all they knew. They had got plenty of practice since their early teens.

Coco Joeliene asked Kid McCall if he wanted her to work in the brothel.

'Of course not,' he said. 'Don't be silly. I love you, Coco.'

The big Jamaican girl cried. She was so in love and so happy. Kid McCall was the only guy she had ever met who didn't want to whore her.

The Kid put it this way to Suzi and Coco, 'You're management now. I don't sell my arse, and you don't sell yours. Ya might have to kill a few now and again, but you certainly won't have to root 'em. OK?'

Kid McCall got out of bed and went to take a shower. He could hear Coco Joeliene in the kitchen cooking him breakfast. The Kid and Suzi ate a lot. Suzi was in the garage pumping weights. She had turned it into her own personal gym.

'The bloody cars can park outside in the rain,' said Suzi. 'If they rust, we get new ones.'

Fair enough, thought McCall, as he passed the second bedroom. The door was a bit open and he looked in and said good morning to Kerry, Lee Lee and Yolanda. The three girls were all up and proceeding to have their first blast of smack for the morning. Greedy pigs, he thought. Junkies. The sooner we put them to work the better. They were nice girls but Suzi was right. They cluttered the place up.

Johnny went into the kitchen and kissed Coco good morning, then headed to the shower and turned the water on. The shower always steamed up the bathroom. He soaped himself up and the door opened and big Kerry walked in and lifted the toilet lid and vomited into it then rinsed her mouth out with mouthwash. She was a good girl like that. On the way out she pulled back the shower curtain and said, 'How ya going, Johnny?'

Her eyes dropped to the kid's dick. She reached her hand over and grabbed it. 'Wow,' she said. Her eyes grew bigger as he did. She started to rub soap all over it and with a lather she proceeded to get the boy to stand to attention.

'Wow,' she repeated in an excited whisper. 'Look at it. Is it real?'

Silly question, really, you don't get one of those in a show bag.

Just then Yolanda and Lee Lee both walked in. One vomited into the toilet then flushed it, and one into the sink. They gargled. It was a routine after a blast of heroin. Not good for the teeth but good for the waistline. They joined Kerry for a look at Johnny McCall. It was like a freak show.

'Bloody hell,' they whispered.

Then Kerry took out her false teeth and bent down and engulfed the lad and to the Kid's surprise she nearly deep throated his full length on the first go. Then she choked and gagged and went back to it. After about 30 to 40 seconds she was engulfing the full lot. Kerry was a mental case but a sword swallower of quite uncommon experience. It was a skill like anything else.

Then Coco yelled, 'Breakfast ready, baby,' and Johnny pushed

Kerry's head away. Kerry had a real gleam in her eye and Lee Lee and Yolanda looked as if they wanted to go next. But the Kid felt guilty, as if he had betrayed Russian Suzi and Coco Joeliene and he knew he'd have to confess what had just taken place.

He got out of the shower and dried himself. He wrapped a large towel around himself and went into the kitchen and sat down. Coco Joeliene was serving a massive helping of ham and eggs to Suzi, who had just finished her workout. He told her what had just taken place like a guilty little kid.

Coco picked up a large carving knife and went to walk out of the kitchen but Suzi said, 'Leave it, let me handle it. We don't want any blood. This is our home.'

The Jamaican put the knife away. The Kid felt a bit frightened without his gun, which was in the bedroom. Both Coco or Suzi would beat him in a fight and he thought for a moment that Coco would use the knife on him.

Suzi gave him a savage look then called out sweetly, 'Kerry, wanna cup of coffee, hon?'

The big shaggy-haired hooker walked into the kitchen. Coco poured a hot cup for her and she sat down and said 'Thanks'. She gave Johnny a look like the cat who had just swallowed the cream, or nearly had.

Suzi said, 'You look a bit rough this morning. Did you sleep OK, Kerry?'

'Yeah,' said Kerry. 'I'm OK.'

'You look like you could use a nice massage, baby,' said Suzi.

'Ohh yeah,' purred Kerry. She was still as horny as hell from the unfinished work in the shower.

Russian Suzi got up and walked behind Kerry who was sitting with her elbows on the table drinking coffee and Suzi began to rub her hands into Kerry's neck and shoulders.

'Ohh yeah,' said Kerry. 'That's nice.'

Then Suzi said, 'Your neck's a bit tight, honey. Hang on, let me click it for you.'

She put one hand gently on the girl's head and the other under her jaw. The twisting motion was so fast it took the Kid and Coco completely by surprise. Kerry's neck went snap, deep down her spine and she went limp.

'Oh my goodness,' said Suzi. 'She's fallen asleep.'

Then Suzi picked up Kerry's dead body and heaved it over her shoulder like a sack of spuds, walked out and opened the back door and vanished down the back stairs to the garage. Kid McCall reminded himself not to ever let Russian Suzi anywhere near his neck, or his dick for that matter.

Lee Lee and Yolanda were lying in bed in their room watching TV. They were totally stoned.

Poor Kerry, thought Kid McCall. He didn't know much about females but he had just learned a big heap that morning. Coco Joeliene and Russian Suzi considered McCall to be their bloke and had a simple solution for any girl who thought different.

This was a small point in manners he would remember. Sexual misconduct could result in death. His guilty feelings and honesty had caused the death of a lady for little more than an oral party trick. It had nothing to do with love. Kid McCall was 17 years old and matters of the heart still puzzled him. He loved Coco and Suzi and they loved him – but broken necks at breakfast over a bimbo and a blow job was a little too much to take in. He felt ill at ease. Poor, poor Kerry. It was enough to put a young man off his ham and eggs. Well, almost.

Saturday night was to be a big night. The morning's unpleasantness with Kerry was soon forgotten. Suzi didn't want Yolanda and Lee Lee around and the two whores were packed off to stay with Danielle Davis, who ran a brothel in Raglan Street, South Melbourne.

Danielle was loyal to Suzi and Karen and would put the two girls to work at once and be grateful for the extra help. The Kid's birthday night was to be enjoyed by Suzi, Coco and Karen and no outsiders. They were all going out to the Strippers and Whores Ball at Jamie Nazzerone's nightclub in the city.

The Midnight Machine Night Club was a high-class sleaze palace for the rich and famous and their hangers-on. The Rocky Horror Show dance contest was first on the card, then the Miss Melbourne Erotica contest.

Both Russian Suzi and Coco Joeliene had entered the erotic-dance contest. No one could out-dance Russian Suzi with maybe the exception of the Rabbit Kisser herself, but Coco Joeliene would win any contest she entered.

At nearly six feet tall, with a body made by the devil and a set of boobs that bordered on the totally outrageous, she was a natural born killer when it came to the dark art of erotic dancing. The amazing thing was that no plastic surgeon had ever been near her. She didn't need implants. She could have had two left feet and any male judge would still cheer himself hoarse. As Karen would say to Suzi, 'She was like a black Raychell Van Gogh.'

There was a bit of girlish comedy over who would win.

'God, Coco,' said Suzi, 'they could carry your dead body on to the bloody stage and you'd still win.'

'No, Suzi, you're the best dancer I've ever seen,' replied Coco.

'I want you to win,' said Suzi.

'No, I want you to win,' said Coco.

The truth was that each girl was planning to outdo the other and win – all for the sake of the Kid's entertainment.

Night had fallen and the gang of three were getting dressed to go out. Johnny the Kid put on an Italian-made $3,000 double-breasted suit and a pair of handmade $1,200 Italian slip-on shoes. He wore a black crew-neck thick cotton T-shirt that stood out against the shiny silver-grey suit. He would have looked like a former prime minister if he was a tad more sleazy.

'God, I look like Johnny the Wop,' complained the Kid.

'No, baby, you look gorgeous,' said Coco.

The Kid looked in the big wall mirror. The scar across the right side of his face and the spider's web tattoo covering his left hand did give his angelic little boy face an evil look. He tightened his belt and put his matching pair of chrome-plated gold-cup .45 automatics into his Burns and Martin clip holsters that fitted snugly on the inside of his pants' waistband. The big double-breasted suit coat covered the hardware nicely.

Next, the Kid stuck a thick roll of hundred-dollar bills in his pocket, put on his gold and stainless-steel Rolex wristwatch and the solid gold necklace that he'd paid four grand for. He put it under his T-shirt so only the top parts of the chain would show. He didn't want to be thought of as a show-off. He knew his suit and jewellery were worth more than most people's whole wardrobe. He was as flash as a rat with a gold tooth. The 'Je Ne Regrette Rien' tattoo across his neck was large and thick and added to his sinister young gunnie look. He loved it.

You don't have to be told what Suzi was wearing. Her favourite fashion accessory – the famous white high-cut thong G-string. This left little to the imagination, but then again she wasn't usually dancing for the Mensa social club.

Coco's panties could have been put together with about three pieces of string, and that's if they were double stitched. Suzi went for a pair of white leather thigh-high boots with a 10-centimetre heel. Coco wore a pair of white stilettos with 10-centimetre heels and that was it. Less was more was her motto. With their gold chains around their necks, and several pounds of assorted solid-gold jewellery, rings, watches, bangles, wrists chains, necklaces, ear rings and (for Coco) ankle chains, they looked quite sexually outrageous. The look they cultivated was to wear nothing but dancing knickers, footwear and personal gold jewellery that must have cost a king's ransom.

The Kid didn't ask where it all came from. Sometimes a gentleman knew when to remain silent.

They both put on long white double-breasted soft woollen silk-lined ladies' overcoats and they were ready to go.

Johnny looked a little stunned. 'Is that it?' he asked. 'Is that all you're wearing?'

'Well,' said Coco, a little puzzled, 'the coats come off when we get inside.'

'Is Karen coming?' asked Johnny.

'She'll meet us there,' said Suzi.

They all went in the Kid's new car, with the Kid at the wheel. If it wasn't his idea of heaven, it was close.

Chief Inspector Graeme Westlock sat in a car parked in Inkerman Street, St Kilda. With him was Abdul Yurenc, head of the biggest Turkish criminal family in Melbourne.

'So it's on?' asked Westlock.

'Yeah,' said Abdul, 'that Jew dog Guzzinburg. After you kill her I will kill him.'

Westlock nodded. 'Whatever you like, Abby. As long as I get her.'

'You no want arrest her?' asked Yurenc.

The hard old copper shrugged. 'Sometimes, Abby, a shot in the skull solves a lot of problems. There's no Court of Appeal from a bullet.'

'I no like kill woman. It bad luck, like running over a Chinaman,' said Yurenc.

'I don't like it either, but, as a young kid I used to know was fond of saying, needs must be met when the devil calls. Ahh, Abby, some people die too early and others live too long.'

Westlock was thinking of Blueberry Hill, and for some odd reason he felt a touch of sentimental feeling for the tough young kid and he felt a bit sad at the fate that he knew awaited Karen Phillips. While Hollywood told the world that their bad guys did it better, in Collingwood criminals who would make Bonnie and Clyde look like Mickey and Minnie Mouse lived and died in silence with no one remembering their names outside the bar rooms of Melbourne and the drunken yarns passed down from crooked father to crooked son.

The Kray Brothers killed two, three, four or five men and reigned over a little bit of London for ten years and wrote themselves into the pages of British and world criminal history.

John Dillinger killed one man and robbed 20 or 30 banks and is world famous.

But an Aussie called Ray Chuckles killed at least a dozen and led a gang of drunks on a raid that took six million from the bookies and no one knows his name outside of a handful of old coppers, newspaper hacks and a few old-time crims who bother to remember.

God, thought Westlock, if the Rabbit Kisser was in America she'd be public enemy number one with a book deal and a movie contract, but in Aussie we hide our crims. Only when they are dead do we raise a glass to them in the bar rooms of the nation's hotels and drunkenly cry into our beer about what good blokes they were.

Ned Kelly was only a horse thief. Squizzy Taylor was just a little battler who shot a few scallywags. Poor old Ripper Roy, he just cut people's arms and legs off. Boo hoo for Raychell Van Gogh, she was just a little girl who cut a few dicky birds off with razor blades.

Let's sing a sentimental song for the Rabbit Kisser. What about the men, including police, who vanished into the mist and were never seen or heard of again. All last seen heading in Karen's direction.

Enough is enough, thought Westlock. Yeah, when she's dead she can go up there with Ned and Squizzy and Ripper Roy and Mad Raychell and Mickey the Nut, along with a dozen or so lesser lights. And, yes, I too will raise a sentimental glass to her, thought Westlock. That's life, and that's Melbourne. In Melbourne people fall in love with their gangsters after they die. Which is the way it has to be.

• • •

The Midnight Machine Night Club in Swanston Street was a ten-minute drive from Collingwood, so there was no great rush for Kid McCall and his pair of beautiful killer whores.

Suzi suddenly had an idea. 'Pull past Bennetts' parlour and let's say hello,' she said softly into the Kid's ear.

Johnny smiled. 'Yeah, why not?' He turned into Johnston Street, Collingwood, and cruised along, with one eye on the footpath and one on the road.

'There she is,' said Coco.

Sure enough, there was Michelle Bennett standing on the footpath in front of the parlour. It was dark but the street was well lit up. She was wearing black stiletto high heels and black elastic top stockings, black high-cut knickers and a little black tank top that covered her curvy body hardly at all. She was standing on the footpath, as bold as brass, talking to Terry Kerr.

'Look at this moll,' said Suzi, 'dressed like that in the middle of the bloody street.' From her disapproving tone anyone who couldn't see her would think Suzi was a Sunday-school teacher dressed neck to knee in flannel.

Kid McCall pulled over and parked. They watched as a carload of oriental gentlemen in a 1992 VP Commodore pulled up and called Michelle over. She left Terry Kerr and strutted over to the Commodore like a catwalk model and bent forward and started talking to the guys in the car. Eager little hands reached out of the open windows to touch her. She didn't object, but then she stood up and went back and continued talking to Terry Kerr, and the carload of Asians drove off.

'Shit,' said Suzi, 'I thought the little cow had just pulled the quadrella.'

'Nah,' said Coco, 'they just window shopping. Thrill seekers with no money.'

'Yeah,' said Suzi, 'dream merchants. What are ya gonna do, Kid?' asked Suzi.

The Kid said, 'Karen wants to see Michelle about that story Yolanda told us. I had better let Michelle know and I want to know what that dog Kerr is doing sniffing about. I don't trust that shifty rat.'

The Kid got out of the car and walked up towards Michelle and Terry Kerr.

'How ya going, Johnny?' asked Kerr, who saw him first.

McCall ignored Terry Kerr and spoke directly to Michelle Bennett. 'Karen wants to see you, Michelle.'

What came next shocked McCall totally. Michelle Bennett spun around and snarled, 'You can tell Karen bloody Phillips to go and get a dog up her. She don't tell me to do nothing no more.'

McCall just stood there dumbfounded at such a public display of temper.

'And you can boot off, too, ya imbecile,' said Michelle. 'Kid McCall, ha ha ha,' she laughed. 'I reckon if we put you in a dress we could make a fortune selling your arse. Go on, piss off, you two-bob punk.'

Michelle Bennett's eyes were blazing. She was as high as a kite on something. Terry Kerr, on the other hand, was white with terror at what he knew would follow, and he had good reason to be. Kid McCall pulled out a gun and shot Michelle Bennett stone dead, then turned the gun on Kerr and pulled the trigger.

Saying 'get a dog up her' about Karen was bad manners, but the remark about McCall being placed in a frock and jack-hammered up the ring gear was simply not on. High on drugs or not, it was a clear breach of etiquette and needed to be rectified immediately.

Jamie Nazzerone's nightclub was in full swing when Kid McCall, Coco Joeliene and Russian Suzi walked in. They walked over to one of the four bars in the club and sat on vacant stools. Most people were dancing. The Rocky Horror Dance contest was about to start.

Russian Suzi saw a familiar face and pointed him out to Johnny and Coco Joeliene. It was Clancy Collins, Melbourne's former Chief Stipendiary Magistrate and at present the deputy state secretary of Alcoholics Anonymous. He was standing at the end of the bar, totally alone, singing. He had his trademark red suspenders on and was drinking a large glass of what looked rather like rum or whisky. According to Suzi, it would be whisky, as he drank only Vat 69 Scotch Whisky and was notorious for holding his glass up to ladies in hotels and yelling out, 'Madam, may I offer you a 69?' Very funny.

Russian Suzi said that she met him once after he had given her a suspended sentence for kicking a mug in the face at the Caballero who was trying to grab her feet while she was dancing, and tripped her over.

'He showed up drunk as a lord later that night at the Caballero and held his full glass up to me as I danced and said, "My dear Miss Polanchoishnavich, may I offer you a 69?"' Suzi said. 'I was so pleased that someone had not only remembered my bloody name but could pronounce it that I jumped down from the stage and said, "Your Worship, I'll sit on ya bloody face any time ya bloody like."

'Well, he nearly fell over. Then he told me he was only joking. He's not a bad old duffer really,' said Suzi. 'C'mon, I'll introduce you.'

Suzi marched over. 'Your Worship,' she said, 'how ya going?'

'Ahh, my dear Miss Suzi,' said the drunken old gentleman.

'You remember me?' said Suzi, delighted.

'Ahh, my dear young lady,' said old Clancy. 'I never forget a blonde. Ha ha.'

'If it's not a rude question,' said Suzi curiously, 'what are you doing here?'

Clancy laughed. 'I'm judging the Miss Erotica contest. What else?'

'Ya joking?' said Suzi delightedly, as if she'd just got word that she had the winning lottery ticket. She slid open her overcoat and said, 'How da ya reckon I'll go?'

The old fellow's eyes nearly fell out. 'My dear girl, are you attempting to make me an offer that I can't refuse?' he spluttered.

Suzi laughed, then Coco moved in and popped the question: 'Your Worship, how you reckon I'll go?'

Poor Clancy nearly fell over as she opened her coat and shoved his face between 48 inches of full-bodied Jamaican marshmallows.

When he came up for air, he took a large swallow of whisky and yelled, 'My dear, there's gold in them thar hills.'

Everyone laughed at His Worship's little jest. He had a great sense of humour, old Clancy Collins.

The Rocky Horror Dance contest was nearly over and Jamie Nazzerone, mine host to the rich and famous and the wannabes, came over and enquired, 'Are you ready, Mr Collins?'

The joint was full of yuppie businessmen and young socialites, all in outrageous dress and all drinking chardonnay. Old Clancy walked off with Nazzerone. Clancy, who had a pair of glasses on the end of his nose and several under his belt, got into the spirit of things by grabbing a microphone and beginning to sing, 'Ohh how would you like to be me, down by the rolling sea, sitting on a rock, playing with my cock, with a mermaid on my knee.' Then he fell over. There were more laughs.

Jamie Nazzerone took the microphone and said, 'Ladies and gentlemen, if the contestants will all go backstage, we will try to sober our judge up and the Miss Melbourne Erotica contest can begin.'

Old Clancy came back to life. 'Can I offer anyone a 69?' he yelled. There's no gag like an old gag.

The crowd roared. They sat Clancy on a chair in front of the stage and Suzi and Joeliene went backstage along with a giggling gaggle of assorted lascivious lovelies.

Kid McCall took a stool and sat back and ordered a double Jamieson's Irish Whiskey and told the waiter to deliver a double Vat 69 to Clancy's table. The music started and out came Saigon Sally, a professional stripper from Hindley Street, Adelaide, who didn't even live in Melbourne and had no right being in the contest. She wriggled her arse in Clancy's face to no avail and then left the stage.

The second contestant was a chick named the Towering Inferno because she was tall with red hair. Her real name was Rhonda something or other, and she was a showbiz hoofer who'd gone wrong and ended up taking her clothes off for living. Big deal, thought McCall.

The third called herself Monique, another pro stripper. She wore the French maid's uniform, the whole works.

The fourth was a former prostitute from St Kilda who had danced at the Caballero before it closed because of Karen's war with the Italians. McCall recognised her. She was Gigi Gascoyne. She was a wet dream come to life and old Clancy sat up and took notice.

Then came Chantelle, another whore from South Melbourne, followed by three or four more non-events. Then on came Russian Suzi and the crowd went insane.

Yeah, she's won it, the Kid thought. No one out-danced the Russian. Any dick that wasn't stiff after that belonged to a dead man or a poof.

But the next one on was the big Jamaican, Coco Joeliene. Her body, the face, the legs, hips and the sheer size of her swinging boobs had a hypnotic effect on the crowd.

She got down off the stage and danced over to old Clancy and jiggled her tits in his face, then sat on his knee. This was cheating. She was tormenting a drunken judge. It was clear she would win when she left the stage. She bent forward with her arse to the crowd and touched her toes, and you could have driven a train up what she was flashing at the punters. Clancy covered his eyes in disbelief. If Coco didn't win, there would be a riot for sure.

As Nazzerone was about to come out on stage, he was pulled back, the lights went dark and a single spotlight came on. This was a turn-up. Out came a fabulous Madonna blonde, and McCall sat up. It was Karen. The crowd took one look and cheered. Karen was notorious. Her face and body had been on the front pages of every newspaper in the land, and on every TV news and current-affairs programme. She was legendary. She was the hottest property in six states, in more ways than one. Every cop in the country was looking for her.

Old Clancy sobered up in about two seconds as the sight of the full-length left-arm spider's web tattoo penetrated his brain. She ran that spider's web up and down her body and it sent the crowd mad. Whatever else she was, or was not, the Rabbit Kisser could dance with the devil and beat him. She was the psycho queen.

McCall looked around and, sure enough, there was Aaron Guzzinburg. I hope no one calls the cops, thought the Kid. He walked over to Guzzinburg and the two men stood and watched and, like everyone else, fell under the spell of this dancing witch. The music died and she vanished.

Guzzinburg said goodbye, then said he had to take Karen to see some people. He vanished. Old Clancy got to his feet and took to the stage and, no longer drunk, he took on a serious but comic tone.

'Ladies and gentlemen,' he began solemnly, 'I'm afraid I've let you down. Honesty tells me Russian Suzi won the contest; lust tells me I'd be a fool not to award the prize to Coco Joeliene, and I will go to my grave happy having seen her perform tonight. But my heart tells me to award the prize to a young lady I cannot name because legally I'm going to pretend I didn't see her here tonight, so I must step down as the judge of this contest and ask our host Mr Jamie Nazzerone to award the prize.'

Old Clancy stepped down, picked up his drink and returned to the bar. Nazzerone came out and awarded the prize to the moll from Hindley Street, Adelaide. She danced as Saigon Sally, was Thai-Chinese, had a silicone boob job, was born and bred in Lipson Street, Port Adelaide, and had never been anywhere near Saigon. In fact, she spoke Chinese with an accent that was a cross between

Henry Lawson and Chips Rafferty. Someone tossed a wine glass at Nazzerone as a small protest against his lapse in taste and judgement and he ran from the stage as the booing started.

The girls returned to the bar to join McCall and Suzi said, 'Thanks, Clancy.'

McCall said, 'You're a shifty old diplomat, Mr Collins.'

Clancy laughed.

Coco Joeliene wrapped an arm around the old magistrate and said, 'Can I offer you a 69? Ha ha.' Then she stepped directly in front of him and whipped open her coat.

'My dear, I'm afraid you'd be the death of me,' he said. Then he stood up and kissed Joeliene's hand, then Suzi's and shook McCall's and said, 'I'm off home.'

He looked at Suzi and Joeliene. 'I will take you with me in my dreams. Good night all,' he said and walked out.

'You're right,' said Coco. 'He is a nice old duffer, like a randy old granddad but he's a gentleman really. He said no thank you in a really nice way.'

'Yeah,' said Suzi. 'He is a bit of an old sweetie.'

The Adelaide moll walked out and came past Suzi and Joeliene. That was her first mistake.

'Bad luck, girls,' she sneered. That was her second.

Saigon Sally didn't see Suzi's right hand flick out. But she sure did feel it chop her in the throat. Sally choked and gasped for air. McCall and Coco turned and walked out. Suzi followed. Sally fell to the floor, still choking, but no one heard her. The music was too loud. The strobe lights flashed and no one saw her writhing on the floor with a shattered windpipe.

'Do ya reckon ya killed her?' asked Kid McCall as they got back into the car.

'Well, if I didn't,' remarked Suzi calmly, 'I'm going to get a shotgun and shoot my bloody instructor. In fact, I might, anyway. He failed me on my last grading and I've been polishing his knob for the last seven years. How dare he fail me. Never trust a Korean with a Yankee Doodle accent.'

McCall was wondering at all this. Kerry got her neck snapped for a teensy blow job, but it was quite clear that both Coco and Suzi would hump who they pleased, regardless of him. He was still a little kid in their eyes, no matter how many he killed.

It was a warm night but rain was falling when the big Mercedes Benz glided up to the corner of Peel and Victoria Street in North Melbourne. Karen sat next to Guzzinburg, who sat at the wheel. It was 2.30 am.

Karen sat with her left hand under her leather jacket holding a .38-calibre automatic handgun with the barrel quietly pointing in the direction of Aaron Guzzinburg. He didn't realise that, although Karen had placed her trust in him, she was taking a bet each way. Force of habit, really.

'Where are they?' she asked.

She was looking over at the Queen Victoria Market. The acres of asphalt were shining wet under the occasional street lamps. The stalls were all folded away and locked up. There wasn't even one of the usual mob of derelicts hanging around, necking a flagon of sherry. On wet nights they all went up to the Gill.

Guzzinburg said, 'It's sweet. They will be here. Your little dance trick made us late.'

'Ah,' said Karen. 'Lighten up. It was the Kid's birthday and if we are late they should be here by now, anyway.'

Guzzinburg moved in his seat. She noticed a flicker of nervous tension in the man who was usually as cold as ice. She'd been making love to him for a while now, and tonight she sensed a distant nervous stranger sitting next to her. What men forget about women is that a man can sleep with a woman for a year and still not know how her insides tick, but a woman can sleep with a man for a night and walk away in the morning with a bloody good psychological profile of the man concerned. It is part of the female gift, part of the survival weapon God gave them.

Karen knew something was very wrong.

Guzzinburg lit a smoke and put it to his mouth, left handed. She knew he was right handed. Where was his right hand? It was dark, but the distant glow of a street light lit the inside of the car with a dull light.

Then Guzzinburg said, 'There he is.'

Karen noticed a short, skinny, evil-looking little man she recognised as Ahman Kuku, bodyguard to Abdul Yurenc. Then little Abdul himself stepped out of the shadows. He stood in Peel Street right near the market.

'Let's go,' said Guzzinburg.

Just then Karen noticed the glow of a cigarette butt as it dropped to the ground in the dark behind Abdul, to his left. Guzzinburg opened the car door and Karen said, 'Hey, Aaron,' and fired her gun three times into the body of the Jew. Guzzinburg lurched out of the car and instinctively returned her fire.

The slug from his .22-calibre magnum automatic cut through her lower stomach and out her back. She fired three more shots and Guzzinburg hit the footpath. She dragged herself into the driver's seat and started the car and screamed off.

Three shots from someone behind the Turk hit the car. Karen's left leg wouldn't work. She felt no pain at all and was totally numb down the left side of her body, but her right foot had enough strength to drive the car, and her arms and hands worked OK. She was pissing blood. She needed help but she had no place to run to for medical attention without being arrested.

The bodgie doctors she knew only patched up minor bullet wounds, knife wounds and sold methadone on the sly. She was in serious trouble and she needed serious help. The rain beat down on the windshield of the car and she tried to make the wipers work. God help me, she thought, and meant it. She headed for the Telford Club.

When Chief Inspector Graeme Westlock walked out of the shadows with his gun in his hand, he spat on the ground in disgust. The two Turks had taken off down Peel Street and jumped into a waiting car.

He walked over to Guzzinburg who was crying in pain and yelling for help. He had taken six direct shots in the guts. Ohh, thought Westlock.

'Help me,' begged Guzzinburg. 'Get an ambulance, get an ambulance.'

Westlock looked down. 'Ahh, Aaron. Six shots in the guts. Ohh, I don't think so. You'll never make it.'

Guzzinburg cried, 'Don't leave me here like this, don't just let me die like this, please, Graeme, please help me.'

Westlock looked down and then he checked the street for onlookers. All was quiet in the still night and pouring rain.

'C'mon, Graeme,' cried Guzzinburg. 'Please, please.' And the ice-cold hitman began to cry.

Westlock bent down and put his gun to the hitman's head. 'C'mon now, Aaron. You know what they say ... no tears for a tough guy.'

Then he pulled the trigger.

When Kid McCall, Russian Suzi and Coco Joeliene walked out of the nightclub and got back into the car, McCall found a wrapped parcel and a card on the driver's seat. It was a birthday present from Karen. He opened it and found a solid-gold pocket watch that played music. Ripper Roy Reeves once owned this watch and it had the engraved inscription inside it which read: 'To Karen, the little Caballero, from Ripper Roy.' On the back of the watch Karen had a new inscription engraved which read: 'To Kid McCall, the little Caballero. Remember me always, Karen.'

The music was Ripper Roy's favourite song. Karen would hum it often. It was a tune by the king of American Blue Grass Music, the great Bill Munroe, a song called 'I Hear a Sweet Voice Calling'.

Kid McCall put the watch in his pocket and drove off, thinking it was the most beautiful and wonderful thing anyone had ever done for him. He had tears in his eyes as he thought of that wonderful lady so alone in the world. The Rabbit Kisser. He would love her until he died, and would gladly die defending her honour.

'I hear a sweet voice callin',' he began to hum to himself.

• • •

Karen pulled up in front of the Telford Club and tried to get out of the car, but her lower body refused to move. How she had even driven the car that far was a miracle. She just sat there. Where was Johnny the Kid? Let me die amongst friends, she thought to herself, her head spinning with pain and loss of blood.

The headlights of a car appeared behind her and she heard Suzi squealing to run out of the rain. Then she saw Kid McCall's head looking through the window and the door opened.

'Karen,' he said.

'They got me, Kid,' she whispered. It sounded like a line from a bad Western, but when you've got a gutful of lead, you're pissing blood and your legs don't work any more it's hard to be deep and meaningful.

McCall called Suzi over and Russian Suzi carried the wounded girl into the club and upstairs.

'Not in the bedroom,' said Karen, shaking with shock. 'I'm not dying in bed like some old lady. Lay me on the couch so I can look out the window at the rain.'

Suzi was in tears. McCall was also crying. Coco Joeliene just sat there and began to sing, almost in a whisper, some sort of strange French-sounding chant or song, like some whacked-out voodoo princess. She was freaking out.

'I can't move my legs,' said Karen. 'And I've messed myself.'

'Don't worry,' said Suzi. 'I'll clean you up.'

'What for?' said Karen. 'I'll only bleed more and mess my pants again. Get me a drink.'

Suzi poured a large Jamieson's and took a giant gulp of the smooth Irish fire water herself, straight from the bottle. So did McCall.

They handed the bottle to Joeliene but she was out of it, rocking back and forth chanting something in a weird dialect that sounded like some sort of black magic prayer to God, or maybe the devil.

'Shut her up,' said Karen, and Russian Suzi slapped Coco hard across the face. But Coco was in some sort of self-hypnotic trance.

'Take her out of the room,' said Karen.

Suzi took Coco into the bedroom and closed the door. The chanting continued, but not so loud this time.

'Give us a kiss and a cuddle, Kid,' Karen said.

He knelt down and put his arms around Karen and kissed her.

'Ya won't forget me, will ya, Kid?'

'I'll never forget you, Karen.'

He kissed the dying girl and hugged her tight. Then she looked out the window and said, 'Listen, Kid, run downstairs and get me one of them icy poles out of the fridge. My tummy is so hot I'm burning up. I like them icy poles.'

'OK, Karen,' said Johnny.

When the Kid walked out, Karen looked at Russian Suzi and said, 'Do the trick with the neck, Suzi, before the Kid gets back. I ain't gonna make it. I could lie here like this for days. Do it.'

'No. I won't,' Suzi said.

'Do it,' Karen ordered. She was breathing raggedly. 'Just do it.'

Suzi bent down and took hold of Karen's neck gently and lifted it, steeling herself for the blow. Karen looked out the window and said, 'Ya know, Suzi, I love the rain.'

Six months later. The war was over and all was quiet. Karen Phillips's body had been discovered the day after Aaron Guzzinburg was found dead near the Victoria Market. Karen had been found wrapped in a snow-white blanket with a pillow under her head, lying on top of the grave of Raychell Van Gogh.

Someone had carried out some sort of bizarre funeral ceremony. They'd lit a small fire at the foot of Raychell's grave and killed a chicken and splashed its blood over the white blanket. Candles had been laid out around the body and lit.

A Miss Muriel Hill claimed the body, as the executor of Karen's will. When she was finally buried just across the little walkway from Ripper Roy, Mickey and Raychell, a heap of unsolved murders were all swept into the grave with her.

It was strange, but the night Karen died, the empty Caballero Club burned to the ground. It was for the best. With the death of Karen Phillips and the destruction of the Caballero came the end of the war.

The sun shone again. The cafes, restaurants, clubs, pubs, parlours and card schools got back to normal. People thronged Melbourne's sidewalks and trendy bars, where mugs and molls, monsters and madmen, millionaires and merchant bankers could all order a second helping of dago muck from the same menu.

Lygon Street, Carlton, was not at all sorry to see the last of the Rabbit Kisser. But, in the immortal words of Ripper Roy, 'No one waves a ghost goodbye. Ha ha.'

Kid McCall, Russian Suzi and Coco Joeliene were highly excited. It was the grand opening of the new massage parlour across the road from the Telford Social Club in Victoria Street. A council permit had been granted in Suzi's name and $137,000 had been spent on flash renovations: spa baths, a king-size sauna, a lounge and small luxury bedrooms with en suites. There was a courtyard garden, a bar, a pool table, hot tub, showers and shit houses. In other words, this, that and the other and two of everything.

Six new top-of-the-range girls had been taken on, and a raunchy collection of saucy little sleaze queens they were. Mammaries seemed to be the order of the day and, of 100 girls interviewed for these select positions, so to speak, only the six were picked.

It is said, and truly so, that 90 per cent of whores and ladies who work in the area of the erotic arts have blonde hair – and if they don't they bleach it blonde. It all came from (according to rumour) the wartime blackouts in Australia and London, when prostitutes bleached their hair so the punters could spot them standing on the streets at night.

It was said that any blonde seen after dark in St Kilda, Kings Cross or Times Square in New York or Soho in London was indeed a lady of the night. Strippers, on the other hand, bleach their hair blonde to stand out in a darkened nightclub. A spot light or strobe looks better with blonde hair than any other, particularly in the downstairs department.

So it was that out of the 100 girls interviewed at least 80 to 90 of them showed up looking like Marilyn Monroe or Madonna on a bad night.

There were two former centrefold girls from leading men's magazines, long leggy blondes with a generous helping of bazoomers. There was a half-Chinese, half-Maltese girl with long, jet-black hair and Latin or oriental looks. She was only a short lady, small and slim, but when she took her shirt off Suzi hired her at once because she had a stunning set of watermelons. There was also a chick who was a bit of a comedy. She walked in the door, undid her shirt, let loose a set of monsters, then she took out her false teeth and put her own hand into her mouth up to her wrist and sucked on it back and forth. When Suzi said, 'You're hired,' Melissa Clarke, the young lady in question, said, 'I take it up the clacker as well.' It was an overwhelming CV.

She was a Collingwood girl with a down-to-earth attitude. She also had the classic blonde hair. The other two girls were sisters from Richmond who specialised in the naughty schoolgirl thing: school tunics, stiletto high heels and stockings. The thing was, they were still schoolgirls and the uniforms they wore were their own. They did the 6 pm to 12 pm shift Monday to Friday, took their stilettos out of their school bags, undid their plaits, slapped on some make-up and they were set to rock and roll.

Legally, Suzi was concerned about hiring them, but they were of legal age and built like Mae West, with tits that would keep the Methodists babies home fed for a month.

Suzi and Kid McCall had decided to call the place 'Coco's Restaurant'. Coco Joeliene was quite touched and wanted to act as the receptionist part-time, as Suzi was also handling that job. The sign on the window read: 'Coco's Restaurant: massage and sauna … you can get anything you want at Coco's Restaurant.'

It was quite comic, but the men poured in by the truckload. It was a licence to print money. At $200 an hour, with $50 bucks to the parlour and $150 for the girls. The girls pulled the mugs on flat out from 6 pm until 6 am. The Collingwood crime families had whacked up and scattered the Rabbit Kisser's empire between themselves, but Kid McCall didn't want any part of it. He had the Telford Social

Club, the 'restaurant' across the road and Coco and Suzi, plus a pile of money and the firepower to protect it. What did he care about anything else? Not a thing.

The Kid and his two girlfriends had even turned quite domestic and bought themselves a pit-bull terrier – a black and white patchy pooch that was also a good guard dog. Coco Joeliene loved to walk the animal every morning. She called it Biff because he could biff and loved to do so. He was so aggro he'd attack his own reflection in a mirror. He hated any other dog or cat he saw. Victoria Street belonged to him.

Coco would put on her joggers and a skin-tight pair of stretchy track and field tracksuit pants and a tight boob-tube bra that did its best to hold her in, then her tracksuit top, and off she would go to walk the dog.

Everything she wore was white and against her dark skin it looked sensational. She was a traffic stopper wherever she went, and these dog walks became a regular perve event for the shopkeepers and the men in the bar of the Terminus Hotel.

A six-foot black chick with long hair, giant boobs, a waist that went in and hips that curved out and legs that went on forever. Coco wasn't a tease, but she couldn't help looking the way she did. She would swing her hips and prance about and let Biff jerk her along, sometimes with her tracksuit top open and her boobs bouncing. No wonder everyone knew Coco. The local kids' gang was a crew of boys aged from 14 to about 16. They were a cheeky bunch of scallywags and when Coco walked past they would yell, 'Hi ya, Coco', and she'd smile and wave.

This friendly banter went on day after day, and then it got a bit cheekier.

'C'mon, Coco – show us ya tits,' yelled the cheekiest kid.

When this started happening, Coco stopped with Biff at her heels and said, 'If I show you my tits, you little boys will all go blind.'

This went on for many days, and the remarks got ruder and cruder.

'C'mon, Coco, show us ya tits! Hey, Coco, how do ya like to suck this?' they yelled.

In the end she didn't walk that way any more, but there was one 15-year-old scallywag kid who was hell bent on getting a look at Coco's tits and this 15-year-old had a brain. His name was Archie Reeves, and he was some sort of third cousin or nephew to Ripper Roy, although young Archie had never met Ripper Roy or Mickey Van Gogh. Archie did know Kid McCall but was too young to knock about with the Kid. He was becoming a much-feared, legendary young gunman and there was certainly no one near the Kid's age in Melbourne who matched his reputation for gunplay and death. McCall was on his way to infamy or an early grave – or both.

In spite of the fact that Suzi treated him like a little kid, most people treated him with a lot of respect. Coco's attitude had changed. She was now accommodating the Kid to his fullest length bedroom-wise, and poor Suzi was still squealing after the first three-quarters of McCall's monstrous offering was implanted. He may have been called the Kid but he was as randy as a billy goat. This caused a tickle of jealousy from Russian Suzi, but Coco Joeliene was secretly loving it.

Coco loved her narcotics and young Archie Reeves was no fool. He knew that he could never tempt such a princess with cash – not that he had much cash to tempt any woman with – but he suspected Coco could be tempted in other areas.

Archie was a thief, a bloody good little break-and-enter

merchant. Like most kids who were destined for a life of crime and violence, they started off small and got bigger. He pulled jobs with his 14-year-old brother Ronnie and two other kids – Fatty Scanlan, a 15-year-old, 200-pound fat kid who could fight like ten men, and Bucky Logan, a tiny little runt who could climb through the smallest opening. No shop or home was safe when Archie's crew was on the prowl. Fatty Scanlan would stand guard with an iron bar, Bucky Logan would climb in, and Ronnie would enter and suss the place out.

Archie could fix alarms and crack locks and the gang ran small-time riot, not for great profit but more for fun.

Coco's tits had been a fantasy for all the lads, but Archie was focused on doing something about making the dream come true. He treated the big Jamaican like a lock he must crack.

One night, a chemist shop in Victoria Street got busted into and a modest quantity of pethidine vials went missing, along with a large tin of morphine tablets and two bottles of methadone. It was just another chemist shop bust, no big news. The chemist got a slap on the wrist for keeping dangerous drugs. End of story. The police stuck it on the list with all the rest.

Joeliene was walking Biff one morning, looking like a wet dream, when young Archie walked up to her and said, 'Hey, Coco, I got something for ya.'

He held out his hand.

'What's this, young fella?' said Coco.

'A gift for ya, Coco,' he said, grinning.

She held out her hand and Archie put a vial of pethidine and half a dozen morphine tablets into it. She looked in her hand, then closed her fingers over the goodies and put them in her tracksuit pocket.

'Thanks, kid,' she said, and turned around and walked back to the Telford Club. Barely fifteen minutes later, she was back on the street without the dog and wearing a white stretch micro-mini dress and a pair of little white slip-on high heels. She had her little white tracksuit top on, as the micro-mini did little to conceal her overflowing cleavage.

She walked up the street and Archie was sitting on a brick fence with his little break-and-enter gang.

'Listen, kid,' said Coco, 'you want to sell some of that gear?'

She was stoned off her head, having just blasted a goodly dose of pure pethidine up her arm. It was fantastic and she was in a very mellow mood.

'It's not for sale,' said Archie.

Coco moved in closer to the boy and bent forward to whisper to him. 'Everything's for sale, baby.'

'Show us ya tits,' said the baby businessman.

'OK,' said Coco. 'But I want more of that. I'll take all ya got. Ya got much?'

Archie held out a handful of pethidine vials, about 1,000 morphine pills and two big bottles of methadone.

'Ahh,' said Coco. 'The chemist shop.' She knew exactly what sort of deal Archie wanted to cut. 'OK, let's go. You can't come to my place – Johnny's home and Suzi is over in the restaurant doing the books. You got some place to go, kid?'

Archie was dumbfounded. His dream was not only coming true but also impatiently demanding accommodation. He had no place to go. He lived with his mum up the laneway.

Coco could see what was going on in his head. 'OK,' she said, 'a quick feel-up.'

She headed up the laneway and stepped into a doorway, undoing a button and a zip. The micro-mini fell open. 'OK, kid, go for ya life,' she said.

She was wearing a white thong G-string and no bra and Archie and his gang just stood and looked in amazement. Then Archie touched her and she shivered a bit and he pulled his hand away.

'C'mon, kid, knock yaself out.'

Little Ronnie Reeves and little Bucky Logan both reached out and grabbed Coco's tits.

'Hey,' said Coco, 'this ain't no gang-bang.'

Fatty Scanlan spoke up: 'Yes it is, we all did the chemist shop and we all get fair shares.'

Coco thought for a split second. 'OK, give us what you got.'

Archie handed over seven vials of pethidine and the boys hurriedly ransacked their pockets for morphine tablets. The little white pills were dropping on the cobblestone laneway.

'Be careful,' snapped Coco, 'now pick them all up.'

The kids scattered to collect them.

'OK,' said Coco, doing her dress up again. 'Give it all here.'

The kids handed over several hundred morphine tablets and Coco stuffed them into the pockets of her tracksuit jacket.

'Right, you little shits, wait here. I'll go and grab my car.'

'You're going to lash us,' said Fatty.

'No, kid, I'm going to doodle shake you little buggers till ya pimply little heads cave in,' she said. 'Now wait here.'

139

Joeliene vanished for several minutes, then came screaming up in a cherry-red 1994 Oldsmobile Achieva.

'Shit,' said Archie. 'Look at the car.'

'Fantastic,' said Fatty.

'Get in!' yelled Coco.

'There's not enough room,' complained Bucky.

'Yes, there is,' she snapped. 'Get in.'

They all piled in and Coco sped off down Victoria Street and drove over to a certain motel in North Carlton.

'Wait here,' she said. She came back in a few minutes with a motel key and a dozen cans of beer.

'OK, you little gangsters, let's rock and roll.'

She had her clothes off before Fatty could close the motel door. Bucky started jumping on the bed, Ronnie turned the TV on, Fatty opened a can of beer and Archie stood in stark nervous terror as the big Jamaican undid his belt and ripped his jeans open. But he soon got the hang of it. They all did.

One month later, there wasn't a chemist shop in Collingwood, Victoria Park, Clifton Hill or Abbotsford that had not been hit. Coco had been off heroin for a month, as was Kid McCall's and Russian Suzi's wish, and had switched to pethidine and morphine tablets. Besides which, she had 27 large bottles of methadone stashed away for when she began her own private programme.

McCall and Suzi were pleased at Coco no longer using heroin. She was paying the little gang of thieves cash for the goodies and allowed them to run riot with her on a sexual basis, as a sweetener. They learned they could sell the drugs for twice as much elsewhere, but you show a 15-year-old kid a million dollars or a set of big tits and he will take the bazoomers every time. It's nature's way. Survival of the species and all.

The young fellas were over the moon. They had heaps of dough, or thought they did. And they were all in love with Coco, or thought they were. She became the tactical and strategic head of the gang, planning the burglaries and buying all the goodies at 5 to 10 per cent of their value and a two- or three-hour gang-bang session.

'You'd better watch them little scallywags,' said Suzi. 'The papers and the police are starting to think these bloody chemist shops are the work of an organised professional gang.'

Coco laughed. 'Four school kids with sticky fingers, pimple problems and dicks like baby carrots. Ha ha. Some professional gang.'

'The police estimate the stolen drugs to date to have a street value of over a million dollars. It's getting serious.'

Coco thought. 'OK, I'll tell them to cool it for a while.'

Kid McCall had been spending more and more time going over to visit Lennox Street, Richmond. Young Melanie Wells would take baby Mickey out in his pram for a walk and Johnny McCall would walk with her. Melanie was a big 15-year-old beauty, a really sweet lovely girl and, when McCall watched her with the baby, he started feeling things for this young girl. He would take Melanie and baby Michael on drives to the beach and when Melanie stripped off to reveal her G-string high-cut bikini the kid could see that she was built for sin, even though she had a sweet innocent face.

He was feeling very, very drawn to this beautiful girl and she thought the world of this young bloke who was starting to look a touch evil-faced. To Coco and Suzi he was just a cute kid with a big gun and an even bigger thingamajig, but to Melanie he was a man. She looked up to him, not down on him. The two were falling in love.

They would walk, pushing the pram, holding hands and kissing and cuddling. Johnny used to think what he imagined were poetic thoughts. He thought Melanie was clean and fresh, like a clear summer's day after a sun shower. And he saw a little rainbow inside her eyes and her smile.

The Kid knew he was in love, but there was a bit of his brain that never lost sight of harsh reality. That bit told him that he must not allow Suzi to find out about this romantic development. The big Russian beauty had become quite paranoid and was growing more dangerous.

She had conned Coco into sleeping in the other room, and it was clear she thought Johnny was her guy and no one else's. Yet Kid McCall knew that when she worked at the restaurant that she would kidnap any good-looking client who took her fancy and service him.

Coco didn't mind sleeping in the other room. As soon as Suzi walked across the street to go to work, she would bang the jukebox on and start dancing and proceed to seduce a very willing Kid McCall. If McCall walked out of the shower once, he walked out a hundred times to find Coco standing naked, except for high heels, with her back to him. Touching her toes.

'Ya don't get past me, Kid, till ya pay the toll,' she'd say. Hardly original, but it got him in every time.

Coco and McCall were friends, real friends, and they loved each other, although not the way he loved Melanie. With Coco it was like a mateship with sex involved, and doing it behind Suzi's back was naughty and fun. Sex for Coco was fun. It was no big deal. She loved it. She no longer whored herself, so she did what she did with men and boys she fancied. Even when the chemist-shop kids put the hard word on her, it appealed to her sense of humour to give the little buggers a time they wouldn't soon forget.

Suzi's attitude of trying to kidnap the Kid all to herself only meant that, when Suzi went to the bathroom, which took a timed eight to ten minutes, then Coco spent a timed four to five minutes over the billiard table or the kitchen table or touching her toes. This was the stupid situation Suzi's jealousy had put her into, but it was good for the hamstrings.

It was all giggles and secrets, but it was a dangerous game and both Coco and Kid McCall knew it. The life and death nature of the game aroused them both.

'You're spending a lot of time over at Lennox Street,' said Russian Suzi one day. She was getting more bitter, superstitious and paranoid all the time.

'I just go over to see baby Mickey,' said Johnny.

'Ya not plonking that little chick Melanie, are you?' asked Suzi.

'No, I'm not,' said Johnny, which was the truth. Suzi could sense that.

'Well, make sure ya don't. I'll cut that dick of yours right off if I find out you're playing up on me,' she warned. 'I might need an axe to do it but I bloody well will. I'll do a Jack O'Toole on your O'Toole if you backdoor me.'

Coco sat drinking her coffee. The Kid had just rammed her ring gear so hard for the last five minutes while Suzi took a shower.

Coco was glad she was sitting down because she doubted she'd be able to stand up for a while. While considering this, Coco couldn't help but giggle.

'What are you laughing at?' snarled Suzi.

'You,' said Coco. 'Relax, Johnny loves you. Jesus, Suzi, I'm the one on drugs and you're a health nut, but you're the one that's paranoid outta ya brain. Have a morph pill and relax.'

Without thinking, Suzi picked up the tablet and swallowed it down with a glass of orange juice.

'Yeah, well,' she said, her voice softening a bit. 'I'm sorry, it's just that I love ya, Johnny.' She wrapped her arms around him.

'I love you, too,' said Johnny, as Coco ran her big toe up his leg and winked at him.

Sir Leopold Kidd sat in his seventh-floor office on Collins Street. At 70 years of age, he was fighting fit and still headed one of the biggest merchant banks in Australia. A millionaire many times over, he looked 20 years younger, and felt at ease with life despite being alone. His wife had passed away 11 years before and his only son had wasted his life with wine, women and song before putting a gun in his mouth and taking a shortcut to the place we're all going.

Why did Sir Leopold still work? Because it was all he had. All his friends and social connections came from his work. At this mansion in Toorak, he had millions of dollars' worth of art and luxury but it was a cold and empty castle. He could travel the seven seas in his own yacht, or fly the seven skies in his own jet. He had luxury homes in six countries and he dined each night with captains of industry and the princes of state and federal politics on both sides of the house. He

Above: The family Jag… I do like class.

Below: I prefer indoor sports myself…

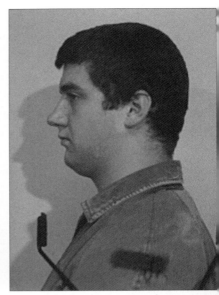

Two years for assault… five for the cardigan.

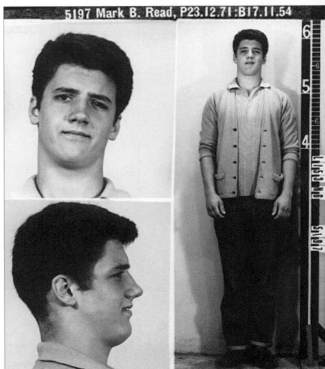

5197 Mark B. Read, P23.12.71:B17.11.54

Left: Between a rock and a soft place – me and Mary-Ann at Risdon.

Right: A nice place to visit, but I wouldn't want to live here.

Above left: I'm allowed out to collect road kills for the birds… but it's nothing to carrion about.

Above right: Me and car. What every prisoner without a driver's licence needs… a V8.

Below left: Born free … *Inset*: No ears for a tough guy.

Below right: Me and Mary-Ann. I do like high heels.

was strong and eager to go but he had no place he wanted to visit, and no one to go with.

He was, quite simply, bored out of his brain. He picked himself up and, as was his wont of late, wandered his building putting his head into offices where he wasn't wanted.

'All correct?' he'd ask brightly, like some Boer War general touring the lines to keep up morale. And some civil young silk suit, with slick-back hair and a small coke habit with only seven more years to go before he paid off his Porsche and 30 to go before he paid off his house in South Yarra and the holiday home he didn't need in Mornington, jumped to his feet and smiled and said, 'Yes, Sir Leo. All correct.'

Leopold Kidd liked people to call him Leo. As he reached the fifth floor, he heard raised voices.

'But you're a fucking investment broker, this is a fucking merchant bank, isn't it?' came a shrill angry female voice.

'Yes indeed, Miss,' said some silk suit. 'But the trouble is ...' He didn't get to finish.

Sir Leo put his head around the door. 'All correct?' he said.

'Yes, sir,' replied the slimy silk suit.

'No, it bloody well is not,' replied Coco Joeliene.

The sight of her stirred something in the old knight he hadn't felt in years, and he wished someone else could feel it too. This black girl was tall, very tall, over six feet in her white high heels. She wore no stockings. Why would she, indeed? Her skin was like dark, rich coffee-brown silk. Her legs ran all the way up to heaven, or very close to it. She wore a tightly cut lady's business suit, all in white with a skirt that cut off about a dick's length from a pair of lovely knees. She wore a lovely collection of solid-gold jewellery that really stood out. The suit coat cut to a deep vee at the neck to reveal – oh so tastefully – the slightest peek of a white lace bra, putting up a valiant effort to act as support.

But the job at hand was simply too much for any bra and, although the expensive well-cut suit did its best to conceal, it was clear to a blind man that this black creature with the white smile, the long black hair and the big wide eyes was built by the hand of God. The eyes caught him and held him. They were green, no doubt the ghost of some white blood in her veins from a generation or two removed. It gave her a haunting look.

'I'll handle this one, young man,' Sir Leo said crisply. 'What's your name?' he said to the silk suit.

'Miller, sir,' the suit said, looking like a whipped dog. 'Wayne Miller.'

'Well, Miller,' said Sir Leopold, 'be careful how you address a lady in future.' He turned his 24-carat manners to Coco. 'Miss, my name is Leopold Kidd,' he said smoothly. 'Chairman of the Board of Kendall, Kidd and Corbott. Alas, Kendall and Corbott are no more and you'll have to suffer with me.'

He held out a splendidly manicured hand.

'I'm Joeliene Gascon,' said Coco.

'Ahh,' said Sir Leo appreciatively, as if she'd just said something clever and witty and interesting. 'French.'

'Yes,' said Joeliene archly, 'by way of Jamaica.'

He was already leading the way to another part of his kingdom. 'This way, my dear,' he said solicitously, like something between the trusted family lawyer and Casanova. 'Dear girl,' he continued, 'I'm sure we can sort out whatever it is that you need sorting and, my dear, if I can't fix it Saint Paul's is always open.'

Joeliene laughed. She was quick on the uptake. What he meant was that the next step up from Sir Leopold Kidd was God. Joeliene smiled big and her eyes danced and her hips swung with just the hint of an extra swing, as if they had been recently well oiled, and when Sir Leopold opened the door to his office and showed her in she swept past him close enough to touch. His left hand rested for a moment in the small of her back against the fine material of her suit. He invited her to sit and he took a chair near her to the left front side. Ignoring his huge blackwood desk, she slowly crossed her legs and the skirt, as it was designed to do, crept up her thighs at a great rate of knots.

Sir Leopold looked at her body from head to toe and, 70 years old or not, found himself with a bone a dog wouldn't chew. He was forced to cross his legs as well. It surprised him, but not her. She had been having that effect on men of all ages since she was 13. All the while her green eyes danced at him.

Kid McCall and Melanie walked baby Mickey in his pram, arm in arm. They were in love. Melanie had cried the night before, telling Johnny that she wasn't a virgin, then she screamed the roof down as the Kid entered her, for she was truly an innocent. She had found the one man she truly loved. The ghost of Blueberry Hill would always haunt her memories, but the flesh and blood reality of Johnny McCall was what she really loved.

'I love you so much, Jackie,' she said.

Johnny noted that he had spent years asking people to call him

Jackie and only two people ever did. One had been Karen Phillips, and that only a few times. And now Melanie.

A car screeched up on to the footpath and Russian Suzi got out. She had a baseball bat. 'You dog,' she screamed. 'I knew it, I knew it, you and this little trenchmouth slut. I'm gonna kill her in front of you. Go on, ya slut, get a bit of this into ya!' She swung the bat at Melanie.

Johnny the Kid was in a state of fear and panic. His brain raced from his own safety to Melanie's and then to Mickey in the pram. He was sworn to protect baby Mickey, the ghost of Karen Phillips would haunt him forever if he didn't. Before Suzi could take a second swing with the bat, he pulled out the small .38-calibre snub-nose revolver he was carrying and fired. The bullet hit Russian Suzi in the centre of the chest and she stopped and looked down then back up to Kid McCall.

'But I love ya, Kid,' Suzi said.

Then she fell backwards and lay there crying. 'I love ya, Kid,' she said three times, and died.

The Kid stood there with Melanie and baby Michael and a crowd gathered. The police came and for some reason McCall didn't run.

'Madam,' cried a drunken Clancy Collins, 'may I offer you a 69?'

Coco Joeliene looked around and there he was in all his wild old Irish glory.

'I've been looking for you,' said Joeliene. 'How ya going, Mr Collins?'

'My dear girl,' said Old Clancy. 'Don't call me Mr Collins.'

'What should I call you?' she asked.

'Well,' said Clancy, 'call me next please, and get that dress off.'

Clancy laughed loudly at his own comedy, while Coco tried to straighten him up.

'C'mon, Mr Collins, this is serious. I need help.'

'Well, first, my girl, you'll call me Clancy. Then you'll tell me what help a lady in distress needs. Have no fear, my dear, Clancy's here.'

They stood in the bar of the Santa Fe Gold nightclub in Russell Street, and Coco told him her story.

'My dear, I haven't acted as a lawyer for anyone in years,' he protested.

'But I don't know any other lawyers I can trust,' said Coco.

'But, my dear, it's a murder charge and I'm out of touch. I'm no longer the man I once was.'

'Bullshit,' said Coco Joeliene. 'You're Clancy fucking Collins. Jesus, you're a living legend.'

'True, true, true,' said Clancy, 'and you say self-defence was involved. A jealous Amazon with a black belt in karate and a 17-year-old lad defending a 15-year-old girl and an infant child. Another drink, my dear, a double.' Clancy handed the waitress his empty glass and stuffed 20 dollars into her garter belt.

'Yes, yes, yes,' he said in deep thought, totally ignoring the bevy of dancing babes on the stage. 'You know, I reckon old Clancy could do it.'

Coco threw her arms around the old gentleman's neck and his hands fell on to her hips and bottom and he didn't remove them.

'Now, my dear, as to my fee, I'm a bit out of touch. Let's say two grand a day and lunch and drinks at half-time.'

Coco laughed. 'Let's say four grand a day and lunch and

drinks at Coco's Restaurant every day of the week after work,' she replied.

Clancy looked surprised. 'My dear, I didn't know you were in the catering trade. How very convenient. Ha ha. Yes, my dear girl. Clancy Collins rides again. And if I may say so I've never lost a murder case.'

Coco was impressed. 'How many murder cases have you won?' she asked, as they left the club arm in arm.

Clancy coughed and cleared his throat. 'None, my dear. You see, I've never actually defended anyone on a murder charge. In fact, the last time I appeared in court was 1969 Richmond Court of Petty Sessions, O'Connell versus the Crown. A nasty case of wrongful arrest involving a man with a goat. We'll say no more on that topic. Distasteful business.'

'Did you get him off?' asked Coco.

'Yes, of course,' replied Clancy. 'But the goat had to be put down. As I said, my dear. Nasty business.'

Coco Joeliene was putting a suitcase full of drugs into the back of her car, along with another bag containing $500,000 in cash. She had given Johnny the Kid's mother another 500 grand, and invested a further half-million with her dear friend Sir Leopold Kidd, who had doubled her investment in three months. Somehow, Russian Suzi and Johnny the Kid and Coco had blown the other half million that made up the two odd million in the secret cellar, but who cared? It was time for Coco to go.

She'd been someone else's slave girl since she was ten years old and now she was a woman with her own money and truckloads of it, and a man who truly loved her. Yeah, Sir Leopold was old enough to be her granddad, but he loved her and if she took it easy on him he could last a good few years yet. She didn't really love him, but she liked the old guy. He was nice and he knew that she was God's little goodbye gift before he went to the big boardroom in the sky.

How many old pops get to sail off into the sunset with a woman most young men would commit suicide over? He was in seventh heaven and he knew it and she'd keep him there. Why not? Old Leo was a good old guy and she was 48 inches of Jamaican marshmallow all alone in the world.

'How ya goin, Joeliene?'

She looked up. It was young Archie Reeves, the teenage thief who entertained her with chemist-shop goodies in return for a little cash and a whole lot of Joeliene. He was a scruffy, cheeky-looking scallywag with a cute look. Joeliene had a soft spot for this streetwise young ragamuffin in spite of the fact he was a hopeless tealeaf and a pants bandit who'd up-end anything in a skirt, given half a chance.

'How ya goin', baby?' said Joeliene.

'Are you going someplace, Coco?' said Archie.

'Yeah, baby,' said Coco.

'Where?' asked Archie.

'Oh, on a yacht, far away,' she said.

'Can I come?' said Archie. 'Please.'

Coco looked and thought why not take a little bit of Collingwood with her. In a world of death and tears, this scruffy little sneak thief was probably the happiest, cheekiest memory she had next to Clancy Collins. Why not?

'Yeah, OK, kid,' said Coco. 'You want to go pack something?'

Archie jumped in the car. 'Nah, I'm right. I got nothing anyway,' he said.

Joeliene jumped in the car and started the engine up and drove off slowly. As they passed the terminus, a laughing and very drunk Clancy Collins staggered out with his arm around a scantily clad Melissa Clarke. He'd grown quite fond of Melissa. He raised his glass in a salute and yelled, 'A 69, my dear?'

Coco laughed and waved. The old boy would have won Johnny the Kid's case had he not fallen asleep during his own summing-up. In his final address to the jury he had nodded off, dead drunk, and still got a not guilty verdict on the murder charge, but poor Kid McCall went under on manslaughter and copped a quick three years.

Melanie had been in tears, swearing to wait for the Kid with undying love, and Coco believed she would.

It was all over. There was nothing left for her in Australia.

'Where we going again?' asked Archie.

'Montego Bay, baby. Montego Bay. Now you gotta promise to be a good kid, no go getting yaself full of piss and bad manners. I'm gonna introduce you to the man I'm going to marry. He won't mind you coming along. He said he'd buy me another pet. I'll just get him to buy me you, OK, baby?'

Archie smiled. 'I'll be on my best behaviour, Coco.'

'Just keep ya sticky fingers in ya pockets and ya fly zipped up,' said Coco.

As they drove through the dusty streets, Archie was looking out the window. Then he turned and with a curious puzzled expression he said, 'Hey, Coco, can I ask a question?'

'What's that, baby?' she said.

The puzzled expression stayed on the young lad's face. 'Did Snowy Cutmore really come from Collingwood?'

PART 4

A SWEET VOICE CALLING

IT was 1956. Russian tanks had invaded Hungary to put down a revolution. British troops went in to sort out the shit fight over the Suez Canal. Rocky Marciano hung up his gloves after proving to the world he was the greatest heavyweight boxer to that date after taking the crown from Jersey Joe Walcott in 1952.

In Melbourne, Frank Sinatra's latest movie had just hit town, the 1955 classic *Johnny Concho*. It was the year a no-hoper horse named Evening Peal won the Melbourne Cup. And, of course, it was the year of the Melbourne Olympic Games, the 16th games of the modern era. The Duke of Edinburgh was in town, the Russian runner Vladimir Kuts was winning heaps, the Olympic great of past games Czechoslovakian Emile Zatopek was on a downhill slide, and two NSW coppers, Merv Wood and Murray Riley, won bronze in the double sculls rowing. They, too, were on a downhill slide. Wood won gold in the single sculls in London in 1948 and silver in Helsinki in 1952, but was to end up a villain and not a hero.

Betty Cuthbert and Shirley Strickland were winning everything, and Brigid O'Shaughnessy was watching it all on her TV set. The only TV set in all of Easey Street.

Hell, if it comes to that, it was the only TV set in all of Collingwood, full stop. Brigid was a big, tall girl of 24, with long legs and curves in all the right places. She did her best to look and act just like her Hollywood B-grade movie-star heroine Jayne Mansfield. Brigid really did look like Jayne Mansfield, with her gorgeous pouting face, bleached-blonde hair, narrow waist and swinging hips. Her extra-large set of jugs set the whole fantasy off very nicely, if you don't mind and she certainly didn't.

Brigid did look the part and acted it as well. Most of the prostitutes in Collingwood modelled themselves on Hollywood film stars – although the one that looked like John Wayne didn't get all that much work, especially before the pubs shut.

Brigid's 20-year-old sister, Colleen, looked like Shelley Winters. Carol Pepper looked like Kim Novak. Bonny Brown did her best to copy Marilyn Monroe. Young Kay Kelly, who was only 14 years old but big for her age, looked like Grace Kelly. Rayleen Bennett did a fantastic Marlene Dietrich. Val Taylor, a vivacious 15-year-old, looked for all the world like Googie Withers. It was fair to say that Jenny Phillips and Cathy Reeves both looked like Betty Grable – and that's only the whores who lived in Easey Street.

The Olympics had done one good thing for the local prostitution industry. The prices had gone from ten bob a time to a straight pound. Yes, a quid a pop, that's inflation for you. But for Brigid

O'Shaughnessy, who was already charging two pound a time, it meant putting her price up to three quid. She handled six to nine mugs a night after the pubs shut at six o'clock. That's why she could afford a brand-new television set as well as the 1954 Pontiac she drove. Now she could tiddle the nobs for a change.

Brigid and the rest of the girls in Easey Street never had to fear the police or the standover men who robbed the rest of the whores in Melbourne. The vice squad from Russell Street Headquarters was headed by big Bluey Westlock, an old third-generation copper. He and his right-hand man Bull Kelly, a second-generation policeman, both took their slings out in trade. At least there was no problems with tax, that way.

As for the crims, thugs and gangsters, Easey Street was ruled by a tough teenage kid and his gang. Young Roy Reeves was not only the leader of the toughest street gang in Collingwood but he was also Brigid's nephew. The last bloke to try it on with a girl from Easey Street was Desmond Costello, and young Ripper Roy had shot him dead in Fitzroy the previous year. It was his first murder and it took the young tough with the Gary Cooper looks from a nobody to a local legend in less than 12 months.

One killing did that in those innocent days.

It was Sunday night, Brigid's one night off. She sat watching her new TV set with a large glass of Gilbey's gin and lemon in her hand. It was her seventh drink for the evening and she was feeling the effect, and loving it. She wore a white pure-silk dressing gown and a pair of white high-heeled slippers. She had the TV turned down and just sat looking at the black and white picture.

The electric record player blared out the sound of Brigid's favourite singer and music man, the king of American bluegrass music Bill Monroe and his mandolin. She was looking at a record by Earl Scruggs and Lester Flatt, pondering whether to put it on next. Or maybe she'd listen to Hank Snow or Leon Payne singing 'I Love You Because'. Or maybe Bing Crosby or Frank Sinatra, or maybe Tommy Dorsey's Band or what about that new bloke, what was his name again? Elvis Presley.

Brigid laughed to herself. Elvis Presley. Shit, she thought. Ya won't get too far with a name like that. Sounds like a real duffer. But he did sing nice. His voice did something to her. I might get some more of his records if I can find any. But for now Hank Snow singing 'I Don't Hurt Any More' would do very nicely, thank you.

Bang, bang, bang.

Brigid's head shot up. 'God,' she said to herself. 'Who's that?'

She looked at the clock on the mantelpiece. It was 7.30 pm.

'Who the hell is that, at this hour?' she grumbled.

Brigid got up and put her cute .22-calibre handgun into the pocket of her silk dressing gown and held it as she walked down the gloomy hallway of her little single-front, two-bedroom house to open the door.

She turned the outside light on first. The flyscreen door was shut, but offered little protection. She peered through it at the shadowy figure on the veranda.

'God,' she snapped, sounding relieved and annoyed at the same time. 'It's you, Roy. What the hell are you doing? You gave me a fright. Sunday's my night off. Bloody hell, I'm a bit pissed. I'm sorry, darlin', come in.'

'Hi ya, Auntie Bee,' said Roy, using the pet name he'd always called her. He pulled the old flyscreen door open and gave the big blonde a kiss on the cheek.

She was still holding her pistol in one hand and her glass of gin in the other. Suddenly, she giggled. 'Sorry, darlin', I was in dreamland.'

'Oh great,' said Roy, hearing the music playing as he walked down the hallway. 'Bill Monroe, I love Bill Monroe,' he added. 'He's the best.'

'Do ya want a drink, Roy?' Brigid asked.

'Ya got a beer?'

Brigid went into the kitchen and opened her fridge. It was brand spanking new. Most people around Collingwood still had ice chests. She had everything, Roy thought to himself.

'Shit, a fancy electric fridge,' he said.

Brigid pulled out a Richmond Bitter and handed it to him. The kid ripped the cap off the bottle with his teeth and swallowed. He was not Rex Harrison from *My Fair Lady*.

'I wish you wouldn't do that, Roy,' said Brigid.

'What?'

'Take the cap off with ya teeth,' she said. 'It sets my nerves on edge watching you do that. Anyway, sit down.'

Roy sat and fixed his eyes on the TV set. 'It's bloody amazing, isn't it?' he said dreamily. 'What they can do now days. Bloody fantastic.'

Brigid sat beside him on the couch. 'Yeah,' she said. 'I can't get over it.'

'How the hell did ya get one, Auntie Bee?' asked Roy. 'Ya gotta order 'em a year in advance. I heard they cost a mint, then ya got to get the bit of wire thing set up on the roof.'

Brigid thought for a moment. She'd screwed not only the bloke who owned the shop but the two who delivered it and fitted the aerial, and it had still cost her nine pounds to get it all fitted in time for the bloody Olympics. But she didn't want to share this info with young Roy.

'Oh you know, Roy, a bit of cash and a bit of luck.'

Ripper Roy snuck a sideways glance at his Auntie Bee's enormous set of tits and smiled. Roy thought she might have been using rhyming slang, but what rhymed with cash? He had a fair idea how she got the TV set, the same way she got the flash car. A bit of cash and a bit of hanky panky. The mugs would fall in love after the first knee trembler and she'd soon get her money back. Her trick was to bung on the dumb blonde, cute and pouty Jayne Mansfield routine – it worked every time.

Some things never change.

'Oh, I've only got two pound. Oh, and I really wanted that watch, could you hold it for me.' Big smile. She had a way of wiggling and jiggling about when she talked to men, even when she stood still, and she always spoke to the manager or owner of the shop. She had screwed most of the shopkeepers in Smith Street, Collingwood, and the married ones spoiled her rotten for the sex, but most of all for her silence.

Roy had polished off his bottle of beer and they both sat watching the box. The record had finished and the arm with the needle in it came up and back and rested all on its own. Roy was amazed.

'Jeez,' he said. 'That's a fancy gizmo. How much did that cost?'

Brigid smacked Roy on the leg and said, 'Don't always be asking the price of things, Roy. It's bad manners.'

'Sorry, Auntie Bee,' he said.

Brigid looked at the electric radiogram record player. 'Anyway,' she said. 'It was a gift.'

Roy burst out laughing. 'I bet it was,' he roared.

'What are you trying to suggest?' said Brigid. She was finishing off her eighth gin, and getting a little bit elephant's. 'Look, Roy, ya know ya Auntie Bee's a bit of a scamp, so don't be a shit stirrer. Who cares what this cost or how I got that. Ya know that handgun I gave you last year for ya birthday?' she said. 'Do ya think I paid for it? Nah, of course not. Ronnie West, the gunsmith, practically wets his pants whenever I walk past his shop. I spent a quick ten minutes face down over his kitchen table to get you that handgun, so don't have goes at me,' she snapped.

Roy was shocked at this outburst. 'I'm sorry, Auntie Bee.'

'Yeah, well, so ya should be, ya cheeky little tacker. I'm your auntie. Your mother is my big sister, so treat me with proper respect.'

She poured herself another gin to go with the wounded dignity.

'I'm sorry,' said the chastised Roy, who put his arm around his favourite relative and kissed her on the cheek again. For a bloodthirsty killer, he was really a nice boy underneath.

Her mood softened at once. 'I'm sorry, Roy. I'm a bit drunk. I'm sorry, baby.'

'Anyway,' said Roy. 'It's about Ronnie West that I come to see ya. I need you to talk to him for me.'

'What about?' asked Brigid. 'Some bloody new gun, I expect. I don't know, Roy, you and ya guns, you're a real little Audie Murphy, aren't ya, darlin'?' she said with a smile and a cuddle.

She stood up and wove her way over to the record player

and put on a Frank Sinatra disc. 'Well, go on,' she said. 'Tell me about it.'

Roy poured her a large gin. A large gin for Bee was enough to blind the average Indian elephant.

'Ronnie West has got an Owen submachine gun,' he said. 'I offered him ten quid for it, then 20 quid. But he won't part with it. Jeez, Auntie Bee, with a bloody Owen gun, me and my gang could run Collingwood. Bloody hell, I've got to get that gun.'

Brigid thought to herself for a moment. Her young nephew and his gang were more feared in the local area than even they realised, but with an Owen gun in Ripper Roy's young hands her own control over the Collingwood street whores would be secure.

The Murrays and the Bennett Brothers and the rats from Fitzroy and Carlton had been threatening to slash Brigid's face if they caught her outside Collingwood. If she wanted to build and expand her own power, she had to support the up-and-coming career of her nephew. She knew why Ronnie West was holding out on the sale of the gun to young Roy. West knew Roy would come to Brigid, and in turn Brigid would go and see Ronnie and the randy gunsmith would not only get his 20 quid but he'd get to run rampant over every inch of Brigid's body for however long it took, which wasn't long, as Brigid remembered.

Yes, she thought, if there is a machine gun going spare, then Roy must have it before it falls into the wrong hands.

She took the glass of gin from her nephew and held it up to her mouth and took a large swallow and her dressing gown fell open. She was only wearing panties underneath and her bosoms were on show, but she didn't move to cover herself.

'Don't worry, Roy,' she said as she swayed to the music, 'that gun is yours.'

Young Roy looked at his Auntie Bee swaying to the music with her silk dressing gown open at the middle and he flushed red in the face and felt himself swelling in an area that he didn't want his auntie to know about. Brigid, however, took a certain evil delight in teasing her young nephew and knew what effect her dancing and swaying body was having on the boy. He was only human, after all.

'I gotta go now,' said Roy.

All he wanted to do was get out. He felt embarrassed that he could get into such an excited condition over his own auntie. Brigid was lost in a seductive dance routine. Roy stood up to leave and his excited condition was making itself evident. The bulge in his trousers was ridiculous, as Roy had backed up for a second helping when the good Lord was handing out the dicky birds.

'God, Roy,' giggled Brigid, pointing to his groin. 'Every time you come to see me of late, you sit on my couch and crack a bone that a dog wouldn't chew on, then get up and run out the door. Does your mum know you want to do it with your own auntie?'

'I do not,' protested Roy, trying to cover his condition with both hands in his pockets.

'Well, what the hell do ya call that thing you're trying to hide?' she said, pointing again to the area in question. 'They haven't seen a monster like that outside of Loch Ness.'

Brigid was still dancing as Sinatra sung. She had an almost hypnotic effect on the lad.

'I'm sorry,' said Roy, almost in tears with embarrassment. 'I'm sorry, Auntie Bee.'

Brigid smiled and walked over to Roy and put her arm around him. 'Don't be sorry, darling,' she cooed. 'It's nothing to be ashamed of. Don't worry, baby. This will be our little secret. Ya mum will never know.'

A group of big, mean-looking teenage boys stood across the street from Ronnie West's gun shop on Johnston Street, Collingwood. Irish Arthur Featherstone, Terry Maloney, Benny Epstein, Mocca Kelly, Bobby McCall, Tommy Pepper, Ray Brown, Normie Bennett, Kenny Taylor, Paul Phillips, Eddy Bradshaw and Mickey Twist, all of them were waiting for the head of their street army, Ripper Roy Reeves, and his wet dream in high heels of an auntie, Brigid O'Shaughnessy.

'Here they come,' said Mickey Twist, pointing at the big white 1954 Pontiac.

'Shit,' said Bobby McCall, 'I'd love to get into that car.'

'Yeah,' said Normie Bennett, 'and I'd love to get into what's driving it. I'd love to get into her glove box.'

They all laughed, as young men with more mouth than experience often do.

'Don't let Roy hear ya say that,' said Irish Arthur.

The mention of Roy's name stopped all laughter. Most of the boys who stood in the group were older than Ripper Roy. Between 16 and 19 years old compared to Roy's humble 15, but the murder of the gunman and standover man Desmond Costello by Roy when he was only 14 put him above them all. They knew Roy carried a loaded .38-calibre revolver his auntie had given him, and he'd use it at the drop of a hat. Roy was a serious young man who would not hear a slight against his auntie without immediate retribution.

The big Pontiac pulled up. Roy got out and ran around and opened the driver's side door to let Brigid out. He was well mannered, was Roy. Brigid wasn't pleased, and she pulled Roy to one side.

'What are these whackers doing here?' she whispered to him, scowling.

'That's me gang,' he said.

'Yeah, I know that,' said Brigid. 'But let's not beat about the bush. You and I both know why you asked me to talk to Ronnie West, and you and I both know that ten seconds after I walk into that shop he'll lock the door and hang the closed sign in the window and in about half an hour's time I'll be walking out with your blinking Owen gun.'

'Yeah,' said Roy, 'and I love you for all you do for me, Auntie Bee.'

Brigid smiled and said, 'I love you too, Roy, but you don't expect me to walk in there and do the business with this team of wombats hanging about outside clutching their tossles and giggling like a pack of silly buggers. It's bloody embarrassing.'

Roy was puzzled. 'But, Auntie Bee, where I go, me gang goes,' he said.

'Look, Roy,' continued Brigid, 'ya know the Saint Patrick Hotel around the corner? Tubby Phillips runs it. Tell him I sent ya and he'll let ya in.

'Shit,' said Roy, 'we're all under age.' He could kill a man in Bourke Street without blinking an eye, but he was concerned that he might be seen in a pub drinking something stronger than red lemonade.

'Oh, don't be silly,' said Brigid. 'You're carrying a gun and ya all look heaps older than you are. Besides, when Tubby finds out you're my nephew, he'll do what he's told.' She winked.

Roy got the picture. 'Oh yeah. Ha ha. OK, Auntie Bee. C'mon, boys,' said Roy. 'We're all off to the Saint Pat.'

'Hang on,' said Brigid and handed Roy a quid. 'You'll need some money. Stick this in your kick.'

'Thanks,' said Roy and gave her a big hug and a smooch on the cheek. The gang waved her goodbye as Brigid walked across the street to the gun shop. Every one of the pimply-faced gangsters would have given a year of his life to be in Ronnie West's shoes. Or his undies, anyway. Brigid was thinking to herself, I hope this doesn't take long. The things I do for young Roy. I deserve a Brownlow bloody medal for the best and dirtiest.

Most of the gang already drank in pubs in Collingwood, but for Roy the drinking caper was all a bit new. Then there was the shock of finding the great and feared Aussie boxing champs Redda Maloney and Jackie Twist going hell for leather in the bar of the Saint Patrick. It was a sight to behold.

The two pugs were both covered in blood, and the sawdust on the pub floor was such a bloody mess it looked like a butcher's shop after a big day. Tex Lawson stood at the door. He was a tough young dockie, about 20 years old. Next to him stood the lovely Colleen O'Shaughnessy. Roy called her Auntie Coll.

She might have looked like Shelley Winters, but she didn't look happy. In fact, she was in tears and her big bazoomers heaved up and down as she sobbed.

'What's going on?' asked Roy. 'What's going on, Auntie Coll?'

She flew into his arms. 'Twist tried to stamp me for ten quid and then he hit me, and Redda jumped in.'

Roy went for his gun, but a big man stopped him.

'Ease up, kid,' he said. It was Fred Harrison. 'Twist will keep. Besides, there's no way in the world he'll beat Redda Maloney.'

Freddy 'the Frog' Harrison was an underworld legend and without a doubt the most feared man on the Melbourne waterfront. He was also no friend of Twist's and had smacked Jackie about in public several times to prove the point.

'You're a dog and a hoon, Twist,' yelled Harrison. 'C'mon, Redda, into him.'

And with that Maloney sent Twist to the floor with a flurry of upper cuts, leaving the heavyweight champ out cold.

Freddy the Frog walked up to the unconscious Twist, opened his fly and pissed on to the boxer's puffy face. 'There you go, Jack,' he sneered. 'Have a drink on me.'

Everyone in the pub broke out laughing. Freddy the Frog, young Tex Lawson and Redda Maloney swaggered out.

'Are ya coming?' Freddy yelled to Colleen.

She looked at Roy. 'See ya later, darl. Here ya go,' she said, giving him a quick hug and a kiss, and stuck a five-pound note in Roy's hand. 'Have yourselves a drink on Colleen.' Then she swayed and wiggled over to Harrison's 1952 Chevrolet, and got in it.

The big man waved at Roy Reeves. 'Hey, Roy, your dad was one of the greatest. Take care of yaself, son.'

'Yeah, Mr Harrison,' yelled Roy as the car drove away. He didn't know it would be the last time he'd ever see the great Freddy Harrison alive ever again. The Frog got croaked soon after. The funny thing was, although there were dozens of men on the wharf when it happened, not one was able to tell the police who did it. Even the ones with bits of blood and brains splashed on them. But some of them reckoned later that, if they had seen the bloke with the shotgun, it was just possible he might have looked a bit like Jack Twist. Of course, that was probably foul slander and innuendo.

Evelyn Owen was a motor mechanic from Wollongong. He invented the Owen submachine gun in 1938. At first it looked like a small Thompson machine gun. The first production models were issued to Australian troops in New Guinea as replacements for the much heavier American Thompsons in 1942, and in time the Owen even replaced the sten gun. It had a 33-round vertical-fed magazine and fired ten shots a second.

Brigid O'Shaughnessy didn't really need to know all this detail, but she listened politely, anyway. She was lying on the single bed in Ronnie's bedroom above the gun shop. He had just spent a fast and furious ten minutes of heavenly happiness tooling the Jayne Mansfield lookalike and was now standing stark naked, holding the Owen gun, and explaining the finer points of the weapon. Brigid could afford to listen for a while – she'd talked him down from 20 quid to a fiver and a bit of the old funny business. Ronnie jumped at it, but he wanted another ten pounds for the 1,000 rounds of ammo that went with the gun. She was trying to work that down to five pounds with another ten minutes of slip sliding away between the sheets, but Ronnie West was a one-root wonder. He fired a shot quicker than the Owen gun.

After a while, Brigid got sick of the firepower lecture. 'Ahh, bugger you, Ron,' she said, getting off the bed and tossing the gunsmith his ten extra quid for the ammo. 'I haven't got all day. Stick all that in the boot of my car, will ya? And the next time you get horny it will cost you a handgun and a box of shells every time. I'm sick of you messing me about.'

'Don't be like that,' said Ronnie.

'One more word out of you, ya ten-minute pansy, and I'll tell young Roy ya hit me and you'll be pulling bullets out of ya bum by teatime.'

Ronnie West took a serious tone. He wanted to hit the arrogant slut for the way she talked to him, but she was right. Roy Reeves would gun down anyone who messed with any member of his family. 'Let me get dressed,' he said, biting his tongue. 'And I'll pack it all up carry it to the car for ya.'

'OK,' said Brigid. 'Snap it up, will ya. I don't have all day.'

It was 1958 and Roy Reeves was driving a lovely FC Holden his Auntie Brigid had bought him. He was 17 years old and growing, and so was his gang. There were now 30 young hoods who'd do anything for Roy, and they weren't the only ones. Roy had a way of inspiring respect.

He was collecting a flat two quid a week from every prostitute in Collingwood, Victoria Park, Clifton Hill and Abbotsford. He collected another ten quid a week from every brothel and a fiver a week from every sly grog operation. He was also standing over every SP bookie in the area for a fiver a week.

It all added up. Roy was pulling in 300 quid a week. Every man in his gang got five quid a week. That was 150 quid a week gone in wages. Every gang member had his own criminal interests and raised their own funds, with a flat 10 per cent going into a general gang kitty held by Auntie Bee. In two years that kitty had grown to 3,000 pounds, a small fortune. At the time a new car cost about 600 pounds.

Auntie Bee's problems with the Bennett brothers had been solved when Ripper Roy came walking through the swinging doors of the Peppermint Lounge jazz club in Smith Street, Collingwood, with a handgun in each hand. He looked for all the world like Hoot Gibson and shot like him – gunning down the three brothers with seven shots. They all lived but held true to the Collingwood code of silence. Two days later Ripper Roy and his newfound friend Stanley Van Gogh did the Murray brothers over with broken beer bottles in Blood Lane. The Van Goghs lived in Collingwood Lane, in the worst and most evil part of the old slums – the part of Collingwood that all the politicians reckoned they would pull down later and put all the people in new Housing Commission high-rise flats. They were saying the same about Richmond and Fitzroy but no one believed them at the time. Stanley Van Gogh said to Ripper, 'The pollies are full of shit and it'll never happen.'

Ripper Roy wasn't so sure about that. As the world grew more la-di-dah, the old slums seemed more like London's East End before the war than Melbourne in the modern 1950s. Sooner or later, he reckoned, they would pull half of Collingwood down and rebuild it. Most of the children in old Collingwood, the dark side, where they didn't even have street lights at night, had spent their first years of life fighting for food with the rats who lived with them. Easey Street was rough, but it was posh compared to where poor Stanley lived.

'Let's head over to Auntie Bee's place to watch telly,' Ripper Roy said to Stanley.

'Nah,' said Stan. 'Them TV things is bad for ya eyes. My dad reckons that they send out radio waves that can send ya blind.'

Ripper wondered at this. He didn't seem convinced. 'Oh well, OK then. See ya,' he said.

He started up his new FC Holden and went over to Gipps Street to collect his two faithful right- and left-hand men, Irish Arthur Featherstone and Terry Maloney.

When he got to the house they shared with Bobby McCall and Ray Brown, he walked in to find Bobby McCall chock-a-block up Helen Hill, a Richmond prostitute who was another Hollywood lookalike. Helen was a big, well-put-together brunette who prided herself on looking like the movie star Jane Russell. Bobby McCall had failed to notice that the big girl was totally unconscious.

'Hey, Bobby,' yelled Roy, 'she's out like a light. What's going on?'

Bobby paid no heed and continued to jack-hammer the poor girl. 'It's this stuff,' said Ray Brown, holding out a glass vial of white powder.

'What is it?' asked Roy.

'We got it from Chang Heywood over in Richmond. He got it from the Chinese. Them dagos in Carlton are selling it to the molls.'

Roy looked sour at the mention of the dagos. There weren't many of them, but the pocket of Italian criminals in Carlton had already made their presence felt around the Victoria Market area with their secret society and dago-versus-dago shootings. They were yet to try the Aussies on for size, but Roy knew it would only be a matter of time. He had already shot two of them in the legs for drinking in hotels in Collingwood. They were a couple of dagos named Corsetti and Carrasella. At least they told the police nothing, which was something to their credit.

The Chinese were harmless. They stayed around Chinatown in the city and had done since the 1850s and had broadened the Aussie culture. After all, Roy reasoned, hadn't they introduced chiko rolls and dim sims to the delicate local palate. But what made Roy ill at ease was the influx of what he and everybody else called 'these reffo immigrant bastards' with their slicked-back oily hair and their charm with the ladies and their waving hands around as they talked their languages you couldn't understand.

'Yeah, well,' said Roy, looking at the white powder Ray Brown was holding out.

'It's called mortine powder or something,' Ray told him.

Arthur Featherstone laughed. 'Morphine powder, you idiot,' said Arthur. 'You mix it with water in a spoon, heat it, then suck it up into one of these.' He showed Roy a glass needle plunger thing, like one he'd seen in a hospital once. 'Then you inject it into your arm or your hip in the muscle or the vein.'

'Shit,' said Roy, 'sounds a bit rough. What's the big deal?'

'Well,' said Arthur, 'a lot of the crackers, the working girls, love it and they pay five pounds for half an ounce, ten pounds an ounce.'

'Shit,' said Roy, 'ten quid an ounce? How much does it really cost?'

Arthur said, 'About ten bob an ounce from the Chinese, 15 bob an ounce from the dagos, but the trick is if you cut it up into small portions and sell it in little packets you can charge five bob a pop.'

'And how many little one-person packets can you get out of an ounce?' asked Roy.

'From 100 to 112,' said Arthur.

Roy couldn't quite believe it. He was doing mental arithmetic as he spoke. 'How much?' he muttered. Then, as if answering himself, he said, 'Five bob 100 times … that's 25 pounds. Shit! Have you got some of this stuff? I'll show Auntie Bee this.'

Arthur handed Roy a one-ounce glass vial and a needle.

'Nah. I won't need that thing,' said Roy, handing the needle back. 'She can taste it by sniffing it up her nose or swallowing it with a cup of tea.'

'But don't drink grog on it,' said Arthur. 'Cos I think that's what killed young Helen over there.'

Suddenly Bobby McCall stopped humping. 'Whadya mean killed?' he said.

Arthur smiled. 'She's been dead for the last ten minutes, Bobby, only I didn't want to be a party pooper.'

Bobby McCall checked her breathing. There wasn't any. 'Geez,' he said, looking sick. 'But she's as warm as anything. What the hell are we gonna do now?'

Arthur kept going as if nothing had happened. Roy looked shocked. 'As I was saying,' said Arthur, 'morphine and alcohol is a fatal mixture, so tell Brigid, OK.'

'I sure will,' murmured Roy as he walked out, forgetting why he'd come to visit in the first place.

As Roy drove over to Easey Street, he wondered about the dead Helen Hill and hoped she wasn't related to the Richmond crew. All the Lennox Street Hills had green eyes and blonde-brown hair, but the dead girl was dark. Anyway, there were at least three Helen Hills he knew of in Richmond and two in Collingwood, and they were all knob polishers.

Shit, I hope the boys dump the body well and keep it secret from young Chang Heywood, he thought. Chang's a bloody gossip. Apart from being the best car thief in Melbourne, Chang was also a loyal Richmond boy.

As Roy pulled up out the front of Auntie Bee's place, he noticed Ronnie West ducking around the corner in a hurry. What's that shifty bugger up to? thought Roy. He got out of his car and walked up to his auntie's front door and knocked. After about two minutes Brigid O'Shaughnessy answered the door. She was in a black silk dressing gown with black high-heeled slippers. She was also in tears. The gown was torn open, revealing teeth marks on her breasts. She had a swollen eye and blood on her lip.

'He raped me,' cried Brigid. 'Ronnie West raped me.' She collapsed into Roy's arms, howling.

'C'mon, Auntie Bee, c'mon,' Roy said gently. He took her into the bedroom and sat her down. He didn't know what to do. She was in fits of tears.

'He did it to me, up my bottom as well and he hit me, and look,' she said, holding her tits for examination, 'he bit my boobs as well.'

'I'll fucking kill the dog,' said Roy. 'But first I'll make you a nice cup of tea. Wait here.' But when he went to the kitchen to put the kettle on she followed him.

'And he put it in my mouth as well, the dirty bastard. That is something I only do for special men I love.'

Roy was shocked.

She wrapped her gown around herself and sat down, trying to control herself, and explained what had happened.

'Have you had your morning gin yet?' he asked.

'No,' replied Brigid.

'Well, don't,' said Roy. 'Try this.' He pulled out the vial of morphine powder and put half a teaspoon of it into her cup of tea. He added three spoons of sugar the way she liked it, then milk. 'Now,' he said, 'drink that and tell me how you feel.'

The sobbing lady drank her tea in four large swallows. 'Ahh,' she said, 'nothing like a nice cuppa. What was that stuff?'

'Magic powder,' Roy said. 'Tell me when you feel something, but remember – you can't drink no grog on it or you'll die.'

Half an hour later Brigid said, 'What on earth have you given me?' She had vomited in the outside thunder box dunny three times and once in the sink, but she felt the best she ever had. As if she was floating on a sea of cotton wool, as if every part of her body and being was wrapped in heaven and all pain physical and mental was gone. She felt wonderful and was running herself a nice bath. The unpleasantness with Ronnie West was not just finished, but forgotten. At least where Brigid was concerned. Roy had a long memory and a loaded gun.

'Jeez, Roy, that is fantastic stuff you put in my tea,' she gushed. 'This is the best I've felt in my whole life.'

The beautiful woman was lying back in her bubble bath, luxuriating.

Roy warned her again. 'Don't drink on it, Auntie Bee, or it can kill you.'

'OK, baby. I won't. I don't even feel like it.'

She looked over and spoke to Roy as she soaped her body. 'You're a good boy, Roy. You're my favourite nephew and my best mate. I love you, Roy. You're a bloody good kid to your Auntie Bee, hey?' she purred.

'Yeah,' said Roy as he sat on a chair in the bathroom.

'Take me to the movies, will ya? I love the movies.'

'Let me guess,' said Roy patiently. 'Humphrey Bogart.'

'Yeah,' she said. '*The Maltese Falcon*.'

Roy knew why his auntie loved this movie so much. *The Maltese Falcon* made in 1941 with Humphrey Bogart, Sydney Greenstreet and Peter Lawrie. The female leading lady was Mary Astor and, you guessed it, she played the role of none other than Brigid O'Shaughnessy.

The Bogart character, Sam Spade, spends the whole movie running from the bad guys or chasing after them and making love to Brigid O'Shaughnessy. At least that's how Auntie Bee saw it. Forget Lauren Bacall, as far as Auntie Bee was concerned, Humphrey Bogart loved her and only her.

'Jayne Mansfield should have played that role,' said Brigid. 'Bloody Mary Astor, she looks like the blinking barmaid at Dan O'Connell's pub. Jayne Mansfield would have gone much better next to Humphrey Bogart.'

Roy knew what to say and when to say it. 'You would have made a good Hollywood movie star,' he said. 'You're beautiful, Auntie Bee.'

'And you look like bloody Gary Cooper,' said Brigid, and they laughed like a pair of kookaburras.

At Auntie Bee's pleading, Roy had decided not to kill Ronnie West, on the logic that a tame gunsmith was worth his weight in gold. But he didn't get away scot free for putting such a serious hole in his manners.

Irish Arthur and Terry Maloney were dispatched to collect Ronnie West from his shop. They borrowed a stolen 1952 Vauxhall from Chang Heywood for the princely sum of ten bob, pulled up with a squeal of drum brakes, dragged a terrified West from his shop and threw him into the car.

They drove to the front of the Royal Melbourne Hospital and parked. Roy Reeves got into the car, and Ronnie West went white.

'I'm gonna hurt ya, Ronnie,' Roy said. 'Now, you can give me up to the police and I'll go to jail but the rest of the gang will kill your mother and father. Ya know Frank Kerr, don't ya? Ya know how he's got one arm? Well, I took the other one. Now which arm do you want to lose?' said Roy.

Ronnie West was in tears of terror. 'No, Roy, not my arms,' he begged. What was the use of a one-armed gunsmith?

'All right,' said Roy, and he pulled out a meat cleaver. 'Hold the dog, Terry.'

Big Terry Maloney held Ronnie West as Roy Reeves smashed the meat cleaver down hard across West's left kneecap. West tried to struggle and kick but Ripper Roy brought the cleaver down a second time. West was screaming and tried to make for the car door but a third blow from the meat cleaver severed the leg. 'Open the door,' yelled Ripper Roy, and Ronnie West was pushed out on to the footpath.

'You'll live, dog, but talk to the cops and your mum and dad will die like dogs,' Roy spat as Arthur Featherstone drove away.

Ripper Roy took the leg and wrapped it in a towel. It looked funny with the shoe still on the foot. He got Irish Arthur to drop him off at Auntie Bee's place and he knocked on the door. Brigid answered and said, 'Hi ya, Roy, what's that you're hiding behind ya back, a present for me?' She said it with a smile, jiggling and wiggling all over with girlish excitement.

'Yeah,' said Roy, deadpan. 'I went to see Ronnie West for ya. He said he's very sorry and he's sent ya this.' Roy held out the severed leg and unwrapped it from the blood-drenched towel.

Auntie Bee fell to the floor in a heap. She'd fainted dead on the spot.

'Well,' said Roy to himself. 'There's bloody gratitude for ya. That's the last leg I'm cutting off for you.'

He bent down and picked up his fallen auntie, while still holding the leg. Brigid woke up and saw it in his hands as he was carrying her down the hallway. She let out a little scream and fainted again.

'Jesus, Auntie Bee,' he grumbled, 'it's only a bloody leg, for God's sake.'

Roy Reeves and Irish Arthur stood looking at a large framed photograph hanging above Roy's fireplace in Easey Street. They were waiting for Terry Maloney and Stanley Van Gogh and a new member of Roy's gang – a 15-year-old kid named Johnny Go Go.

'Who's that in the photo, Roy?' asked Arthur.

'That's my old dad, Johnny Reeves, but they called him Roy the Boy and the little bloke in the bowler hat is Squizzy Taylor. My dad was Taylor's right-hand man,' said Roy proudly. 'Yeah, Johnny Reeves was the bloke who tried to shoot Phar Lap before the 1930 Melbourne Cup.'

Arthur looked impressed. 'Shit,' he said. 'Now, there's a bit of dinky-di Aussie history for ya.' He looked thoughtful for a moment, then continued. 'But between you, me and the gatepost, Roy, I'm glad ya old man didn't kill Phar Lap.'

Roy nodded in agreement. 'Yeah, me too. How would I be as the son of the man who killed Phar Lap?'

'Bloody oath,' said Arthur. 'Not too bloody popular.'

Roy's mum let Terry Maloney in, along with Stanley and Johnny Go Go. They were all off to the footy to watch Collingwood play in the 1958 Grand Final.

'Another Premiership for us,' yelled Terry.

'Of course,' said Roy. 'I don't even know why we bother going. We all know who's gonna bloody win.'

'Did ya hear Ronnie West is out of hospital?' said Johnny Go Go.

'Nah,' said Roy. 'That's news but I do know he stuck staunch.'

What Roy didn't know was Auntie Bee had quietly paid Ronnie a visit in hospital and instead of giving him grapes she slung him a thousand pounds of her own money. She told him to take the cash and shut up, and if he mentioned Roy's name she'd scream rape on him. It was a fair exchange, sort of the crims' version of Worker's Comp. Also, Ronnie was by nature a solid Collingwood boy and never gave people up. Besides which, the passing threat from Ripper Roy re his mum and dad had stuck with him.

Roy seemed like a man of his word.

Brigid swore to herself that it would be the last time she went crying to Roy when some bloke upset her. God, she was still having bad dreams about that leg.

'Shit,' said Brigid. 'No one misses a slice off a cut loaf and crying over getting up-ended once in a while isn't worth it.'

If her nephew intended to thrust severed limbs in her face, she wouldn't be sharing her troubles with him in future. The cut-off leg was more of a mental and emotional shock than the rape.

'Never again,' she said.

When the boys went to the footy, Brigid went to church to do a bit of plea bargaining with God. She knelt before a statue of Holy Mother Mary, surrounded by candles. She lit a candle for Ronnie West's severed leg and crossed herself, then prayed.

'Hail Mary, full of grace, the Lord is with thee. Blessed art thou among women and blessed is the fruit of thy womb Jesus. Holy Mary Mother of God, pray for us sinners now and at the hour of our death. Amen.'

Then she opened her eyes and looked up at the Madonna and said, 'And please watch over Roy, Lord, and we are sorry about Ronnie's leg. I know I'm a fallen woman and probably deserved what I got for all my sins, but I reckon Ronnie West had that coming to him. Nevertheless, please forgive us. I'd tell the priest, but Father Gillis is a bad drunk with a big mouth and between you and me, Lord, I reckon Father Gillis would give ya up in a police station, so this is between us, hey, Lord. You, me and Mother Mary.'

Brigid crossed herself, then stood up and walked out. She had once been, if nothing else, a good Catholic girl. Somewhere along the way, she'd mislaid the 'good' bit. But she was still a Mick at heart.

It was 1962. Ripper Roy was driving a brand-new Chevrolet Belair, which suited his style as a wealthy man. He'd put 3,000 pounds on Hi Jinx to win the 1960 Melbourne Cup, and the result made him one of the biggest landlords in the inner suburbs, as well as running all the other standover rackets. He was on easy street, and he was on his way to Easey Street after a visit to the cemetery. He and Neville Griffin, Tex Lawson, Redda Maloney, Bobby Rebecca and Stan Twain had put flowers on Freddy 'the Frog' Harrison's grave, as was their habit since Twisty had blown his head off a few years earlier down on the docks.

Ripper Roy remembered Freddy fondly. 'One of the grand old men and a better chap you'd never meet in a day's march,' he used to say.

He pulled up to Auntie Bee's place. Brigid had put on a few pounds over the years around the hips and tits area, but she was still a small boy's wet dream.

He walked in to find Auntie Bee on her knees in the lounge.

'What's goin' on, Auntie Bee?' said Roy.

'Father Della Torre told me to go home and say an act of contrition,' said Brigid.

'Who the hell is Father Della Torre?' asked Roy.

'He's the new priest at St Mary's' she answered.

'Holy Mother of God,' said Roy. 'A dago priest. Shit, Banjo bloody Paterson would roll over in his grave if he could see this.'

'No, Roy,' protested Brigid, who was a soft touch in more ways than one. 'Father Della Torre is a lovely man.'

That would be right, thought Roy.

He was ashamed to admit it, but he knew his esteemed auntie had a weakness for these Latin types, especially since Norman Bradshaw had taken her to Perry Bros Circus and Zoo down at the Burnley Oval in Richmond. Old Normie had been shaggin' the guts out of young Brigid since she was 16 years old, but it wasn't love. She did, however, fall in love when she met the Great Caballero, a Spanish acrobat and trick rider who performed at the circus.

She was 17 years old and she was head over heels over the acrobat. The smooth-talking Spaniard promised her the world, then left her at the altar a year later, pregnant and broken-hearted. She lost the baby in childbirth, which was about right, as nothing the oily dago gave her ever worked right. But, afterwards, she still had this thing for cowboys like Gene Autry, Roy Rogers, Hoot Gibson, John Wayne and Audie Murphy. If they rode a horse and carried a gun, she loved 'em all, but her favourite was the Mexican Caballeros on the movies. The Spanish horse riders. Did she love them Latins.

Now and again Brigid would use silly Spanish expressions, like her favourite: 'Uno momento, senor, may I have the money first please?' Or 'Come on, Caballero, ride me like the wind.'

It was all very cute, but Brigid's love or lust for these dago movie cowboys made Roy a bit sick.

'Anyway,' Brigid was telling him, 'I went to confession this morning and Father Della Torre told me to go home and say an act of contrition.'

Roy laughed. 'Confession, hey, Auntie Bee? That must have taken a while.'

She gave Roy a sharp look. 'Don't joke, Roy. Now kneel with me while I pray.'

So Roy knelt down facing his Auntie Bee. They both crossed themselves and Brigid began: 'Oh my God, I am sorry and beg pardon for all my sins and detest them above all things because they have crucified. No, no that's wrong,' she said. 'Hang on, yes, I remember; because they deserve the dreadful punishments because they have crucified my loving saviour Jesus Christ and most of all because they offend thine infinite goodness and I firmly resolve by the help of thy grace never to offend thee again and carefully to avoid the occasions of sin. Amen.'

'Amen,' said Roy, as he stood up. But Brigid remained on her knees. 'Well, come on Auntie Bee, up ya get. Ya know, Auntie Bee, between Hail bloody Marys and doodle shaking half the world, the good Lord is going to have a bugger of a time figuring out what to do with you.'

Meanwhile, a 1957 FE Holden with five men in it was parked a hundred yards up the street from Brigid's place. Tuppence Murray sat at the wheel. Big Twisty was next to him, with a loaded .38-calibre handgun in his hand. Titchy Turner, Normie Green and Con Hardgrave were in the back seat. No one wanted to be left out, so they all had .38s.

'He won't be in there long. Probably still staring at his auntie's tits,' said Twist.

'Ya joking,' said Turner. 'He's not, is he?'

'Well, why not?' said Twisty. 'Colleen O'Shaughnessy is getting shafted by Billy and Ray Reeves and they are her cousins, and old Herb "the Hat" O'Shaughnessy is her own uncle and if he isn't plonking her I'll bare my bum in Myers bloody window.'

'Shit,' grunted Con Hardgrave, 'it's all a bit sick, isn't it?'

'Yeah, the whole Reeves clan have been a sick pack of killers and whores for as long as anyone can remember.'

'Ripper Roy's mad dad was the bastard who tried to kill Phar Lap, for God's sake,' said Titchy Turner.

'Yeah, well, Ripper Roy killed my dad and that's all I'm interested in,' said Tuppence Murray. 'My whole family will have to find a new place to live if we don't fix Roy. He's been hounding us for years.'

'That's fair enough,' said Con Hardgrave. 'But, your problems aside, we've all got our own scores to settle.'

Hardgrave was thinking about his younger brother, Danny, who'd been shot dead outside the Cricketer's Arms Hotel in Cruickshank Street, Port Melbourne, the previous year. It had Ripper Roy's fingerprints all over it. As far as he was concerned, Reeves had to go.

As Brigid walked Roy to the front door, she was chattering on about helping old Father Harrigan down at the Sailors' Mission. They were putting on a fund raiser.

'So what does the old drunk want you to do, Auntie Bee?' asked Roy.

'Oh, Father Harrigan wants to put on a fete and he wants me to get some of the girls to bake cakes.'

'I knew a few of them had buns in the oven but I didn't know the girls could bake cakes,' said Roy, smirking at the idea.

Brigid giggled. 'No, I guess we'll just pitch in a fiver each and get Quinn's Bakery to knock up a few hundred, and we'll probably toss Father Harrigan a lazy hundred quid to go with it,' she said. She was a soft touch, all right.

Roy shook his head. 'These two-faced priests condemn you in public for being whores and fallen women, then stamp you for a quid when the honest people won't chip in. If it wasn't for the crims and crackers slinging these priests money half the poor people who go to the church for food and warm clothes would freeze and starve. Christ, ya must hand over a grand a year to the priests, Auntie Bee.

And what about the other girls? I saw old Harrigan stamp Sally Wingate for a fiver yesterday, and she's a bloody Protestant.'

Brigid scowled suddenly. 'Roy, don't speak ill of Father Harrigan,' she snapped. It was the Irish in her. She was as game as Ned Kelly about everything else, but scared of crossing the priests.

'Speak ill of the old dog!' said Roy. 'When he's not stamping the girls for money, he's trying to pants them.'

'Oh, nonsense,' said Brigid, 'that's just a rumour.'

'Ha ha,' laughed Roy. 'You ask Bonny Brown about Father Harrigan. He's been pantsing poor Bonny for the last ten years.'

'Bullshit,' said Brigid. 'You can't believe Bonny, she just loves to gossip. I'll see her about that.'

The two stood on the footpath just behind Roy's car. Roy put his arm around Brigid and said, 'I'll see ya later, Auntie Bee.'

He didn't see the FE Holden as it cruised towards them, but Brigid did. She screamed, 'Look out, Roy,' and threw herself in front of him. She grabbed him, putting her body between Roy and the line of fire. A stream of bullets hit them. Roy tried to push her out of the way to protect her, but she clung on tight. She had three slugs in her back, and there were more coming. They whistled past Roy's head and smacked into the front of the old red-brick house.

He clawed for his gun and returned fire, hitting the Holden with six slugs as it tore away. When it turned the corner, he laid Brigid down on the footpath. She was bleeding badly and coughing blood.

'Auntie Bee,' Roy yelled. 'Don't die, Auntie Bee.'

But she was. It didn't matter how much he yelled. The dying woman was still holding Roy's shoulder with her left hand and she looked up at him with her big eyes.

'I'm gone, Roy,' she said.

'No, ya not, Auntie Bee. No ya not,' cried Ripper Roy.

'Yes, I am, darlin',' said Brigid. 'Via con dios, caballero,' she said, coughing blood. 'Via con dios.'

'No, Auntie Bee, no,' cried Roy.

Brigid O'Shaughnessy looked at the crying Roy Reeves and said, 'Bill Monroe's the best, hey, Roy?'

Ripper Reeves held his Auntie Bee. 'Bill Monroe's the best,' he said.

The dying woman started to sing, 'I can hear a sweet voice calling,' then she closed her eyes and died.

Ripper Roy stood up slowly. He emptied the spent shells out of his .38 and reloaded as if he was in a trance. He didn't look at the pistol, but down Easey Street with a faraway stare. For a while, he was lost in space and time. Then he spoke to the body on the footpath.

'They'll be hearing some sweet voices calling tonight, Auntie Bee, I can promise ya that. They'll be hearing some sweet voices calling tonight.'

Oh, an Irish girl's heart is as stout as shillelagh,
It beats with delight to chase sorry or woe,
When the piper plays up then it dances as gaily,
And thumps with a whack to leather a foe.

Brigid O'Shaughnessy, 1962

• • •

Late 1976. Van Der Hum had won the Melbourne Cup and you'd think Ripper Roy Reeves owned him and backed him as well, with the amount of cash he had quietly invested around Collingwood.

Ripper Roy was sitting in one of his investment opportunities, the newly named Caballero Night Club, in Smith Street. It had formerly been the Peppermint Lounge, but that ended as soon as Johnny Go Go bought the place, fronting for Roy.

Things changed fast. Whereas the club had once bopped along to the jazz sounds of Jelly Roll Morton, it now rocked to the sound of striptease music while a young hot pants from Richmond named Muriel Hill popped fly buttons all over the joint.

Ripper Roy was travelling pretty well. He was about to tuck into a big feed of baked lobster with oyster sauce, which was the kind of tucker he had only heard about when he was nothing but a dangerous kid. Now he was rich and choosy, but still dangerous.

'Holy shit,' he yelled as he spat out a mouth full of roast lobster. 'What's this shit? Who cooked this crap?' he said to Arthur Featherstone.

Irish Arthur hurried over to see what the matter was.

'Taste this crap!' Roy demanded.

'God,' said Arthur, spitting it out. 'That's off. That would kill a brown dog.'

Terry Maloney and Ray Chuckles came over along with Veggie McNamara and Marco Montric.

'What's wrong?' they asked.

'Who cooked this shit?' asked Roy.

'Bunny Malloy,' said Terry. 'He was head cook at Pentridge for the last seven years. He got out three weeks ago.'

Arthur broke in, trying not to smile. 'Excuse me, Terry, but is this the same Bunny Malloy who told young Muriel Hill a few days ago that Cordon Bleu was a French bank robber?'

As laughter broke out, Roy snarled, 'You sack him, Terry, or I'll shoot him.'

When Reeves threatened to put someone off, he didn't mean to the unemployment office. It's hard to get a new job with a hole in the scone.

'But, Roy,' protested Terry.

Ray Chuckles jumped in, trying to defend poor Bunny. 'He's a good bloke and a hard man,' he said.

'Well, then,' said Roy, 'pull him out of the kitchen and give him a job as a bouncer, but he's to stay out of the kitchen. OK, Terry?'

'Yeah, Roy,' said Maloney, smiling.

'If he can slaughter load-mouthed drunks like he did a job on that overgrown yabbie, then he'll be the toughest doorman this side of the East End,' Roy said.

'Now,' he said to Chuckles, 'what do you wombats want this side of town? Sit down, boys. Sit down.'

Ray Chuckles, Veggie McNamara and Marco Montric all sat down at Ripper Roy's table.

'Tex Lawson sent us to see ya, Roy,' said Ray Chuckles.

'But he's in jail,' replied Roy. 'Doing 13 years for murdering Pat Boon down the docks.'

'Brian O'Flanagan spoke to him for us. They're in H Division together,' said Ray Chuckles.

'Yeah, yeah, I know,' said Roy. 'Only testing. Go on, what's the go?'

'Well, Roy,' said Ray. 'It's like this. We need six machine guns, and you're the only man in Melbourne with his own personal collection of machine guns.'

'What's it all for?' asked Ripper Roy. 'And tell us the truth or ya can all piss off right now. I know you're a good bloke, Ray. I know ya used to be Tex Lawson's bodyguard. I know you're a solid and staunch Caballero – but lie to me and I'll kill ya right now, OK?'

He meant it. Ray Chuckles continued very politely. 'It's like this, Mr Reeves. Remember the old bookmaker Bert Shaw? He's dead now. Remember old Bert went to Tex about an idea he had and Tex went to Teddy Kidd and his crew, but Kidd knocked it back?'

'Shit,' said Roy. 'Not that old chestnut. Tex Lawson has been trying to interest people in that numb-nut idea for years.'

Ray Chuckles nodded solemnly. 'Yeah, Mr Reeves, the bookies.'

Roy started to look interested, in spite of himself. He was a natural born thinker when it came to planning any sort of larceny, especially if it involved a bit of the old firepower. He would have made a great general if there'd been a war handy. 'You'll need at least six to seven men,' he said suddenly.

'We've got seven in the crew,' said Ray. 'Six will do the job.'

'You'll need heavy-duty firepower,' said Ripper Roy, which was no surprise. If there was one thing he liked, it was the smell of gunpowder. Even after 20 years.

'Well, that's why we came to see you,' said Ray Chuckles.

Ripper Roy was looking into space and thinking aloud. 'The bloody Victoria Club,' said Roy, lost in thought. But he looked doubtful. 'Shit … could it be done? Nah, you'll never pull it off.'

'But,' said Ray, 'if we do, we could net millions. If we don't, that's our risk.'

'Yeah,' said Ripper Roy sourly, 'and I lose six machine guns. Do you know how hard it is to put together a collection of machine guns?'

'Ya right, Roy. But you're a punter,' said Ray. 'If we win, you're there for a slice of the pie.'

'How much?' said Ripper Roy.

Ray Chuckles looked at Veggie McNamara and Marco Montric. 'We have all discussed it. How about 100 grand if we pull it off?' said Ray.

'Right,' said Roy. 'I can let you have one sten gun, two Owen guns and three Stirling submachine guns. How's that sound?'

Ray Chuckles smiled. 'Thanks, Ripper. I mean Mr Reeves,' he added hastily.

Roy laughed. 'Forget the bullshit. False courtesy and politeness will do.'

'OK, Roy,' said Ray Chuckles.

'What about the Kanes?' said Roy.

'Ahh, piss on them,' said Ray Chuckles. 'They have been talking to that copper Skull Miller for so long now they think they're policemen. I betcha they've got flat feet to match their flat heads. I'll handle them,' said Ray.

'We can kill 'em for ya,' said Roy.

'Nah,' said Ray. 'The Kanes are our problem. We can catch and kill our own mice, as they say.'

Ripper Roy thought about Brian and Les Kane. They had always stayed clear of Collingwood. As long as Ripper Roy got his hundred grand, Ray Chuckles and his crew and the Kanes could drown themselves in their own blood, for all he cared.

Roy then wondered if Tex Lawson was copping a sling out of all this. After all Bert Shaw was dead and it was Tex who'd taken the bookie plot to Ray Chuckles in the first place.

'OK,' said Roy, slapping Chuckles on the shoulder. 'Ya got yaself a deal.'

He turned and yelled, 'Terry, grab the key to the gun cupboard, will you?'

Roy had 60 machine guns in storage, oiled, ready and waiting. What was six more or less? It was a hundred grand for jam, raspberry jam.

The ghosts of 1962 had been laid to rest, more or less. Ripper Roy hadn't seen the faces of the men in the car who shot at him in Easey Street and killed his Auntie Bee, so he simply put the names of his worst enemies into a hat — all 70 of them — and got Terry Maloney to pull six names out. By the end of the month three totally innocent men were dead, and three more who had nothing to do with the shooting had vanished off the face of the earth.

'When in doubt, shoot everybody,' was Roy's thinking. Whether they did it or not, it made Roy feel much better. And it made people think twice about crossing him.

As Ray Chuckles and his two offsiders drove their 1973 Ford Falcon through the streets of Collingwood with six machine guns and ammo in the boot, they had to stop for a gang of kids playing cricket in the street.

Ray Chuckles tooted his horn, then wound his window down. 'C'mon, you rug rats, move yaselves,' he yelled.

'Who are youse talkin' to?' yelled a skinny little kid who stood knee high to a grasshopper.

'You, ya little bastard,' growled Ray Chuckles. 'Move yaselves out of the way or I'll run over the lot of you.'

The kid picked up a rock and hurled it at the car. It smashed the side window and hit Veggie McNamara in the face, where he was sitting in the back seat.

'You little turd!' yelled Veggie.

Ray Chuckles got out of the car and so did Marco Montric and Veggie. Next thing, about 30 kids aged from five years old to twelve armed themselves with rocks, stones, broken bottles, fence palings and cricket bats and surrounded them. The little kid, who didn't seem to be any more than six or seven, seemed to be boss.

'Go on,' yelled the little kid, 'make a move, dogs, and we'll kick ten shades of shit out of ya.'

Ray Chuckles laughed and said, 'Where's your mother, you little bastard? You need a foot up the arse. I'm goin to tell ya mum on you.'

The little kid spat on the ground. 'Yeah, that would be right. Dob me in, ya dog. All you buggers from Footscray are give-ups.'

Ray was puzzled at this Footscray remark, then realised there was a Bulldogs football sticker on the back window of the car. The reason for that was it was Jockey Smith's car. He barracked for Footscray.

A girl came up and took the little kid by the hand and said, 'Come on, Mickey, let's go.'

'Nah,' said the little kid, 'if these dogs want to start, let's rip it in to 'em. Let 'em have it!'

Broken bottles, rocks and fence palings rained down on the car and the three men. Ray Chuckles, Marco Montric and Veggie McNamara jumped back in and took off, but not before every window in the car was broken.

Little Mickey Van Gogh looked up to Raychell Brown and said, 'Them bastards from Footscray won't be trying to mess up our cricket game no more, will they, Raych?'

'Nah, Mickey,' said Raychell, with a giggle. 'I don't reckon they will.'

Meanwhile, in the car, Ray Chuckles was thinking. 'I hope we make a big heap of dough out of this job,' he said to the other two.

'Why's that?' said Veggie, still amazed at what had just happened.

'Because,' said Ray, 'people with big heaps of money don't have to drive their cars through bloody Collingwood. That's why.'

It was 1979, the year Hyperno won the Cup. But, at the Caballero Night Club, other interests were on the agenda.

Terry Maloney, Edgar Duffy and Phil Scanlan sat at the bar talking to a new girl who was working at the club as a dancer. She was a big blonde named Kerry Griffin.

'Ya see, Kerry,' said Terry Maloney, who was a talker, 'it's like this. The 17th of March, St Patrick's Day, isn't to celebrate St Patrick's birthday the way everyone thinks. The 17th of March is the day St Patrick died.'

'Oh,' said Kerry, fascinated with the history of the saints according to Terry the Collingwood hoodlum. At least, if she wasn't fascinated, she was doing a bloody good job of pretending she was.

'Now,' said Terry, 'you're Bonny Brown's niece, aren't ya?'

'Yes,' said Kerry.

'Well, then, the Browns are related to the Callaghans and the Gradys, and the Gradys are related to the Bradys, and the Bradys are related to the Reeves, and the Reeves are related to the

O'Shaughnessys. For God's sake, my dear girl, you're a blood relative to St Patrick himself.'

Terry Maloney held his arms wide open and said, 'Cead mile failte.'

Kerry Griffin was puzzled. 'What does that mean?' she asked.

'It's Gaelic,' said Terry. 'It means "a hundred thousand welcomes" – and now you say "Cead mile failte" back to me and give me a big cuddle.'

Kerry Griffin said the ancient words and fell into big Terry Maloney's arms. 'Ya mean I'm really related to St Patrick?' she asked.

Irish Arthur walked up and Terry muttered something to Arthur in the ancient Gaelic language. Arthur smiled and recited an ancient Irish poem out loud to a star-struck Kerry Griffin.

'St Patrick himself was a gentleman. He came of decent people and in Dublin town he built a church and on it he put a steeple. His father was a Callaghan and his mother was a Brady. His aunt was an O'Shaughnessy and his uncle was a Grady.'

Kerry Griffin clapped her hands in delight and Terry said, 'So ya see, my little darlin', you're as Irish as Paddy's pig and a blood relation to old St Patrick himself, and on 17 March you must wear green and you can never take a penny off an Irishman on St Patrick's Day. OK, princess?'

Kerry kissed Terry Maloney, and walked away as happy as Larry.

'God,' said Edgar Duffy under his breath, 'where the hell did you find her? And where did you get the gift of the gab? I don't reckon you kissed the Blarney Stone – you took a bite out of the bastard.' Edgar shook his head in admiration at Big Terry's form in the wagging department.

Roy Reeves sat at the other end of the club at his private table. It was a quiet afternoon. The club was closed all except for a handful of live-in strippers and a dozen or so members of his crew, along with a few invited guests come to talk business.

Ripper Roy smiled as he overheard Terry's verbal nonsense to the tits and legs stripper, but at the same time he was trying to pay attention to what Victor 'Vicky' Mack was saying to him. Victor was talking nineteen to the dozen. He was excited about something, and that something was Ray Chuckles.

'Mate, I've spoken to Geoff Twain and Brian McCormack, and they all agree. George McKeon, Eugene Carroll, Lou McMahon, Donny McIntyre, Frank Lonigan, Terry Scanlan, Bobby Fitzpatrick, Pop Kennedy, Liam O'Day, the whole friggin' crew. Mickey Burke, Larry McDougal, Jamie O'Callaghan. They all agree. Ray Chuckles has gone too far.

'Les Kane is dead, which is fair enough, and no skin off anyone's nose, but Chuckles has lashed a lot of people. He stamped a lot of people for a lot of up-front cash, guns and goodies so he could pull the bookie raid. Now he's six million bucks the richer and not a penny repaid. We know he got the machine guns from you. He's using his legal problems and his war with the Kanes as an excuse not to repay debts. I'm tellin' ya, Roy, he's gotta go. Jesus, this bloody war he started with the Kanes has pulled both our crews into it and not a penny for either of us.'

Ripper Roy sat in silence for a few seconds after Vicky Mack's outburst. Then he spoke quietly. 'You've done a deal with Brian Kane, haven't ya, Vicky?'

'So what if I have?' said Vicky Mack, on the back foot all of a sudden.

'Well, why come to see me?' asked Roy. 'OK, so Chuckles lashed on the machine guns. Big deal, I got plenty more. Why come to me about Chuckles?'

Vicky Mack took a big swallow on his large glass of Glen Heather scotch. 'We want your blessing, Roy. We know Chuckles was close to Tex Lawson, and Lawson is part of your crew.'

Roy broke in, 'We are all Aussies together, all Irishmen. We shouldn't be killing each other.'

'But we have been for years,' said Vicky Mack.

'Yeah,' said Roy, 'and while we kill each other the bloody dagos sit back and grow stronger and richer.'

'I know,' replied Vicky Mack. 'But what do ya do, Roy? Do we have ya blessing, because none of the crew will agree to move without your final nod.'

'And what about Brian?' said Ripper Roy.

'Ha ha, that's the good part,' said Vicky Mack. 'Ray Chuckles's own crew will kill him after we kill Chuckles.'

Roy smiled. 'Everyone dies and six million just vanishes. Hey, yeah, only the Irish would consider that to be a fabulous plan of attack.' Ripper Roy shook his head in his own comic self-disgust.

'Ha ha. Yeah, to hell with it, piss on 'em all. Why not kill him?' said Roy. 'But let Chuckles know it came from me, hey, Vicky?'

'And how will I do that, Roy?'

'Yell out, "Hey, Raymond, Roy Reeves said to say hello," in front of plenty of many witnesses.'

Then Ripper Roy bent forward and whispered into Vicky Mack's ear.

Victor Mack smiled and said, 'OK, Roy, I'll do that. Ya got yaself a deal.'

• • •

On St Patrick's Day the Caballero Night Club was a wondrous sight to behold. Edgar Duffy and Phil Scanlan and young Megan O'Shaughnessy had spent all night decking the club out for the big day. The full membership of the Collingwood branch of the friends of Sinn Fein were due to attend and the Collingwood chapter of the Fenian Brigade were also coming along with the Sons of St Patrick. Just to make sure every street fighter and gunman in Collingwood was there, every member of Ripper Roy's gang and his extended family and the relatives of his gang members were also on the invite list.

A big Irish flag with the Golden Harp of Tara on it hung from the ceiling. The green, white and orange flag of Ireland also hung down. A giant golden harp of Erin stood at the end of the bar and a seven-man Irish band was all set up. The only non-Irish thing in the place was a giant Collingwood Football Club flag, a big white affair with a magpie in the middle.

The club was filling up with people. By 10 am green beer and Jamieson's Irish Whiskey was being served as if it would go off if it got warm. Liam Lynch and Bunny Malloy took care of club security, with the aid of two concealed AK47 assault rifles.

Because Father Harrigan was coming, the club strippers were not allowed to perform, which didn't please a lot of the men, but Kerry Griffin, Muriel Hill and Megan O'Shaughnessy were all set to jump into their green stiletto high heels and green high-cut bikini bottoms, with little green shamrocks stuck to their nipples, the moment the Reverend Father had drunk his fill and passed out or pissed off.

Arthur Featherstone had also arranged a jelly wrestling contest – using lime jelly, naturally – between Lizzie Bennett and Marion Taylor, a couple of voluptuous harlots of low moral rectitude from Wellington Street, Collingwood. So getting the good Father drunk and in a cab and back to the Sailors' Mission was the first plan of attack.

Nearly every prostitute in Collingwood, Abbotsford, Victoria Park and Clifton Hill had decided to come and, in spite of Father Harrigan's attendance, it was damn hard to prevent hanky panky. Human nature, green beer and Irish whiskey being what it is.

As the booze flowed, the general conduct grew a little lax and some of the ladies and the more drunken gentlemen were getting a bit disorderly.

'I'm back in the saddle again!' cried Seamus O'Brien, as he proceeded to put the ferret through the fairy hoop with a drunken middle-aged lady who looked like the local school teacher. Seamus was at least 60 years of age, and the lady he was tooling at the far end of the club was no spring chicken – she wasn't even a spring roll.

'Drag that drunken pair of idiots into the street,' ordered Ripper Roy. 'Sorry, Father,' said Roy, as he stood at the bar with the old priest.

Arthur Featherstone and Terry Maloney and young Kerry Griffin stood with him. All had large glasses of Irish whiskey in their hands.

'So you are a Catholic, my girl,' said Father Harrigan.

'Oh yes,' said Kerry Griffin, 'I went to St Monica's.'

'Ahh, good,' said Father Harrigan.

Kerry had on her virginal butter-wouldn't-melt-in-her-mouth face, in spite of the fact her green 'Give Ireland back to the Irish' T-shirt did little to conceal her tits. She was wearing a faded pair of denim jeans so tight they looked like they had been painted on. It was true to say that poor Kerry was built like a porno queen, and even fully clothed in jeans, runners and T-shirt she was hardly the sort of girl you'd expect to see talking to an aged priest.

About 20 feet away, Roy noticed an unconscious man with a large piece of cutlery stuck in his face, which was covered in blood. He whispered to one of his men to remove the gentleman in question, and ordered the band to play. Irish jigs broke out all over the club.

The place was now in full swing and packed full of Irish drunks and ladies being molested by Irish drunks. The various fist fights that broke out got little attention due to the music and dancing. Then, at midday, the club was called to order by Arthur Featherstone so the 'Amran na Bhfiann', the Irish national anthem, could be sung in Gaelic by the members of the Sons of St Patrick. A soldier's song, sung in Gaelic.

When that ended Terry Maloney jumped on to the bar and yelled in Gaelic 'Dia's muire agus padraig duit,' which translated means 'God and Mary and Patrick be with you.' And, with that, the celebrations continued on.

Mick Sheehan and Sean Danaher pulled out handguns and fired shots into the ceiling and were promptly attacked for misconduct by Bunny Malloy and Liam Lynch, much to the amusement of Father Harrigan, who was taken up in what appeared to be deep religious and political conversation with Kerry Griffin.

The big white-haired old Irish priest looked like Boris Karloff, the old horror-movie actor, as he stood next to Kerry at the bar bending his head down to hear what she was saying. As she chattered into his cauliflower ear, he rested his right hand on the small of the girl's back so as to push her that little bit closer. The music was a touch loud, and he had trouble hearing her, of course.

Kerry was quite taken with the old fellow, and was overwhelmed that he should spend his time talking to her and listening to her. Her big tits strained against her T-shirt, and as she spoke into his ear she couldn't help but press herself against the grand old man. However, being a gentleman at all times, and a man of the cloth, the priest gave Kerry no sign that he either noticed or minded.

Meanwhile, Arthur Featherstone, Terry Maloney and Johnny Go Go had moved over to Roy Reeves's private table. Mad Lizzie Bennett was eager to get the jelly wrestling under way, as the winner would collect $500 and a dozen bottles of whiskey. The loser would collect $250 and half a dozen bottles of whiskey. The luckiest spectator collected either the winner or the loser, according to taste.

'Mudguts' McNally was already dragging the children's swimming pool full of green jelly out on to the dance floor. Both girls had their green high-cut bikinis on, ready for action.

'C'mon, Roy,' said Lizzie, anxious to get into action. 'Piss on the priest – the dirty old bastard's got a hand full of Kerry's arse, who's he to complain?'

Roy looked over through the crowd and sure enough it looked as if Kerry was standing rather close to the old fellow as they talked, but he couldn't see any hands on bums.

'Nah,' said Roy. 'We'll recite the pledge first, then I'll get Kerry to pull the Father's coat and get him out of the way.'

The pledge for them was the Collingwood version of the old Irish pledge of allegiance.

Roy called for order and the whole mob stood and faced the Collingwood Football Club flag, and the room broke out with nearly 400 voices swearing the pledge to Collingwood.

'We are willing to fight for the club that we love, be the chances great or small;
'We are willing to die for the Collingwood Club, be the chances nothing at all.'

Then a massive cheer went up and the band played the Irish national anthem again.

Roy went over and spoke to the priest and Kerry and the two walked away with a full bottle of Irish whiskey and two glasses, and Kerry seemed to be leading Father Harrigan in the direction of a booth table at the left-hand side of the stage. This would face the good Father away from the jelly wrestling and give the Father and Kerry greater privacy for the conversation they were involved in.

Three drunken Irishmen and a semi-clothed young miss who were in the full throes of a rampant exchange were promptly dragged from the rear booth by Bunny Malloy, and Kerry and the holy man took their seats.

'Right,' declared Roy, as if he was Boutros Boutros Whatsisname at the United Nations, 'let the fun begin.'

So, while Lizzie Bennett and Marion Taylor tried to kill each other in a pool of green jelly, to the wild roars of the crowd, Kerry kept talking to the good Father.

'It's nothing to be ashamed of, my dear girl,' said Father Harrigan with great compassion and understanding in all things. 'Why, our Lord Himself mixed with killers, thieves, tax collectors and whores. Yes, my dear, whores. You have heard the story of Mary Magdalen. She bathed our Lord's feet with the most expensive oils, then dried His feet with her own hair.'

Kerry was wide-eyed as the priest poured himself yet one more large whiskey and continued his spiel.

'Well, my child, Mary Magdalen was a whore just like you. So, you see, you have no reason for guilt or shame. Just confess your sins, come to mass and donate to the church and say a Hail Mary before bed and all will be well.'

The priest still had his hand around the girl's back as if he didn't even realise it, and Kerry without even thinking placed her hand on Father Harrigan's left leg and squeezed in a show of affection.

'You're a really lovely old bloke, Father,' she cooed. 'I wish I had a real father just like you.'

The old priest smiled. 'And if I had a daughter, my child, I'd want her to be just like you.' He gave her a nice little squeeze with his hand.

'Is it wrong for me to want to give a priest a kiss and a cuddle?' asked Kerry.

The old Father thought about this. 'Oh, I see no reason why not, my girl,' and with that Kerry melted herself into Father Harrigan like marshmallow.

'Do ya reckon that priest is OK in there with Kerry?' asked Terry Maloney.

Roy was remembering old rumours about the good Father and Bonny Brown, but had previously dismissed them due to his Auntie

Brigid's anger at such nonsense. After a while the suspense was killing him.

'Go over and stand on a chair and peek over the top of the booth,' he said.

Terry Maloney walked over and, as instructed, found a stool and stood on it. He peered over the top of the darkened seating area. Then he came back. 'Nah,' he said. 'She's sweet. They're just sitting together.'

'Well, in that case, we'll join them,' said Roy. 'It's a bit insane out here.'

The three men walked over to the private booth and said, 'Mind if we join ya, Father?'

The priest gave a weak and very strained smile and a nod of his head. He didn't look well. He was flushed, red in the face and his right eye was sort of flickering.

'Gee, Father,' said Arthur. 'You don't look too good.'

The three men slid into seats and poured themselves a drink. 'Here, Father,' said Terry. 'Have a drink.'

The priest took the glass with a shaky hand and put it to his mouth, and began dribbling whiskey as he drank.

'Shit, Father, you look like you're gonna have a heart attack. Do you reckon we should call a doctor?'

Father Harrigan didn't reply. Kerry sat in silence, blind drunk, with one hand holding her whiskey glass and the other hidden under the table. You don't have to be told. She had the old bloke unzipped and was slowly and with the skill of a snake charmer giving him a nice old workover.

Roy looked at the priest, then at Kerry, and a strange thought crossed his mind. Then both Arthur and Terry picked up on it. Kerry couldn't contain herself. She put the glass to her lips to drink, then winked at Roy and gave a little giggle. Father Harrigan's face looked like it was about to explode, and his eyes glazed over. For a moment Roy thought that he was about to drop dead. Then Father Harrigan let out a groan like a man in great pain and began to jerk his shoulders and chest. Then he groaned and jerked again.

Ripper Roy, Terry and Irish Arthur looked on in total amazement. Then the priest collapsed and tears welled up in his eyes and he hid his face in his hands and cried.

Kerry lifted her hand from under the table and moved away. 'Let's get away from the dog, boys,' she said. 'Bloody priests. I've been hearing that God loves a whore. Bullshit. Since I was old enough to do it, I've never meet a bloody priest who didn't want to do it to me. Has anyone got a hanky?'

Terry handed her a hanky and the girl wiped her hand. Ripper Roy and the boys were still in a state of shock.

'I'm a whore,' said Kerry. 'But I'm not a liar or a false pretender, I'm not a hypocrite. He's no priest. He's just another mug who wants to get his prick pumped. I should have charged the two-faced dog, but, like you say, Terry, you can't take a penny off an Irishman on St Paddy's Day. Ha ha.'

With that, the big buxom girl walked away.

'Ya know,' said Roy, 'I reckon she's been stooging us all. She might be a bit dippy, but I've got a funny feeling young Kerry ain't totally stupid.'

Muriel Hill walked out of Pentridge. She had been in to visit Ray Chuckles. The governor had allowed a special contact visit and Ray had made the most of it. One good thing about being built like a blow-up doll is that men think you're stupid and this, if played right, can be a winning advantage.

In between a rather frantic session of being slipped on like a wet soapy sock when the screws weren't looking, followed by Ray Chuckles's scallywag idea of Muriel bending over the visit table while he pretended he was a Greek Orthodox priest, he had told her he'd be facing Chief Stipendiary Magistrate Clancy Collins for committal proceedings in three days' time.

The case was crap and Ray reckoned it wouldn't get past the committal. Being rogered twice in the space of an hour while keeping both eyes out for the screws and both ears open for gossip was not Muriel's idea of a good time, but people didn't say no to Roy Reeves. If Ripper Roy told her to do the locomotion with the local Collingwood boy scout troop or a herd of elephants, her reply would be a big smile followed by 'OK, Roy.'

People who said no to Roy Reeves may as well hit themselves in both eyeballs with a broken whisky bottle, because if they didn't do it themselves someone else certainly would do it for 'em. When it came to business, Roy had respect, because he was hard but unfair.

Roy Reeves had noticed the way Raymond Chuckles had looked at Muriel Hill when he had come to ask for the machine guns and, when Ray received Muriel's letter while he was in jail, he never suspected for a moment that this hot-arse, gorgeous sex machine was part of some master plan. Muriel Hill was just a knob junkie from Richmond, one of the Lennox Street Hills, a family of criminals – solid, staunch and dumb. She was just a slippery bit of mischievous nonsense.

While Raymond was in jail, he thought he'd won the lottery when she first came in to see him. God, she was built like Babylon and did anything Ray asked her to. On one contact visit, Brian O'Flanagan was having his birthday two tables away so Ray sent Muriel to the toilet and about 90 seconds later Brian O'Flanagan walked into the toilet. It only took about five minutes and Brian was back at his table talking to his mother and friends and Muriel was back on Raymond's knee. Muriel was a bicycle with a better than average face and a lavish body, but a moll was a moll and Ray Chuckles was not a sentimental person.

But that didn't make him invincible. What he didn't know was that the moll was also a mole.

It seemed to Ray that Muriel was in love with him and he just played her along. Hell, thought Ray, Muriel's whole life was one big perverted unnatural act. She was there to be used, not loved. She ran on a diet of cash and KY Jelly, the bloody whore.

'He goes to court in three days' time,' said Muriel, looking a bit down.

'What's wrong, princess?' asked Roy.

Muriel was a bit frightened but spoke up. 'Well, Mr Reeves, I'd rather not visit that bloke no more if it's OK with you. I'm a good girl. I do like I'm told, but I'd just rather not.'

Ripper Roy patted Muriel on the head. 'You're a good kid. You done me a big favour, OK. You don't need to visit him no more.'

Muriel smiled.

Ripper Roy picked up the phone and rang Victor Mack.

• • •

Ray Chuckles sat in the cells of Melbourne Magistrates' Court. Muriel had promised to visit him by 9 am. He had gone to some lengths to arrange the visit, but she hadn't shown, and he was filthy on her. 'Bloody molls,' he said sourly. 'Ya can't trust 'em.'

Two policemen came to collect him. He had to face the legendary Clancy Collins on the bench. He was sure he'd beat the blue, because he had Steve Stratton representing him. The Crown had no case at all. Once he beat this crap, he was home free, he thought to himself. He had just over a million dollars put away and he was heading for sun, sand and surf. To hell with bloody Melbourne and its never-ending wars. His whole crew was heading a long way north.

Veggie McNamara had his girlfriend living in Spain already, in a rented villa. A million bucks in Spain was like ten million in Aussie land. He had the dim sim factory and the restaurant in Brunswick and the massage parlour in Fitzroy. He had the car yard in Footscray and the block of flats in Richmond. He had a half-share of the pub in Coburg and $75,000 worth of shares in BHP. He had a solicitor managing the whole shooting match for him and monthly cheques would be sent to him anywhere in the world. He also had hard cash in various bank accounts and building societies, and some on hand as well. He could walk away – or keep fighting mindless wars and power struggles. The smart thing was to hit the toe and never come back.

As the two coppers walked Ray Chuckles through the court corridors, he noticed neither of them had guns. Nah, he thought, I'm not falling for that ... being shot by police who are carrying guns while escaping from police who don't have guns. Anyway, why bother? He would beat the murder blue over Les Kane. He'd won.

As he walked along, he noticed that the cop on his left was sort of humming and singing a tune to himself. Ray thought he recognised it.

'What's that?' he asked.

The young copper answered, 'It's an old Bill Monroe tune.'

'Shit, yeah,' said Ray. 'Bill Monroe. That's it. I know a bloke who's always whistling or singing that tune. What's it called again?'

'I forget,' said the young copper, and the three of them walked along in silence until Ray Chuckles started to hum the old tune, all the time wondering what the name of the song was, and marvelling that it really was a very small world indeed.

Victor 'Vicky' Mack sat on a bench in a crowded corridor outside Clancy Collins's court room, upstairs in the old magistrates' court opposite Russell Street police station. People were milling about. There were a lot of tits and legs. A whore in a micro-mini skirt and high heels was sitting next to Vicky trying to make conversation.

'I told the bastard to just leave me alone,' she said. 'My life is my life, but would he listen? No way. If I want to go out and have a good time, I bloody well will.'

She lit up her tenth smoke for the morning and offered Vicky one. She noticed he was wearing a wig. At least it didn't look like his own hair. It was long and not the same colour as his eyebrows. He was probably trying to pull a shifty in court, she thought. Good luck to him.

She wouldn't shut up. 'Anyway, I said to him, "It's not my fault if your mates keep putting the hard word on me."' She crossed a pair of legs and the micro-mini ran up to reveal nearly all she had, but Vicky Mack was looking down the corridor.

'I said to him, "Just cos I'm your bloody wife don't mean ya own me," and it's not my fault his brother and his best mate got me pissed at Leo's party. What am I meant to do? Now he's calling me a slut and a moll and his dad is calling me a moll. Ha ha, that's rich. That dirty old bastard. I could tell the court a few things about him, but I won't.'

Vicky Mack saw two police escorting Raymond Chuckles down the corridor about 30 feet away through the crowd. The long-legged lady with the big mouth was crossing her legs the other way around now, with every man in a ten-yard radius casting wide eyes in her direction.

All except for Vicky Mack. He quietly stood up and walked down the hall. As he walked he could hear the dragon with the long legs bellow out some more personal detail about her domestic troubles.

'His mum's just a drunk and both his bloody sisters are junkies and they call me a moll, if you don't mind. He should tell his dirty old dad and his prick of a brother to stop trying to root me before he points the finger.'

As Ray Chuckles walked up the stairs from the courtyard with the two cops, he was in daydream land.

'What's the name of this bloody tune? Jesus, that's annoying. Ripper Roy's favourite song. God, what is it?'

As Ray Chuckles and his two young police escorts walked towards Vicky Mack, Ray scratched his nose with his handcuffs – and remembered. 'Yeah, that's it,' he said to the police escort. '"I Can Hear a Sweet Voice Calling." That's the name of that tune.'

At this point, Vicky Mack pulled out his .38 handgun. 'Hey, Caballero!' he yelled.

Ray Chuckles's eyes shot towards Victor Mack as the gun went off. It's true what they say: you never hear the shot that kills you. Ray never heard the sound. All that was inside his head as he fell was the song he'd been humming.

As he hit the floor, he could sense the panic around him but he felt numb. Everything was soft. He could hear everything but see and feel nothing. Everything was dark, but he could still hear. 'He's got a gun!' he heard some woman scream.

People were running all around him. He could hear them, standing over him, yelling for help. Then the old song came back and all else faded.

'I can hear a sweet voice calling.'

Ray Chuckles smiled and drifted away. He was dead on arrival at St Vincents.

> 'Ya never hear the shot that kills ya.'
> Ray Chuckles, 1979

PART 5

GREAT DAY FOR A SHOOT 'EM UP

GREAT DAY FOR A
SHOOT 'EM UP

EVERYBODY has to believe in something. Earl Teagarden believed he would sit on the back steps of his home in Peel Street, North Melbourne, and pass the time. As usual, he was playing with his Jack Russell terrier, Pig.

Mind you, to call Pig a purebred Jack Russell would be a slight exaggeration, as his mother was a bull terrier-Staffordshire terrier cross. But Pig's dad was a prize-winning Jack Russell show dog, all right. The result of this cross-breeding was a short, thickset little animal with a head on it like a sledgehammer with teeth.

Pig moved as frantically as a speed junkie who had to be some place in a hurry and didn't know which way to turn. The dog darted up, then down, side-stepped to the right, then to the left. Back and forth, to and fro, he went.

Just to make life interesting, Earl would occasionally toss a slice of hot Italian salami into the air and Pig would hurl himself up, three feet off the ground and into the air. His jaws would snap shut on the hot tasty titbit.

'You're a bloody dago, Pig,' Earl said one day after watching Pig do his salami trick for the hundredth time. 'You love that bloody Italian sausage, hey, boy?'

Pig licked his lips, showing off about a yard of pink slobbery tongue and darted about, then stopped still and readied himself for another leap in the air to catch another slice of hot salami.

Then they were interrupted.

'Oi!' yelled Evil Hadley.

Earl Teagarden looked up to see his next-door neighbour, whose real name was Nigel Hadley, pop his head up over the back fence.

'How's it going, Evil?' Earl enquired politely. 'What's new?'

'What's new?' said Evil Hadley. 'I'll tell you what's new, all right. John Harding just shot himself.'

'What?' exclaimed Earl in surprise and disbelief. 'Not Detective Inspector John Harding, the copper?'

'Yeah,' said Evil. 'It just come on the radio. Put a gun in his mouth sometime last night.'

'Hey, Earl,' said Evil. 'Wasn't he one of Westlock's henchmen?'

Earl Teagarden cut another slice of salami and tossed it high into the air. Pig jumped for it and missed, landed, then spun about like a top trying to locate the fallen slice of meat.

'Yeah,' said Earl looking intently at Pig as he located the slice of salami. 'He was one of 'em. He was the one who drove the car when Rocky Roy Wilson blew Marc Michieletto off the motorbike after he did the bank in Footscray.'

'Rocky Ray Wilson transferred out of the armed robbers after the Michieletto shooting. The armed robbers are falling apart,' said Evil Hadley.

'Shit, half of 'em are up on shooting charges, murder blues, suspended from duty or putting guns in their mouths. You know the Victoria Police motto is only three words … bang, bang, bang.'

Earl Teagarden sneered. 'Graeme Westlock and Doc Holliday are still safe and secure. The rest of the police can go down the brasco. Westlock and Holliday are the ones that count.'

'Yeah,' said Evil Hadley as he climbed over the fence. With only one good leg it wasn't easy.

'When are you getting ya new leg?' asked Earl.

Evil hit the ground with a thud, and he winced as his ill-fitting false leg sent a shock wave of pain up into his kneecap.

The police, led by the famed Detective Sergeant John 'Doc' Holliday, well-known friend and right-hand man to police legend Detective Chief Superintendent Graeme Westlock, had raided Evil Hadley's Peel Street home two years before, looking for an underworld figure called Gary Armagh. They didn't find Gary Armagh, but they found Evil Hadley's right leg. In fact, they put a shotgun blast into it for good measure, claiming Evil had pulled a gun on them. Which he had, but later denied, naturally.

The police, led by Westlock, shot and killed Gary Armagh two weeks later – exactly a year to the day after Westlock and Holliday had shot Jimmy Jetson to death. Jetson had been the head of the crew Armagh ran with.

'Shit,' said Evil under his breath as he held the top of his stumpy leg. 'Shit, that hurts.'

'Don't worry,' said Earl with a smile, 'time heals everything, Evil.'

Hadley hobbled over and sat down on top of an upturned five-gallon drum near the back door, then pulled out his pipe and began to fill it with tobacco.

'Not everything, Earl,' said Evil. 'Time doesn't heal everything.' He tapped his false leg with the pipe. 'I don't notice this growing back.'

Pig began to growl, then let out a yap as the front-door knocker crashed several times against the wood.

'Hang on, Evil,' said Earl. 'I'll go and see who that is.'

Jerry 'Pancho' Moran stood on Earl's doorstep. He wasn't alone. He had a large bottle of Earl's favourite drop with him, a clear brown fluid called Hankey Bannister Scotch Whisky.

Pancho was an up-and-coming street fighter and gunman from Grosvenor Street, St Kilda. He was not an overly popular figure in the criminal world, as his cosy relationship with the Italians was well known. He was, in fact, widely considered too shrewd for his own good.

Pancho lived with the sister of a notorious Italian crime boss. Her name was Angela Dellacroce. Her big brother, Gaetano, controlled heroin sales throughout the western suburbs and was the power behind the throne of one Ivan Markovich, known throughout the Melbourne underworld as 'Doctor Chicago'. Pancho's only saving grace in the eyes of the old Aussie crooks was that he was best mates with young Cisco Van Gogh.

Earl Teagarden opened the front door with his left hand. His right hand was behind his back. In it was a small sawn-off double-barrel .410 shotgun. A very useful weapon for snakes, particularly the two-legged variety – which there were more of around North Melbourne.

'How's it going, Pancho?' said Earl.

'OK,' said Pancho. 'Can I talk to ya please, Earl? It's important.' He held out the bottle of Hankey Bannister.

Earl took it with his left hand as Pancho stepped into the hallway. It was then the visitor noticed the sawn-off shot gun with both the hammers pulled back in his host's right hand. It wasn't the sort of reception advised in Emily Post's book of etiquette, but Pancho understood a different set of manners. And he wasn't about to put any holes in them while the little .410 was looking his way.

'No trouble, Earl,' he said pleasantly. 'I just want to talk.'

'OK, kid,' said Earl. 'Out in the backyard. Evil is out there. Go through.' He indicated the way by waving the barrel of the cut-down shotgun.

As Pancho Moran walked on ahead of him, Earl Teagarden thought to himself, What does this shifty rat want? This speed junkie little turd has got more twists and turns than a Simpson washing machine.

You could say that Earl didn't really trust Pancho – even if he was Cisco Van Gogh's best mate.

Pancho pulled up a large wooden box from the various piles of rubbish in Earl's backyard, and sat down. He looked out of place, dressed in his Armani suit, sitting on an old wooden box in Earl's shit pile of a backyard.

Earl handed his visitors a glass and poured each man a full glass of whisky, then poured himself an equally big drop. Teagarden was no teetotaller, that was for sure.

'OK, Pancho,' he said, 'what is it?'

Pancho looked at Evil Hadley and hesitated.

'It's OK,' said Earl. 'I trust Evil.'

'Well,' said Pancho, 'it's about Little Cisco. He's planning to knock Graeme Westlock and Doc Holliday.'

Angela Dellacroce and Sherrie Gangitano stood at the bar of the Sports Bar nightclub in King Street, Melbourne. The two girls had just been turfed out of the Crown Casino for glassing a Vietnamese lady in the face during a heated argument at the roulette table. This was not considered good manners by the management. Only the bouncers in some shifty joints were allowed to get away with maiming punters – and they never used broken glasses. It didn't look good on the security film.

The two girls were in fine form. They were dressed to kill – showing as much leg, arse and tit as was legally allowed in a public place – and roaring drunk to go with it. Sherrie stood with a large glass of Bundaberg rum in one hand. The other hand was up her tight black skirt and down her high-cut black panties, giving her bum a good scratch. She was a toff, our Sherrie.

'Jeez, I gotta itchy arse,' she complained, raking her long red-painted fingernails over the hard-to-get-at spot.

'I reckon I know what you need,' said Angela with a grin.

'Yeah, and I'm just the bloke to give it to her,' said Jungle Jim Zoocos. Jungle Jim, known as Jimmy the Greek for short, was part of Doctor Chicago's crew, and lived just three houses down from Sherrie Gangitano in Castle Street, Jolimont. Jimmy Zoocos was a tall, thickset, good-looking knockabout with a big smile and a winning way with the ladies.

Sherrie Gangitano gave Jimmy the glad eye and pulled her hand out of her knickers and wrapped it around Jimmy's neck. 'Hi ya, Jimmy,' she purred.

Not one to waste time, he began to rub her arse up and down. 'Let me know when I've hit the right spot, baby?' he said.

Then everything went black for Jimmy the Greek. All he could hear was the screaming of Sherrie and Angela as he fell to the floor with a pool cue buried in his skull.

This was no accident. It was a classic sneak go from some very sneaky customers from Footscray – two blokes called Boe Duc No and Ronny Kee, supported by at least ten of their gang from Footscray. They were ripping into Jimmy and the two women like a re-run of the Vietnam war, bar the napalm.

A broken beer glass tore Sherrie's face open from her top lip to her left ear, and Angela was stabbed in the face and neck with knives from several different directions. A meat cleaver smacked across the base of Jimmy's spine, and everything from the waist down went numb. Then, as fast as the Vietnamese attack squad hit, it vanished.

The club bouncers seemed to appear about ten seconds after the Vietnamese had left, but it was all a bit too late. Funny about that.

The war between the Footscray 5T gang and Doctor Chicago had begun. The 'White Rat Mafia', as the Footscray Vietnamese crime gang was comically nicknamed, was 200 strong. The war between the gooks, the dagos and the Aussies had been on the boil since the murders of Con Tu Vu and Boe Cop Nam.

Italians were real good at making money, and the newspapers described the Italian criminal drug lords and money men as 'Mister Bigs'. This was the common outsiders' point of view, from the outside looking in. The reasoning was that the crooks with all the cash must be on top — and the top crooks in charge of the crooks with all the cash must be the Mister Bigs. But, as the song says, it ain't necessarily so.

Within the criminal world, everyone knew that cash was only fairy floss. Because, when the shit hit the fan and the shooting started, all the money in all the world couldn't do anyone much good at all.

Gaetano Dellacroce had a problem. Doctor Chicago had a crew of 60 heroin dealers who had all scattered for cover as soon as the Vietnamese hit Jimmy Zoocos. Dellacroce's whole multimillion-dollar drug empire was geared for money, not war.

Of course, death and violence were dealt out to the weak scum who owed money and who broke the rules, but this was schoolyard-bully stuff. Break a leg here, hand out a pistol whipping there, set up the odd hot shot as a lesson to the other junkies not to push their luck with the man. But the Dellacroce crew grew and grew using cash and connections and agreements, not guns. Violence against mice was just by way of public relations. Agreements with police, connections with other criminal crews and gangs was their stock in trade. Agreement, cash and considerations. It was, after all, a business. What it was not was a blood and guts crew geared for war, when the Irish nutters called the dago heroin dealers 'powder pussies'.

Here was a multimillion-dollar empire, based on white powder, held together with bluff and bullshit. What the media didn't know was that any crew of nutters with the arse out of their pants and a few sawn-off shotguns and a heap of dash could gut any multimillion-dollar drug empire in two or three nights with two or three dead bodies.

The richer a crook gets the more he has to lose, and the more he has to lose the less he will be inclined to risk it with serious gunplay. No drug empire can survive a blood war without coming out of it crippled, and there was no way in the world Dellacroce would win against the Vietnamese.

There was only one crew of psychos in Melbourne whose taste for sheer bloodshed outshone the Viets. Gaetano Dellacroce picked up the phone and rang his friend Pancho Moran.

Detective Chief Superintendent Graeme Westlock sat in the passenger seat of the unmarked police car. Doc Holliday was at the wheel.

'Watch the bloody road, Doc,' Westlock growled. 'You nearly side swiped that bloody taxi, ya cranky mad bastard.'

'Sorry, Graeme,' said Doc.

The police radio was turned off. Doc was listening to his cassette player. Carrying a ghetto blaster in a police car was not quite within police standing orders but, as Doc was fond of asking Westlock, what was the bloody use of being a bloody Detective Chief Superintendent if you couldn't toss the police standing bloody orders out the bloody window?

Perfectly correct, Westlock agreed. Which was why he was also sucking on a cold can of beer as the cop car sped through a lazy Sunday afternoon's traffic with a gospel singer called Mathalia Jackson blasting her lungs out on Doc Holliday's tape deck.

'Great afternoon for a quiet drive, hey, Graeme?' said Doc.

Westlock tossed an empty can out the window and reached over and grabbed another one out of an esky on the back seat. They were off to Charlie Ford's place to have a BBQ and raise a glass or two to the memory of their late comrade John Harding.

'All the boys will be at Charlie's place, won't they?' asked Doc.

'Yeah,' said Westlock. 'I got young Frank to ring around and rally the troops.'

'Ha ha ha,' he giggled, after a pause.

'What's up?' asked Doc.

Westlock patted his friend on the shoulder. 'The gooks and the dagos are at it. And that turd Pancho Moran rang the office this morning with an urgent message that he wants to see me. I reckon it's rock and roll time again, Doc.'

'That Moran, he's in with them dagos, isn't he?'

'Yeah,' said Westlock. 'He's also pretty close to Cisco Van Gogh and the leftovers of McCall's old crew. He's a cunning little dog, but he might come in handy.'

Doc Holliday laughed as he swerved to avoid a gas truck. 'It's like the friggin' pixies' bloody parade,' he swore. 'Every junkie mental retard in Melbourne must be out for a Sunday bloody drive.'

'Yeah,' said Westlock, as he jotted down the number of the offending truck. 'That bastard is gonna get a visit. Watch out, Doc — lady with a pram.'

Doc stopped at a red light and a fat woman with a pram pushed her way past the police car.

'Jesus Christ,' said Doc Holliday. 'Cop the clacker on that cow.'

Westlock looked at the woman wobble past. 'Ya know, Doc, it's sights like that that make me wonder if we aren't arresting the wrong people.'

'Too right,' said Doc Holliday. 'Know just what you mean.'

'Bloody hell, Archie,' said Little Cisco, getting a little exasperated. 'It's dead-set easy. Kid McCall told me once about when the Gallo brothers, Crazy Joe Gallo and his two brothers Larry "Kid Twist" and Albert "Kid Blast", walked into the Park Sheraton Hotel barber shop in Manhattan, New York, on 25 October 1957, and blew away Albert Anastasia, the head of Murder Inc., as he sat in the barber's chair. It's a classic way to knock somebody – and Westlock gets a haircut once a month, every month at the same place, Con's Barber Shop, in Gertrude Street, Fitzroy.'

'Con the Greek?' asked Archie Reeves.

'Nah,' snarled Little Cisco. 'Con the bloomin' Chinaman, ya dickhead. Of course, Con the Greek.'

'Ohh,' said Archie. 'So that's it. Ya just walk in and blow him away while he's having a blow wave.'

'Yep,' said Little Cisco. 'He he he.'

Archie smiled at Little Cisco's Tommy Udo laugh. Cisco Van Gogh's favourite film was the old gangster movie *Kiss of Death*, starring Richard Widmark. Little Cisco was yet to push a crippled lady down a staircase as she sat helpless in her wheelchair, but he was hoping to do it one day. He was not without ambition.

Archie Reeves thought to himself how it was odd that so many criminal psychopaths in Melbourne shared several of the same passions and traits with the more gung-ho police.

They were either church-going Bible bashers, Wild West nuts or movie buffs. Some were all three. It was a well-known fact that Graeme Westlock was rumoured to have a giant oil painting of

Hopalong Cassidy on his horse Topper. The story was that the oil painting was hanging above the fireplace in Westlock's home. Then there was the strange inscription written on Mickey Van Gogh's gravestone: 'Proverbs 14.12'. It took a full year before it became known what Proverbs 14.12 meant. It was the same inscription written on the tombstone of Jimmy Gatz in *The Great Gatsby*.

Yeah, thought Archie Reeves, the more serious police and the more serious criminals in Melbourne were all quite seriously mad. Shooting Westlock as he sat in the barber's chair just like the Gallo brothers shot Albert Anastasia, indeed! It was a joke. Archie shook his head. Cisco Van Gogh was as mad as the maddest he'd ever known – Kid McCall and Karen Phillips included. Archie just hoped Little Cisco didn't expect him to join in on the venture.

'Will this be a one-out job, Cisco?' he asked straight-faced.

'Nah,' said Cisco. 'Pancho will give me a chop out on this one.'

'Are you sure?' said Archie. 'I don't know what you see in that bloody Moran.'

'Nah,' said Cisco. 'She's sweet. Pancho's OK, he's a good bloke.'

'Oh well,' said Archie. 'As long as you're sure.'

Cisco Van Gogh smiled and patted Archie on the shoulder. 'Don't worry, Archie, I'm not as silly as everyone thinks I am.'

Archie gave a faint smile and said nothing.

Pancho Moran had taken the Dellacroce contract to Earl Teagarden, Preston Phillips, Geoff Twain, Bunny Malloy, Archie Reeves, Sonny Carroll, Sean Maloney, Johnny Pepper, Billy Burns, Greg Featherstone, Ferdie Taylor, Pat O'Shaughnessy and Little Cisco Van Gogh.

All Dellacroce wanted was for the head of the snake to be removed. But first you had to find the head.

When Kid McCall and his hit team killed Con Tu Vu and Boe Cop Nam, Duc Tu Vu and his cousin Wock Eye Kee, a cross-eyed Vietnamese mental case, had taken control. However, there was a different power behind the throne. It was all very mysterious, but somehow Dellacroce knew that the only way to win a war against the Vietnamese was to kill a local Melbourne Chinese business and political identity, Run Fat Lee, known to one and all as Ronny Lee.

Using Pancho Moran as a middleman, Dellacroce put up the sum of one hundred thousand dollars for the Collingwood crew to hit Ronny Lee and handle any fallout as a result of the hit. Which is why Pancho took the plan to Earl Teagarden. Earl, uncle of Kid McCall, carried some weight, even though he was not part of the Collingwood clan.

Pancho also took the offer to Cisco Van Gogh, who rejected it at once. However, Preston Phillips, Johnny Pepper and Bunny Malloy, along with Geoff Twain, accepted the deal and the hundred grand up front. Then they sub-contracted the whole deal out to the nutbush city limits crew – the Albanian Mafia and their Romanian cousins.

The so-called Albanian Mafia was a mixed collection of Albanian, Romanian, Russian and Yugoslav families, all inter-related and interconnected. Along with a smattering of mad Hungarians and Lithuanians, they were a silent criminal force that rivalled the Calabrian and Sicilian criminal clans.

The Albanian and Romanian criminals would kill God for sixpence and for twenty thousand bucks up front the sky was the limit. Dragan Muskkar and Vladac Dobbroc, nicknamed Johnny Dobro, were only too happy to kill Ronny Lee for 20 big ones.

The Melbourne criminal scene was becoming blurred and mixed. Nothing seemed black and white any more. Preston Phillips was living with a Vietnamese prostitute, Sean Maloney was living with Tina Castronovo, Johnny Pepper was going to marry Barbie Bonventre and already had a kid with her, old Ferdie Taylor had a Chinese girlfriend and Sonny Carroll was going out with a hot-looking black chick. The whole Collingwood crew was changing. If Ripper Roy could have seen 'em all now, he'd turn in his grave.

The whole crew was split in half, with one half chock-a-block up a gook and the other half in love with a dago or a spook. Cisco Van Gogh found the whole thing distasteful and seemed to mix more and more with his inner circle of Archie, Normie and Neville Reeves. He liked Pancho Moran, but Pancho's relationship with the dagos was suspect to say the least.

Mind you, Little Cisco had taken to screwing the pants off Gaja Jankoo, the mad Russian girl who once acted as housekeeper for Kid McCall. It didn't enter his head that Jankoo was in fact Lithuanian, not Russian, and her uncles and cousins were part of the Albanian-Romanian crew.

The whole Melbourne crime scene had become a melting pot. Only the teams, gangs and crews remained. The wars would never end, but the soldiers in each private army could be from any nationality. Hell, the Vietnamese had moved from Richmond to Fitzroy to Collingwood. There were already Vietnamese and Chinese teamed up with the dagos in wars with the Aussies.

Any criminologist who claimed to understand the Melbourne

criminal world was a liar. The whole thing ran on family, friendship and who's up who – and it all kept changing. The friend of my enemy is my enemy and the enemy of my friend is also my enemy. However, the enemy of my enemy is my friend – and the friend of my friend is my friend.

If you kicked my mate's dog 20 years ago, you'll be my enemy until we chop your leg off. In the meantime we smile at each other on Monday while plotting to kill each other on Tuesday. He's on my side, he's a good bloke; he's on his side, so he's a dog. The wars never end, and while everything else may fall the teams, gangs and crews remain. Outsiders looking in never see it like it really truly is.

Graeme Westlock and Doc Holliday stood in the Santa Fe Gold nightclub talking to Pancho Moran.

'When I take a bloody haircut,' said Westlock, looking at Moran in disbelief. 'Are you serious or delirious?'

'No,' said Pancho. 'It's dead set, Mr Westlock. He's gonna get ya next time ya take a hair cut. Ya still use Con the Greek, don't ya?'

Westlock went silent. Doc Holliday was busy stuffing funny money down some wet dream's G-string. The police have always donated generously to good causes, just as they expect other people to donate generously to them. This time it was a donation to the policeman's balls.

'What's in it for you, Moran?' said Westlock.

'Look, Mr Westlock, I help you today, you help me tomorrow.'

Westlock pondered this point. Moran was ambitious. Pancho played every side against each other. That was OK, thought Westlock. Pancho was betraying Cisco. He might also like to betray Gaetano Dellacroce.

'You're sort of Gaetano's brother-in-law or something, aren't ya, Pancho?' asked Westlock.

'I was gonna be,' said Pancho, 'till them gooks give it to poor Angela.'

Westlock pretended to be sad. It didn't come easy. 'Yeah, they don't reckon she will make it,' said the big cop. 'Bloody tragic. Freaking insane animals, them gooks.'

'If she does make it,' said Pancho, 'she will be a veggie.'

Doc Holliday broke in. 'What's Cisco reckon of all this kissy kissy with the dagos then, Pancho? Ha ha.'

Moran didn't like Doc Holliday and the feeling was mutual.

'Anyway, Mr Westlock. I told ya what I told ya. I gotta go now.' He turned and walked away.

'So Pancho betrays Cisco, hey, Graeme?' said Doc Holliday. 'You know, Graeme, I reckon everyone will end up dead.'

The two men walked out of the club.

Holliday burbled on, much to Westlock's entertainment. 'Yeah, Graeme, I can see it all now, every one of us will end up dead. It's like something out of a Banjo Paterson poem.' And with that, he started to recite a verse of a Banjo classic, or at least his memory of how it went.

'By the old Campaspe River, where the breezes shake the grass,
'There's a row of little gravestones that the stockmen never pass,
'For they bear a crude inscription saying stranger drop a tear
'For the cuff and collar players and the Geebung boys lie here.'

Westlock and Holliday roared laughing and together they walked off into the night.

• • •

Earl Teagarden and Little Cisco Van Gogh sat in a car with Archie Reeves outside the Terminus Hotel in Victoria Street, Abbotsford.

'Ya know, Cisco, the Italians have been here for a long, long time. They are part of Aussie land, even if blokes like us don't like it.'

'How do ya mean?' asked Cisco.

'Remember the story of the 1854 rebellion at Ballarat?' said Earl.

'The Eureka Stockade?' said Little Cisco. 'Yeah, of course, with Peter Lalor. Everyone knows that.'

'Yeah,' said Earl. 'But did you know that Peter Lalor's right-hand man, the bloke who stood with him during the whole shit fight, was a dago?'

'Bullshit,' said Archie Reeves.

'No,' said Earl. 'Fair dinkum, an Italian from Calabria named Carboni, Raffaello Carboni.'

'Shit,' said Cisco. 'There are Carbonis living in Collingwood.'

Earl Teagarden shook his head. 'You're getting off the track.' Earl didn't want to get into one of the famous Collingwood conversations about anyone who was anyone coming from Collingwood, from Ned Kelly to Mother Teresa. 'I'm just letting ya know that the Italians have been here for as long as the Irish have – and a damn sight longer than the Dutch,' he said.

Cisco put his hand inside his coat, on to the butt of his .38-calibre automatic handgun. He didn't look happy. 'What do ya mean by that smartarse remark?' he snapped. 'The Van Goghs have lived in Collingwood for a hundred bloody years.'

'Yeah, and Van Gogh's an Irish name, isn't it, Cisco?' said Archie.

The conversation was starting to annoy Earl. Trying to talk common sense to the mentally ill was always a danger. He breathed a sigh of relief when Anne Griffin walked up and tapped on the car window.

Cisco opened the car door. 'How's it going, Anne?'

'Ronny Lee just got blown away in the waiting room of the Royal Melbourne Hospital. It just came on the TV in the pub,' she said.

It had happened like this. Ronny Lee had gone into hiding and was nowhere to be found, so Dragan Muskkar and Johnny Dobro had simply walked up to his 73-year-old mother as she shopped in Little Bourke Street, punched her to the footpath then shot her in both kneecaps.

She was rushed to the Royal Melbourne Hospital, and members of the Albanian crew sat off the hospital and simply waited for Ronny Lee to show up. It was an old trick, but a good one. It took Ronny three days to turn up, but the psychology proved correct. And Ronny proved dead soon after arrival.

The strange thing about this was that when Dragan Muskkar and Johnny Dobro came running out of the hospital after shooting Ronny they jumped into a getaway car driven by Nguyen Cao Ky, the brother of Preston Phillips's whore girlfriend Mekong Kellie. Nguyen Cao Ky and Nguyen Bao Dai were the right- and left-hand men to Le Duc Tho and Ngo Dinh Diem, two Vietnamese gang leaders from Collingwood who were at war with the Chinese and Vietnamese gangs from Richmond, Fitzroy and Footscray. They were nicknamed the Mekong Mafia, and most of the 30-man gang lived in the Collingwood Commission flats.

The Mekong crew had carved out a heroin empire worth between three and six million dollars a year and seemed to be well armed and interconnected with all the old crews – including the old Collingwood crew, yet on the face of it the old Aussie Irish mob and the up-and-coming Vietnamese had nothing to do with each other.

However, this strange and unseen relationship between the two gangs had not escaped the attention of Pancho Moran. Moran reported this vital intelligence to Gaetano Dellacroce, and Dellacroce sent him to see Preston Phillips. So it was that Pancho Moran found himself sitting at the bar of the old Telford Club.

The club had been let go and was rather run down. No one lived upstairs any more and it was now used for general storage and a place to bash, torture and shoot people in private.

Preston Phillips, Johnny Pepper, Bunny Malloy and Preston's moll gook girlfriend Mekong Kellie were all in attendance.

'Look, Preston, all Gaetano wants is to talk,' Pancho started. 'The old days are dead and gone. It's the future we all have to look to and the only way to go is to crew up together. One big solid Aussie, Italian, Vietnamese crew. If the three main crews teamed up, we could control everything. We would have every side covered.'

While Pancho tried to sell Dellacroce's master plan to Preston Phillips, Mekong Kellie stood on the pool table dancing to an old Dusty Springfield song playing on the jukebox. The lyrics went: 'The only one who could ever reach me, the only one who could ever teach me, was the son of a preacher man.'

Johnny Pepper was standing beside the pool table trying to stick the barrel of his gold-cup .45-calibre automatic handgun up the bum of the wiggling Asian beauty.

'Cut that shit out,' yelled Preston. 'Don't worry, Kellie. Johnny's only kidding.'

Preston Phillips returned his attention to Pancho Moran.

'Yeah, Pancho, it all sounds OK, but what about the Albanians? Do we include them?' he asked.

'Piss on the Albanians,' said Pancho.

'Well, what about Graeme Westlock?' asked Bunny Malloy. 'Do we include him?'

Pancho was taken aback. 'What's he got to do with it?'

'Ya know Anne Griffin?' asked Preston.

'No,' said Pancho. 'Not really.' Then he admitted, 'Yeah, well, I do and I don't. I've seen her about.'

Bunny Malloy laughed. 'Have you ever seen her about the Santa Fe Gold?'

'What do ya mean?' asked a now very nervous Pancho.

'Anne Griffin works as a table-top dancer when she's not on her back. She might be a moll and a maddie but she never forgets a face and she don't tell lies. Pancho, you're a fucking dog. You been talking to the police,' said Bunny Malloy.

'Bullshit,' spluttered Moran. 'What? You're gonna take some moll's word over mine?'

Preston Phillips pulled out his .38-calibre police special. 'Pancho, the point is, even if Anne never seen you with the police, we was still gonna kill ya.'

'Yeah,' yelled Johnny Pepper, 'cos the thing is, Pancho, we don't like ya.'

And with that Preston Phillips, Johnny Pepper and Bunny Malloy all took aim at Pancho Moran and pulled their triggers. Bullets from three different directions smacked into Pancho's body and he fell to his knees.

Mekong Kellie got down off the pool table and grabbed a big bread knife and walked over and cut Pancho's throat from ear to ear. Pancho's head fell backwards and blood pumped out like a red oil well from the gaping hole in his neck. The girl was covered in blood.

'Jesus, Kellie,' said Preston Phillips. 'That wasn't necessary. Look at all this bloody mess.'

Preston got up from the stool he was sitting on and backhanded the girl hard across the face. As he did this, Pancho's body fell to the floor.

'You mad cow,' yelled Preston. 'You mad sick cow.' Then he let fly with a second crashing backhander that sent her about six feet backwards and on to the floor.

Bunny Malloy proceeded to undo his fly and said to Preston, 'Hey, Pres, waste not, want not, mate. Don't flog her too hard.'

Preston looked at the dead Pancho with his head almost cut off, and then at the fallen and crying Kellie. The whole party had turned a little sick for his liking.

Cisco Van Gogh sat in Chang Heywood's old 1967 Hillman Arrow car. Archie Reeves had agreed to come along for the ride, much against his better judgement. Neville and Normie Reeves sat in the back seat, highly excited. Cisco was about to gun a copper down in a barber's shop, just like on the old late-night-TV black-and-white gangster movies. They thought it was great.

It was pissing down rain as they waited in the old car across the road from Con the Greek's Barber Shop, in Gertrude Street, Fitzroy.

'Holy shit,' said Archie. 'It's coming down cats and dogs. You'll bloody drown in this, just walking across the bloody street.'

Little Cisco sat in silence checking his H & K 9mm automatic. It was a modern, heavy-duty job, the sort of gear the SAS and anti-terrorist squads use. He'd cut Westlock in half with this thing, Cisco thought to himself.

'There they are,' said Archie.

Sure enough, when Cisco peered through the rain-splattered car window, he saw Westlock and his faithful sidekick Doc Holliday getting out of an unmarked police car.

The two cops wore overcoats, which might have seemed odd, normally. But it was raining, after all. They made their way into Con the Greek's shop and started chatting to the bloke waving the scissors.

'How's it going, Con?'

'Ahh, Mr Westlock,' said Con with a big smile, 'is a shit of a day. Good a day for ducks.'

Westlock smiled as he took off his overcoat and hung it up. 'Yeah, Con, good day for the ducks.'

Above the coat rack was a large photo of Sir Donald Bradman. Con the Greek loved cricket, which was a touch unusual for a Greek. On the other wall was a large photo of David Boon. At least Boon looked a bit Greek.

'Speaking of ducks,' said Doc Holliday, pointing to the photo of Bradman. 'He was gone for a duck in the last game he ever had.'

'Ahh, Mr Holliday,' said Con, 'that's not fair. Don the Batman was the best. He even better than Boonie – not much, but yes, I have to say Don the Batman was Mister Magic with the bat.'

'Ya know,' said Doc Holliday, 'Don Bradman was really born in Melbourne.'

'Bullshit,' said Con, who believed the customer was always right, except when it came to cricket. 'He came from New South Wales, then went to South Australia.' And he looked to Westlock for confirmation.

'No,' said Westlock, sitting in the barber's chair. 'Don Bradman was born in Hoddle Street, Collingwood. Three houses down from David Boon.'

'Ahh, Mr Westlock,' said Con, 'you pulla my leg. Boonie came from Launceston, Tasmania.'

Westlock shook his head. 'Nah, Con. Hoddle Street, Collingwood.'

Con looked at the photo of David Boon in disbelief. 'Collingwood?' he said.

He gave up the argument, and threw the black nylon sheet around Westlock and tied it tight around the policeman's bull neck.

'Boonie come from Collingwood?' Con muttered to himself, still in a state of puzzled disbelief. 'I reckon you tell Con the bullshit, Mr Westlock.'

Graeme Westlock turned to Con and said, 'Con, I'm a member of the Victoria Police Force. Would I tell you a lie?'

Con shook his head. 'No, Mr Westlock. I'm a just surprise, that's all.'

Westlock silently pulled out his .38-calibre police special with his right hand and held it against his stomach with the barrel aimed towards the open doorway, which had red, yellow and white strips of plastic hanging over it, designed, it would seem, to keep the flies in.

Westlock gently clicked the hammer back and held the weapon steady under the cover sheet. Doc Holliday sat on the bench at the rear of the shop. Surprise, surprise, his overcoat concealed a cut-down 12-gauge shotgun with a pistol-grip handle.

'Short back and sides and a bit off the top, hey, Con?' said Westlock cheerfully. He was a tough bastard.

'OK, Mr Westlock,' said the Greek barber.

Doc Holliday pulled the latest copy of Louis L'Amour's 'Hopalong Cassidy' adventure out of his overcoat pocket and began to read.

'Great day for a shoot 'em up, hey, Graeme?' said Holliday.

'Always a good day for one of those, Doc,' Westlock quipped.

Both men laughed at their private joke.

'Listen,' said Archie Reeves to Little Cisco. 'Have you given this enough thought?'

Cisco gave his auto one final check and tucked it into his waistband under his coat. 'Yeah. I'll never get another chance like this, Archie. Now you three wait here. This won't take long.'

Cisco opened the car door and a sheet of rain blew in. Cisco laughed and turned to Archie, Neville and Norm. 'Ha ha, great day for a shoot 'em up, hey, boys?'

He got out of the car. The rain drenched his hair and the drops ran down his face. Cisco turned and looked back at his mates through the open door before he closed it. 'Ya know, boys, I love the rain. Ha ha ha.'

PART 6

A HOT DATE

THE screw had a head only a mother could love, and a temperament to match. 'McCall,' he snarled, 'you're getting out in the morning. Pack your gear.'

'Thanks, sir,' said Johnny McCall, and the prison officer slammed the cell trap door shut.

'Shit,' said Leigh Kinniburgh, 'you won't be getting much sleep tonight.'

Johnny McCall had been sharing a cell in A Division, Pentridge, with this young Richmond tough for the past nine months. And Kinniburgh had spent the whole time regaling McCall with wild yarns of fist fights and shootouts in Richmond and stories of Billy 'Blueberry' Hill and Bobby Boy Michieletto.

He told stories about how his uncle Billy got shot in the jaw by Johnny the Pig back in the wild 1970s, and how his other uncle several times removed bullets from friends with the help of large amounts of grog and some drugs mixed up by a tame local chemist.

He told McCall of a legendary street fighter and gunman from the western suburbs called Harold who hanged himself in the Footscray lock-up some 20 years ago. And how his grandfather once rode the 1965 Melbourne Cup winner Light Fingers, and how he was the great-great-great-grandson of Ned Kelly, and how he had once waved at Ripper Roy Reeves from a distance of 300 yards.

The wild yarns went on and on, in between blasts of heroin. But, all in all, Leigh wasn't a bad young bloke. He had a badly smashed-in face and no front teeth and spoke with a dribble – the result of being in some sort of coma, so he claimed. McCall didn't mention his own 'Blueberry' Hill connection in the form of Muriel Hill and Melanie Wells, as that would expose baby Mickey. And Johnny knew that a secret shared is a secret lost, and that sometimes discretion can be the better part of valour.

'Ya won't need ya colour telly and ya radio and the cassette player or the CD player when ya go, will ya, Johnny?' asked Leigh.

'Nah, you can have the lot,' said McCall.

McCall had served nine months of a 12-month term for unlawful possession of a firearm, a stiff sentence for a first offence. His lawyer, Clancy Collins, had lodged an appeal against conviction on the manslaughter blue and briefed Mr Robert Rouldorff QC at $5,000 a day. The manslaughter conviction vanished, but McCall still had the possession of a handgun bullshit to do.

All in all, thought McCall, things have gone off brilliantly.

Russian Suzi, God bless her, had left Coco's Restaurant and the

Telford Club to him in her will. This made Johnny feel a tad guilty over killing her, but it was too late for all that now.

Coco Joeliene had dropped a pile of cash to his mum's place – about half a million, so his mum reckoned. Joeliene didn't know exactly, because she hadn't bothered to count it. She just guessed.

Auntie Muriel had taken over the management of Coco's Restaurant and sold her flower shop in Lennox Street, Richmond. Johnny's sweetheart girlfriend, Melanie Wells, was acting as live-in full-time nanny for baby Mickey.

Yeah, thought Johnny, as he started pulling the photographs off the ceiling and walls, things have really come together. Here he was, not quite 19 years old, and he was at least half a millionaire. He owned a whorehouse and the Telford Club, which he planned on turning into a sly gambling club. The Crown bloody Casino hadn't pinched all the business. The scallywags and hard men didn't always like flashing cash around in squarehead places with security cameras in case the authorities got nosy about where it came from.

Johnny still had more guns than God in the cellar of the club, and a few other little stashes.

He was a rising criminal star. He had it all. As he pulled down the wedding photos of Clancy Collins and Melissa Clarke, he laughed to himself at how the romance had come about. It seemed that old Clancy had taken to walking about at night, carrying an old antique sword in a cane for personal protection.

He was walking down Lygon Street, East Brunswick, one night about six months before on his way to see his accountant at the Quarry Hotel when up ahead he heard the cries of a lady in distress. Well, maybe not a lady altogether, but she was young and definitely distressed. It was young Melissa being molested by a gang of drunken louts and roughnecks. They had the fair Melissa bent over the hood of a HQ Holden and were giving her a goodly bit of the old ram jam big band up the South Pacific region.

Old Clancy yelled for them to unhand the girl but to no avail. The old gent then drew his sword from his cane and with his overcoat flapping in the wind he charged up the street and entered the field of combat like Basil Rathbone. He slashed to the left of him and to the right of him and to the left again, and dispatched the offenders in grand fashion.

It was at this point that young Melissa fell in love. She so overpowered old Clancy with her charms they were married within a month. It seemed married life was the salvation for both of them. Melissa no longer worked at Coco's or any other restaurant of ill repute, and old Clancy no longer staggered the streets of Melbourne at night and haunted hotels and nightclubs yelling, 'Madam, may I offer you a 69?' as he waved his ever-present glass of Vat 69.

He was too busy at home in bed being physically attacked. Good luck to the both of 'em, thought Johnny. They'd taken their honeymoon in Kingston, Jamaica, at Coco Joeliene's invitation, and her expense, and McCall had the snapshots sent over to prove it.

As for Jamaican Joeliene. Well, well. McCall looked around at his cell walls littered with photos she had sent him including her wedding photos. She had married Sir Leopold Kidd at, believe it or not, Government House in Kingston, with the Governor General of Jamaica acting as best man. She was all tits and taffeta on the day and looking wonderful.

McCall received a letter each week from her with at least six photos in each letter, and she demanded he ring her reverse charges at least three times a week. He would ring and it would be night time in Jamaica and if she was asleep she would just stick her nose in a fat bag of cocaine and chatter away for an hour or more. And could she keep McCall entertained with tales of her high adventure as Lady Joeliene, the wife of a millionaire merchant banker and Knight of the Realm.

No door in the Caribbean was closed to her. She lived in a mansion in Kingston and kept Sir Leopold's yacht, renamed *Lady Joeliene*, in Montego Bay. She opened a bar-restaurant-nightclub affair in Kingston and, you guessed it, she named it Coco's Restaurant. It was the hottest place in town, the star attraction being a former Miss Trinidad and Tobago from Port of Spain who had fallen on hard times. And fallen on a few other things since.

This wanton wench put on a show which would be quite against the law in Australia. She openly bragged of having accommodated the entire touring Australian cricket team between the hours of 9 pm and midnight before attending to the needs of the local side. A sticky wicket all round.

Lady Joeliene would often hand the phone over to the former Miss Trinidad, leaving McCall in no doubt that Isabella Dominquez would be a most interesting lady to know socially if he ever got to the Caribbean.

Kinniburgh was looking at him. 'Can I have a few photos of Joeliene?' he asked hopefully, looking like a smashed-up pig dog wagging its tail for a bone. It was more a case of wagging his bone for a piece of tail.

McCall looked and picked out a couple of Joeliene on the beach on Montego Bay, wearing some sort of saucy bikini, and another of her in some sort of tiny G-string thing. All tits and legs in the sun, surf and sand.

'Gee, I'd love to slip it into her,' said Kinniburgh, clutching himself like a drowning man grabbing a straw.

McCall laughed. 'I'm sure if she was here right now she'd be more than happy to knock the top off it for ya, mate, because she's that sort of lady. But you'll never get the chance, mate.'

Kinniburgh frowned. 'Yeah, but I can still dream.'

McCall thought, Yeah, that's all a bloke in jail has really got – his memories and his dreams. Anything to escape the reality of the moment. McCall remembered the nights he had spent looking at Joeliene's photos of faraway Jamaica and reliving old memories and loving her letters and phone calls. Yeah, Melanie Wells would visit him on contact visits and when the coast was clear he'd empty a healthy load of prison frustration into her, but in his dreams he wanted to be in the sun and surf and sand with his old friend Coco Joeliene.

The truth was, he really missed his old mate and desperately wanted to see her again and planned to do just that when he got out.

On Coco's advice, McCall had transferred a large slice of his funds to a very friendly bank in Georgetown, Grand Cayman Island. His passport was in order and so was Melanie's. His mum had agreed to take over the babysitting of Mickey. He would get out and check on the Telford Club and Coco's Restaurant, then grab Melanie and jump on a plane for Jamaica.

He needed sun, surf and sand after this bluestone hell hole. He looked at a photo of Coco on the beach, with her left arm around Sir Leopold and her right arm around Archie Reeves of all people. The terror of every chemist shop in Collingwood.

Hell, thought McCall. Did that little scallywag kick a big goal when he handed Coco Joeliene a fist full of pethidine way back when. He was behind the bar at Coco's nightclub and didn't ever want to return to Collingwood, and who can blame him?

Archie wanted to open his own small bar and call it the Collingwood Club. Coco was looking at a small place for him on Prince Alfred Street. Lucky bastard, but he did thieve her a million-odd bucks' worth of top-of-the-range drugs and got about ten grand for the lot and blew that on bullshit with his mates. So she sort of owed him.

Sir Leopold ran his business interests from Jamaica now, and Lady Joeliene had become a power of sorts in her local government parish and was a member of the PNP, the People's National Party, as well as a cash contributor to the JLP, the Jamaican Labour Party. She always liked a bob each way.

Sir Leopold loved her desperately, and why not? He spoiled her rotten and gave her 20 per cent of a Jamaican aluminium business, so Lady Joeliene was now a heavy in the metals game. From blow jobs to bauxite.

McCall looked around to see Leigh Kinniburgh stick a heroin needle into his arm for his second plug of the day. God, get me out of here, thought Johnny. Thank you, Joeliene. You have kept me sane, and soon I'll be with you again.

He picked up a photo sent to him by the new girl at Coco's in Abbotsford. She took over when Melissa Clarke bailed out to marry old Clancy. Her name was Kristy Toy. She was a Collingwood girl, a crew-cut neo-Nazi boot girl but built for athletic passion. She came in to visit McCall soon after she started work at Coco's but got barred from the prison after the screws found her bent over a table with the Kid. The screws thought they'd need a crowbar to pull them apart.

As the screws grabbed McCall, Kristy yelled, 'Fuck 'em, Johnny. Keep doing what you do best,' and he did. In the end they left him to it until the finish. Kristy got dragged away by two bull-dyke female prison officers and Johnny McCall spent a month on punishments. Ha ha.

Melanie never found out why he was on punishments and too bad if she did. Jail is jail and wet dreams that produce themselves in the flesh on contact visits cannot be ignored, not when most of the poor bums in the joint are pulling theirs, dreaming about things they will never get.

Yeah, he loved Melanie but being in prison had done something to McCall. Hell, he might even pull Kristy to one side on the quiet when he got out tomorrow. He had to check on Coco's anyway. She was a raving nutter with a heap of guts. McCall also knew a thousand per cent that Joeliene fully intended and expected him to ram her solid, and likewise her double-jointed star nightclub attraction. The Kid was going to make up for lost time. Most women who loved prisoners couldn't understand what happened when they got out. It was like putting a starving man in front of a mountain of food, he ate until he was sick. A prisoner who's been starved of pussy never knocks back a chance again.

Isabella had already told McCall in no uncertain terms that Melanie or no Melanie she wanted him knee deep inside her within the first five minutes of their meeting each other. What was he to do with Melanie? He was a kid with a thousand things to do and places to go and dreams to live, but all Melanie wanted was to get married. He knew he could never be faithful to one woman. That's why he got on so well with Joeliene. He loved her and she was his friend, but sex was just uncomplicated fun. It didn't mean romance, hearts and flowers and till death do us part. Holy shit, bloody Muriel came in to see him with little baby Mickey. She was wearing a tight skirt and bare legs with high heels and he lost the plot and put the hard word right on her. Muriel blushed a bit, looked around, went silent, then said, 'Don't ever let Melanie find out about this.' She was old enough to be his mother, but she had a good memory.

Outside, in the criminal world, he knew life meant sex, drugs and death. In jail, life meant sex, drugs and death. Drugs meant money, sex meant money, and money meant death or murder either to earn it or to defend it. It all meant the same thing.

In jail all he thought of was sex, money and power. It all came back to murder to defend it or earn it. He wanted every woman he saw. Jail was a cess pit: wall to wall junkies, wall to wall bloodshed. Sex was the butter that smoothed things over. If a guy owed money on drugs, he sold what he could to pay the bill. His arse or his mouth, or he begged his wife or his sister or even his daughter to pay the bill. Or he got a knife or an iron bar and paid the bill himself.

Drop ya pants or die. Or your wife or sister or girlfriend or daughter drops her pants or you die. Either that or you kill or cripple. It was all filth and inhumanity. Only the truly evil survived. And he had wide-eyed innocent Melanie looking to him to be her white knight. If he was any sort of knight at all, it was a black knight. He liked killing, and he loved dirty girls and wicked ladies. Melanie was in for a broken heart.

'Hey, Johnny,' said Leigh Kinniburgh. 'Ya won't sleep tonight. Do ya want a bit of speed?'

McCall looked down at the gram of speed Kinniburgh was holding. Yeah, why not? thought McCall. He'd stay up tonight and get ready for tomorrow and have another blast in the morning. He'd be full of beans and as horny as hell when he got out. He'd plonk Melanie then get her to wait at home in Lennox Street while he went to check on Coco's in Victoria Street, then he would bang Kristy and Muriel. Why not? Hell, he'd been away a fair while. Shit, yeah.

McCall put the speed into a spoon and mixed it. He didn't use drugs, but a little now and then wouldn't hurt. Leigh sucked the speed up into a needle and McCall held his arm while Kinniburgh shot him up. Shit, yeah, it nearly took the top of his head off and hit him in the arse at the same time. That was good stuff. No wonder Karen loved it. Poor Karen. His first root and his most sentimental memory. He'd never forget her.

Kinniburgh lay on his bunk and started to nod off. He was full of smack. The lamp in the cell was on and the TV was on with the sound down. McCall packed his letters and personal gear into a box, but couldn't stop going through the photos and his memories. He had become obsessed with going to visit Joeliene in Jamaica when he got out. The whole world was his. He had it all waiting for him. He felt like a young prince on his way to being king. Nothing could stop him.

He held up a photo of Joeliene with a group of well-dressed men and looked at it. She looked a million dollars at some swish party. He looked at the back of the photo. It simply said 'Bridgetown, Barbados' but he couldn't recall the story.

Hang on. That's right. Sir Leo had taken her on a private jet to Barbados for some weekend political do. Sir Leo had taken along a group of Jamaican senators and some members of the Jamaican House of Representatives, including a fist full of cabinet ministers. They had to attend some Caribbean political do. Joeliene had taken along Isabella Dominquez and some other chick McCall had a photo of – a beautiful Hispanic Chinese African mixture who was another beauty-contest runner-up fallen on hard times.

Evidently a fist full of cash and a beautiful sheila sitting on a politician's face could get you anything you wanted in the Caribbean. Whatever Joeliene was now, and regardless of her husband's money which would be all hers one day, she was basically a corrupt and criminally minded miss. McCall knew this was one of the reasons she so much wanted him by her side.

It was clear that she was becoming the Rabbit Kisser of Kingston, with an army of dark-skinned wet dreams at her disposal. She was on her way to being a very powerful woman and very, very wealthy. God, few fit and strong young men could last a long weekend with her. Sir Leo was 70 or 71 years old. He'd be in the cardiac unit any time now, what with 48 inches of Jamaican marshmallow rolling around underneath him every night.

God, McCall, you've got it made in heaven. C'mon, open the cell door. Let me out of here, for God's sake. I want to get out. Joeliene needs me.

McCall was starting to spin out. What was it she said about a bit of trouble with the Marcus Garvey mob? What did she call them? The Haile Selassie Mafia. Ha ha. Yeah, that's right. The bloody Rastafarians. She has to pay them off to keep her nightclub going, regardless of her newfound wealth, status and political influence. She still has to deal with the street people.

McCall held up a photo of Isabella and the beautiful African-Chinese-looking lady standing on either side of a small donkey on a stage inside Coco's club. God, thought McCall, I gotta get outta here and if Melanie gives me any shit I'll leave her behind. Hell, a few months working at Coco's Restaurant in Victoria Street would do her good, so she better not whinge. I'm gonna get out and have a good time ...

The screws were opening the cell doors. Hell, it's bloody morning already, thought McCall. He shook Leigh Kinniburgh awake and grabbed his gear.

'Ya want another blast?' asked Leigh, pointing to the half-gram of speed.

'Nah,' said McCall. 'I'm off my head at a hundred miles per hour already.'

The cell door swung open and McCall heard the noise of 200 men as they came out and ran around having a shower – doing this, doing that, doing a thousand different meaningless things men do in jail in the morning.

'Got time for a quick shower, boss?' he asked the screw.

'Yeah. But hurry up, McCall. You're out of here in half an hour.'

'OK, yeah. Thanks, boss,' said McCall.

'Can I have that photo?' said Kinniburgh, pointing to a big striptease photo of Joeliene he'd forgotten to pack.

'Yeah,' said McCall. 'Keep it, I'm outta here. I'll be with the real thing in a week. Pull yaself silly.'

Johnny the Kid shook hands with Leigh Kinniburgh just as big Frankie Waggels put his head in the door and said, 'If ya want a shower, Kid, ya better hurry up.'

Frankie was a good bloke, doing the lot for a murder he didn't do. At least that's what he told everyone, and no one would dare argue with him, least of all McCall.

'Thanks, Frankie. See ya later.'

'Yeah, Kid,' said Frank, and they shook hands. 'Get one of them beauty queens to write to me, will ya, Kid?'

'Frank, I'll have one out here sitting on ya lap by the weekend,' said McCall. 'And that's a promise.'

'Yeah, well,' said Frank. 'I'm off to sit some breakfast on my lap. See ya, Kid.'

He waved and walked off. McCall headed for the showers, put his box of personal goodies down outside, and took his shower bag and towel and went in. The shower room was full of men and the steam was like a hot London fog. McCall took a vacant shower at the end after stripping off. He cleaned his teeth and had a quick shave under the shower and lathered himself up.

Suddenly, out of the steam came a smashing blow to the nose. His nose shattered and he fell against the shower wall. He stood up. Blood ran down his lips and chin and his chest and dripped on to the cement floor.

'How ya going, pretty boy?'

McCall looked up to see a thickset evil thug of a man he recognised as Chico Della Torre.

'Getting out today, hey, Kid?' said the Sicilian. Della Torre was serving a 14-year sentence for a $250,000-payroll armed robbery. He had served ten years and was awaiting deportation back to Italy.

McCall had politely avoided Della Torre during his time in Pentridge, but now the big Sicilian was standing naked in front of him in the shower.

'Ya know, Kid, I always reckoned you had an arse on you like a little girl's.'

McCall knew what that meant. He tried to run out of the shower but Della Torre grabbed him and pushed him back, then crashed a fist into Johnny's top teeth, mashing teeth and lips. Another punch to the jaw dropped him.

Della Torre stood over McCall and said, 'Kid, down this way we eat chicken and, when we done with that, we eat more chicken.'

McCall looked up and Della Torre looked down like some evil, smiling entrant in an Edward G. Robinson contest.

McCall went to try to stand up but Della Torre bent down and sent another killer punch into the side of his jaw. The Kid was nearly unconscious. Della Torre was soaping himself up and got down on his knees behind McCall and said, 'Kid, this ain't the fucking Limerick Castle and you ain't got no gun. You're gonna remember me till the day you die.'

McCall was on all fours under the shower with his blood pouring out of his nose and mouth. Della Torre slid a substantial Sicilian salami deep into the lower bowel of Johnny the Kid.

McCall let out a scream and he heard laughing from the other men in the shower room. Della Torre withdrew and then thrust himself in deep again and McCall let out another scream, only to receive another smashing blow to the side of the face. The blood flowing from his face was mixing freely with the blood coming from his bum, all running together with the soapy hot water on the shower floor.

Della Torre laughed, 'Ahh, Kid, you're a little virgin. Ha ha.'

He began to thrust himself in and out, faster and faster. McCall felt helpless. He was being shafted like a girl on the shower floor, like some little girl slut taking it up her arse. Della Torre began to moan, 'Yeah, Kid. You're a good fuck. Go on, Kid. Make me come.'

Then he let out a little cheer as he blew his load deep into McCall's body. McCall fell to the shower floor and his bowels gave way and he shit himself and lay there under the shower in his own blood and mess and curled himself up into a ball and sobbed. His tears ran on to the shower floor and mixed with his blood. He heard men laughing and he cried.

Melanie, he thought to himself. And Joeliene. They loved him because he was a man, but he had just been turned into a woman. He wanted to die. He could not stop the tears. As Della Torre wrapped a towel around himself and walked out of the shower, he turned around and looked down.

'C'mon, Kid,' he sneered. 'Cut out the cryin'. Ya know what they say. No tears for a tough guy.'